# The Gospel for Islam
## Reaching Muslims
## in North America

# The Gospel for Islam
## Reaching Muslims
## in North America

Edited by
Roy Oksnevad
and Dotsey Welliver

**emis**
Evangelism and Missions
Information Service

BILLY GRAHAM CENTER
WHEATON COLLEGE

Published by EMIS, a division of the Billy Graham Center
Wheaton College
Wheaton, IL  60187-5593  USA

Printed in the United States of America.

Cover design: Dona Diehl.  Cover photos: Top photo by Roy Oksnevad, other photos courtesy Arab World Ministries.

ISBN 1-879089-36-X

Chapters in this book were originally presented at a conference. Opinions expressed by the authors do not necessarily represent the viewpoint of the Billy Graham Center.

For information about other publications or resources of EMIS or the Billy Graham Center, phone (630) 752-7158, E-mail: EMIS @wheaton.edu or visit the website: www.billygrahamcenter.org

# Table of Contents

# Preface and Acknowledgments

## Preface

Several events shaped the writing of this book. The first one resulted from a personal pilgrimage. In 1985 my wife and I left the United States to work overseas. In 1994 my growing family and I returned to the United States and began looking for a place where God could use us in reaching Muslims.

We were challenged to consider North America. This was a new thought for me to consider. After calling several agencies and interviewing key people referred to us, it seemed that few people knew what types of ministry opportunities existed with Muslims in the North American context.

Secondly, we noticed that little communication was taking place between groups and individuals working among Muslims in North America, resulting in duplication. This was illustrated in two separate incidences.

In 1996 two conferences on Islam were scheduled in the Chicago area at the same time. One group canceled their conference and encouraged their people to attend the other conference. Another incident came from a conversation with then Director for Muslim Studies in Wheaton, Illinois, Dr. Larry Poston, who informed me that a project he was working on was very similar to a project someone else was doing. He sent his research to the other person to help him. It was becoming obvious that organizations, ministries, and individuals working among Muslims in North America needed to meet together to share what each one was doing.

In learning more about the North American context, we discovered that the growth of Islam in North America is relatively new. According to the CAIR (Council of American Islamic Relations) 2001

Mosque Report (Bagby, Perl, and Froehle 2001), the majority of the more than 1,200 existing mosques (87%) have been founded since 1970. They report that the collective Muslim population has grown to between 6–7 million in North America. In major cities from Toronto, Canada, to Houston, Texas, from New York City to Los Angeles, this new population group has grown large enough to be visible through their numerous mosques and ethnic businesses.

At the same time, through a variety of reasons ranging from retirement to personal issues, God is sovereignly bringing experienced missionaries to North America who desire to reach out to the growing number of Muslims. In addition, a growing number of individuals and churches have entered into dialogue with Muslims but do not know of others conducting similar ministries. There is an increasing need to share what is being done in North America, and to share these insights and lessons learned so that others who desire to reach out to their Muslim neighbors would have the tools and information needed.

In 1997, a call went out to a small number of missionaries and professors to meet together to explore whether there was enough interest and need to call together various ministries and individuals to share ideas. From this meeting, the planning started for convening workers among the Muslim population. The common goals laid out were:

◆   to build a broad base of consensus among workers and agencies to ensure maximum participation;
◆   to better understand Islam in North America with its agenda and the response of the church;
◆   to serve as a catalyst for networking of ideas, resources, and personnel for more effective ministry;
◆   to highlight North American working models of outreach to identify strengths and needs of Christian ministries among Muslims in North America.

In 1999 these leaders, missionaries, and individuals shared their wisdom, which is contained in this book. It is our prayer that this book will encourage the body of Christ as we seek to be relevant to the ever-changing population. We trust that the stories told of the varied ways people are reaching out to their Muslim neighbors would encourage others to step out in faith and try similar endeavors to reach people in their neighborhoods.

## Acknowledgments

The committee that came together was without question the best group of individuals that I have had the privilege to work with. Their wisdom, ideas, and willingness to tackle various tasks made this project an exciting venture.

The committee grew from a handful of people in the beginning to 25 in the end, so it would not be possible to mention all the people that have helped bring together so many people from such diverse backgrounds and experiences. However, I would like to mention a few. Robert Douglas and Janet Metzger were an encouragement in the early stages of this project. The collective wisdom and experience of Robert Webster, Larry Kendricks, and Jim Kraakevik was invaluable as we met monthly to go over the details needed to cover every topic. My dear brother Samuel Naaman gave timely advice and invaluable personal support. David Olmsted, Dick Bailey, and Rick Bailey worked tirelessly in gathering information and corresponding with many people. Manny Jose put together an excellent e-mail system to facilitate communication in our modern age of electronic communication. Lastly, a special thanks to the Billy Graham Center and Concordia Theological Seminary who gave unselfishly of their resources, expertise, and personnel to see this project through to the end.

Roy Oksnevad

*Section 1*

*Islam in America*

# CHAPTER 1

# The Current State of Islam in America

*Dr. Larry Poston*

## Introduction: The Muslims of America

As recently as 1960, it would have been difficult to engender a lengthy discussion about Muslims in America. But in the decade that followed, Islam gained an increasingly visible profile through such figures as Cassius Clay (Muhammad Ali) and Malcolm X. By the end of 1973, when an Arab oil embargo (resulting from the latest Arab-Israeli conflict) was imposed against Western powers, all Americans had become aware that a new kind of power was abroad in the world.

It is significant that all three of the above-mentioned examples were highly negative in their impact. For all his boxing skill, Cassius Clay was considered pompous and conceited; Malcolm X was described as an insurrectionist rebel; and the oil embargo created a tidal wave of ill-will towards Middle Eastern people in general. An image was implanted in American minds that has never been eradicated. And while the purveyors of this image—the media—have not been entirely wrong in their presentation of Islam and Muslim peoples, much has been happening of which the majority of the American public has been unaware. This essay is concerned with this behind-the-scenes history.

## Ethnic Muslims, African American Islam, and Converts

The first distinction to be made with regard to the Muslims of America is between what may be called *ethnic Muslims*, *African American Muslims*, and *converts* to Islam. Ethnic Muslims, who comprise about 57 percent of the total Muslim population in America, are those who themselves or whose ancestors came from Islamic nations.

Yvonne Haddad and Adair Lummis outline five separate "waves" of Muslim immigration starting in the last quarter of the nineteenth century and continuing to the present time.[1] The adherents of the Islamic faith who came in the first three waves (all prior to World War II) tended to blend into the American melting pot. They were basically indistinguishable in lifestyle from the Irish, Italians, Scandinavians, and others who came to seek a new life in the New World. Many of these persons have been "Muslims" only in the cultural sense of the term. For instance, to be from Saudi Arabia means more or less automatically that one is an adherent of the Islamic faith. The same is true for someone from Turkey, Iran, Iraq, Syria, Libya, Tunisia, Morocco, Algeria, Pakistan, Afghanistan, and the Gulf States. More often than not it is also true of someone from Egypt, Lebanon, Indonesia, Malaysia, and other North African countries.

To be *culturally* Muslim means that one participates in the Islamic rituals of whatever country one is a resident of. The pressure of society to conform almost always outweighs any desire to deviate from the norm. In such circumstances, one is not a Muslim by choice, but rather by custom and habit. Immigration to a country such as the United States frees one from such pressure and allows one to choose to remain Muslim, change to a different religion, or not be religious at all. The choice that one makes depends to a great extent on the number of Muslims surrounding the individual in his or her new environment, the consistency and regularity of contacts with such peers, and the attitude of non-Muslims with which the individual comes in contact.

This last aspect is particularly important, for a number of previously "nominal" Muslims have been radicalized by negative contacts with outsiders. When an American makes a prejudicial or misinformed remark about Islam in the hearing of a Muslim, the potential exists for that person to become vitally *Muslim* in a way that he or she never was before. This is obviously a dynamic that Christian witnesses must try to avoid whenever possible.

A second group of Muslims in America adhere to what is known as African American Islam, a phenomenon that for many years was classified under the rubric of "sociology" rather than "religious studies." The movement began in the early 1930s in Depression-wracked Detroit, Michigan, where hundreds of young African American males had been idled by factory layoffs.

In the midst of an atmosphere of despair and frustration, a street vendor named Wallace Fard began to preach a startling message that gained an immediate following: African Americans needed to cast off the shackles of Christianity—the slavemasters' religion—and join themselves to the original religion of African blacks: Islam. Fard preached a message of disciplined and ethical living allegedly based on the teachings of the Qur'an. A fellowship was formed leading to the establishment of "The Lost-Found Nation of Islam," complete with secret rituals and a temple structure.

When Fard disappeared in 1933 under mysterious circumstances, his chief lieutenant Elijah Muhammad stepped into the position of leadership. Accusations concerning Fard's disappearance forced Muhammad to flee to Chicago, which he made the headquarters of the movement. Over the next four decades, the Nation became increasingly a Black activist group, devising doctrines about the origin of the "white devils" and the need for African Americans to assume their rightful status as the supreme race within humankind, all couched in terms said to be Islamic in origin.

During this era, the entire movement was denounced by all Muslim nations as having nothing to do with true Islam. This viewpoint was driven home early in the 1960s by the defection of Malcolm X, and his subsequent assassination served only to exacerbate the gap between Black and ethnic Islam. Upon Elijah Muhammad's death in 1975, however, the Black Muslim movement received new leadership and a new direction. Under Warith Din Muhammad, the overwhelming majority of the Nation's members abandoned their political rhetoric and chose to identify with Sunni Islam. In the 1980s, they became members of the Islamic Society of North America, an umbrella organization providing leadership and guidance to a majority of America's Muslims.

In 1977, Minister Louis Farrakhan publicly announced his dissatisfaction with the new direction that African American Islam was taking and called for a return to the original vision of Elijah Muhammad. Farrakhan's official following has never been more than several thousand persons (compared to over a million adherents of Warith Din Muhammad's loosely organized ministry), but his flamboyant style and vitriolic rhetoric have earned him the greater proportion of media coverage. Consequently, the majority of Americans have mistakenly identified African American Islam with Farrakhan, when in actuality his organization contains an almost negligible number of adherents.

The third division of Muslim Americans—Anglo converts to Islam—are as yet a small group, but they are being accorded increasing visibility among both Muslims and non-Muslims. Conversions from among White Americans and Western Europeans have been recorded since the late 1800s; most sources cite Alexander Russell Webb (1846–1916) as the first American convert. Webb was certainly the first of any public stature, having been an ambassador from the United States to the Philippines for a time. Throughout the early twentieth century, sporadic reports appeared concerning others who made similar decisions.

Many of these conversions were the result of the intentional missionary activity of the Ahmadiyya, an Islamic sect which originated in India and was established in the United States in the 1920s. Others came about through intermarriage and through experiences of military personnel stationed in Islamic countries.

It was not until the 1960s that winning non-Muslims to Islam became an objective of the Muslim mainstream. The establishment of the Muslim Student Association in 1963 as a "para-mosque" campus organization[2] similar to Campus Crusade for Christ was significant, as was the conversion of New York resident Maryam Jameelah (née Margaret Marcus). Jameelah has been a prolific writer, focusing on the alleged superiority of Islam to both Christianity and Judaism.

In the 1970s the decision of the musician Cat Stevens to become a Muslim aroused a great deal of comment; Stevens now goes by the name of Yusuf Islam and has recently been involved in producing music for Muslim youth. Islamic publishing agencies appeared which produced materials such as the Islamic Circle of North America's *Manual of Da'wah*, a monograph on how to win Americans to Islam. And in the 1990s, testimonials such as Jeffrey Lang's *Struggling to Surrender* and Carol Anway's *Daughters of Another Path* went a long way toward erasing the taint of "strangeness" associated with the idea of a Westerner converting to the religion of Islam.

### Defensive-Pacifist versus Offensive-Activist Muslims

A second distinction with regard to the Muslims of America can be made between the adherents of Islam who are "on the defensive," so to speak, and those who "take the offensive." *Defensive-pacifist Muslims* are mainly ethnic Muslims who have assumed a "melting pot" mentality, adopting the culture of their new land as quickly as possible. Nearly all Muslim refugees who came to America during the last quarter of the nineteenth century and the first half of the twentieth assumed such a mentality. This is not to say that they abandoned their Islamicity—most did not. But neither did they seek to convert non-Muslims to their faith. They were—and their descendents are still—quiescent with regard to their religious beliefs and practices. And unlike other immigrants, Muslims did not tend to clump together in enclaves such as "the Italian quarter" or "Chinatown."[3] They scattered themselves, and in dress, language, and other cultural aspects became assimilated to their surroundings. Their desire was (and is) to "fit in" and be accepted by other Americans.

From the perspective of the typical American, of course, this acceptance of the cultural and religious pluralism that distinguishes the United States from most other nations is commendable. To live undisturbed, and let others live undisturbed, is the essence of American liberty. But from the standpoint of classical Islamic theology, such an attitude is technically unacceptable. Already during the lifetime of Muhammad, Muslims divided the entire world into two categories. One they called *dar al-Islam*, or "the abode of Islam." Every geographical location where the *shari'a* (Islamic law) is in force is included in this category. It is not necessary that Muslims form a majority in dar al-Islam—although such is the eventual intention. Muslims need only to be in control and enforce their law as the law of the land.

*Dar al-harb*—the "abode of war"—is the second category, applied to every location where Islamic law does not reign supreme. Such places would include Hindu, Buddhist, Christian, Shintoist, and "pagan" (animistic) lands, as well as secular democracies. The goal of Muslims is to eventually make all of dar al-harb into dar al-Islam.

Problematic from the standpoint of the defensive-pacifist Muslim population in America is the fact that Islamic law forbids any long-term residence of a Muslim in dar al-harb. Muslims are to reside in dar al-Islam, where they are subject to the shari'a and where the sociological pressure of one's environment aids in living a Muslim lifestyle. But the majority of those who immigrated to America from Islamic countries came for economic, political, or theological reasons and have given little or no thought to these facts. Nor have their descendents, even though they, too, are technically living in disobedience to Muslim law.

Shari'a does, however, allow for three exceptions to this general rule. A Muslim may live *temporarily* in dar al-harb if he (or she) is engaged in business transactions, in political representation, or in missionary work. The latter category is of increasing significance for the Muslims of America. *Offensive-activist Muslims* often recruit from among defensive-pacifists by appealing to the fact that in order to be in conformity to shari'a, they need to adopt the identity of missionaries. Only then can their continued residence in the American dar al-harb be justified. By taking part in *da'wah* (missionary) activities regularly or even occasionally, the requirements of the law are satisfied.

Offensive-activist Muslims are carrying out what evangelical Christians would consider true missionary activity. Chief among this group are students who have come from Muslim countries to study at American universities. Students are by nature activistic, and they have the liberty to be critical of and seek changes within their host culture for the simple reason that they have no plans to abide permanently or to assimilate into that culture. Consequently one of the earliest activist organizations was the Muslim Student Association (MSA), founded in 1963 at the University of Illinois at Champaign-Urbana.

Student involvement in local mosques has been motivational for some defensive-pacifists who are permanent residents of the United States. Many of these persons, along with students who decided to remain in America, banded together to form the Muslim Communities Association (MCA) as an organization designed to meet the needs of Muslims who were not students but who were not content simply to be absorbed into the American melting pot. In the early 1980s, the MSA and MCA were combined under an umbrella organization called the Islamic Society of North America (ISNA), today the most organized and influential of the activist agencies in America.

Among the many sub-divisions of ISNA is the Islamic Training Center, the purpose of which is to train men and women for *da'wah*, the Arabic word for missionary activity. Other organizations have developed programs for accomplishing the same task, such as the Islamic Circle of North America, the Islamic Information Center of America, and the International Institute of Islamic Thought.

Publishing agencies such as the Islamic Book Agency, Kazi Publications, and the International Books and Tapes Service produce materials for Muslims to use in their missionary outreach. Magazines such as *Islamic Horizons* and *al-Jumuah* keep the general Muslim populace informed regarding advances being made by Islam in North America and around the world. Youth organizations such as the World Association of Muslim Youth (WAMY), prison ministries, and relief and development agencies have provided additional avenues for activists to exert their influence.

What forms do da'wah activities take? As of yet, few Muslims are involved in anything as direct as "door to door evangelism." Most efforts are directed toward prison ministries (particularly among African Americans), literature production and distribution, and formal dialogues and debates with the adherents of other religions—mainly Christians.

One of the chief models for the latter method of outreach has been Ahmed Deedat, a resident of South Africa who founded The Islamic Propagation Centre as a defense against the evangelistic efforts of Christian missionaries. Deedat's booklets (such as "Is the Bible the Word of God?" and "Crucifixion or Cruci-fiction?") and videotapes (highlighting debates between himself and Christian apologists such as Josh McDowell) have become inspirational for an entire generation of Muslim activists. Another influential personality has been Maryam Jameelah, author of several vehemently anti-Christian books and booklets. Increasingly popular in the United States are such personages as Jeffrey Lang, a mathematics professor at the University of Kansas who converted to Islam in the late 1980s and whose books have become famous for their advocacy of Islam for all North Americans.[4]

Islamic activists are not to be trifled with. More than one Christian has made the mistake of not taking them seriously enough, and as a consequence has suffered loss of face in front of others or even a serious crisis of faith within their own lives. Many of these Muslims have mastered problematic portions of the Bible with which Christians are generally unfamiliar and are able to use these passages with devastating effectiveness.

This is not to say that Christians should be intimidated by Muslim activists, but they should definitely be better prepared. They should be able to explain the Bible passages used by Muslims in attempts to prove the Bible unreliable. They should be familiar with the booklets and general arguments of Ahmed Deedat, Maryam Jameelah, and Jeffrey Lang. They should be able to answer these arguments in some coherent fashion, understanding all the while that such answers will not ultimately win a Muslim to Christ but may at least earn enough respect so that the gospel of Christ may be communicated and received. It is toward this end that the Christian activist should direct his or her efforts.

## Conversion to Islam

Who converts to Islam in the West? A number of studies conducted in the past several years have made it possible to present a general profile of the typical convert.

1. *Men and women in equal numbers.* Existing statistics for conversion to Christianity indicate that approximately twice the number

of females as males are attracted to evangelical versions of the faith.[5] But with respect to Islam, the male/female ratio is an even fifty-fifty. Islam has thus never acquired the reputation of being a religion for "women and children," but instead has an air of masculinity attracting both genders.

2.  *Older converts.* The average age of the convert to Christianity is sixteen years. This has been the case since earlier studies conducted in the late 1800s, and it will continue to be so for the foreseeable future. Converts to Islam, however, are on average in their late 20s or early 30s. Their religious pilgrimage has followed a distinctive pattern, starting with a deliberate rejection of the religion of their upbringing or surrounding environment (usually Christianity or Judaism) at about the age of sixteen or so, followed by a period of moratorium with regard to a solid religious commitment. The subjects experiment with a variety of religious alternatives, usually Eastern in orientation (i.e., Hinduism, Buddhism, the New Age, etc.). Eventually they settle for a "middle path;" a religious alternative halfway between the religion of their upbringing and the religions of the Far East. Islam is distinct from both Christianity and Judaism, and yet has a sense of "familiarity" about it, unlike Hinduism or Buddhism.[6]

3.  *Alternative motivations.* Those who choose Islam do so for a number of specific reasons. First, Islam is considered to be **simpler** than Christianity in particular. It is simpler both in terms of what one must do to become a Muslim (pronounce the *shahada*—the Muslim creed—before witnesses; nothing more), and simpler in the sense of including a far smaller number of denominations or factions. Choosing between the enormous number of Christian denominations is a daunting task. While Islam also has its divisions, they are far fewer in number and largely unknown in Western societies.

Second, Islam appears to be more **rational** in its approach to spirituality than does Christianity. Christians speak of God as "three in one" and of Jesus as "100 percent God and 100 percent human," concepts almost impossible to grasp. Teachings regarding the new birth, the miracles of Jesus and his disciples, and other such matters are also included in this category. Islam, on the other hand, denies the Trinity, the incarnation, a "new birth," and other such ideas. It presents itself as strictly black and white, the "thinking man's religion."

Third, Muslims are much more **"this-worldly"** in their orientation toward life than are Christians, who are considered to be too "other worldly." Islam offers a "package deal" consisting of political, economic, judicial, ethical, and religious components, all geared toward enabling one to live a fulfilling life in the here and now. Christianity is said to demand that its followers concentrate on the world to come, preparing to live a life "in heaven," not on earth, while Islam equips a person for both, and is therefore a superior religious alternative.

Fourth, Muslims are said to have dealt with issues of **race and ethnicity** better than any other religious followers in the world. The ritual known as the Hajj, in which a Muslim makes a pilgrimage to the city of Mecca, is held up as a showcase of Islamic unity. In the great square that contains the Ka'ba (the black-draped, cube-shaped building which is the religion's holiest shrine), men and women of every race, ethnic group, and social class meet, worshipping side-by-side. Muslims are fond of pointing out that in the "Christian" West, the most segregated hour of the week is 11:00 on Sunday mornings.

Fifth, Islam is the ultimate **"do-it-yourself" religion**, a fact which appeals strongly to Western individuality. One is not required to attend a mosque to worship; the prayers may be prayed at home, in one's office, or in one's classroom. There is little—if any—accountability to a human figure; one is answerable directly to God alone. There are no priests and no mediators between individuals and Allah. Consequently the religion is much more "open" and much more easily adapted to an individual's lifestyle than, say, Christianity, which requires individual accountability to a priest or pastor and to an institutional structure.

Despite these attractive elements, decisions to adopt Islam are still rare. But perhaps the only thing currently preventing the conversion of significant numbers is the highly negative stereotype of Muslims held by nearly all Westerners. People do not convert to a religious system held in low esteem by friends, relatives, and peers, and the view of Islam as a medieval, backward, chauvinistic, terrorist-spawning faith does not lend itself to general acceptance. Only those who are unconcerned about peer opinion or who are strongly opposed to their sociocultural environments are able to examine the Muslim faith closely and discover the motivational factors listed above. Until this stereotype is altered or abandoned, conversion to Islam will consist of only a trickle of persons.

This is not to say that a momentum will not eventually develop that could produce a much larger influx of Westerners into the faith. An increasing number of Muslim organizations are working to transform the negative image into a positive one, and it may well be that over time they will succeed in their mission.[7]

## The Future of Islam in America: Issues Facing Muslims

For the time being, the number of Muslims in America will grow at a relatively slow rate. There will not be a massive influx of immigrants from Muslim countries, for two reasons. First, the number of persons permitted to immigrate to the United States is somewhat fixed, and while this figure may be characterized as generous, it is not, relatively speaking, very large. Second, the vast majority of the world's Muslims are either so poor that immigration is not possible, or so wealthy that immigration is not desirable.

Nor will there be a significant turning to Islam on the part of African Americans, again for two reasons. First, the rhetoric of Louis Farrakhan's Nation of Islam is racially oriented as opposed to religiously oriented, and as such it appeals mainly to African Americans who still house strong feelings of disenfranchisement and ostracism. Many Blacks, however, have realized that while there is still a long way to go to attain true equality between the races, enormous gains have been made since the 1960s. State and federally-mandated affirmative action programs, for instance, have reduced the levels of frustration that existed previously, with the result that there is no longer a felt need for an enclave such as Elijah Muhammad's movement once was.

Second, African American Christianity remains a strongly viable entity which satisfies the religious needs and aspirations of most Black women and a goodly number of Black men. To put it simply, the exuberant, emotion-filled worship services and community-oriented social disposition of Black churches are far more contextualized to the African American psyche than is the formal atmosphere of mosques. For most, conversion from a vibrant Christian fellowship to a staid and formal Islamic orthodoxy is unthinkable.

It is also doubtful that Muslims will be able to produce a significant number of lasting conversions among Anglo-Saxons. The stereotype that the American media has implanted serves to hinder interest in Islam as an alternative faith system. In addition, there is a decided question as to what a person is asked to convert *to* when committing himself to Islam. This issue will be examined below in depth.

The adherents of Islam are faced with the challenge of "contextualization in reverse." While Christians wrestle with the need to adapt their message, theology, and religious institutions in order to communicate adequately with various people-groups, Muslims are faced with the same task. How can the religion of Islam be made palatable to Americans—in particular, to Americans with a *Christian* background?

Currently, only a few Muslims are dealing with the question, since it is the conviction of most that Islam represents an inflexible standard to which others should adapt themselves. Islam does not change to become communicable to people, but rather it is people who are to change in order to be able to understand, appreciate, and ultimately convert to Islam.[8] But Islam is not Western—it is Semitic (i.e., Middle Eastern). And the Middle East is not regarded by Westerners as being comprised of superior civilizations; on the contrary, it is considered by most to be somewhat backward. It is an established sociological fact that the populations of civilizations which consider themselves superior do not "step down," as it were, to the customs or religious beliefs of "inferior" cultures. While Muslims may well consider their civilization to be superior to anything the West has to offer, they have a huge task ahead of them convincing Westerners that this is the case.

It is, of course, understandable that a religion which considers itself to be the ultimate expression of God's revelation to humankind would be reluctant to alter itself in any way. While many Muslims argue that Islam has already been changed from its original form—making further transformation quite acceptable and even necessary—others argue that Islam is already too compromised by adaptations made in the past. Islamic fundamentalists would prefer to slough off the accretions of the centuries and return the religion to the purity of the original Muslim community.

Thus Muslims are divided, and those who wish to contextualize the religion for Westerners are severely castigated by those who seek to return Islam to its roots. In turn, fundamentalists are criticized for advocating an Islam which to modern Westerners appears medieval and archaic. As long as this situation continues—and there is no sign that a resolution is anywhere in the offing—communication of the "gospel of Islam" will be hampered, and few conversions will occur.

A second issue that contemporary Muslims face is that of determining precisely what "conversion to Islam" means. Evangelical Christians, for instance, speak of a "new birth" as the hallmark of the conversion experience. Contained within this event is the rebirth of the human spirit, a specific part of one's person (see John 3:6–7). Other effects include the opening of the mind to communication from and understanding of God and his revelation of Himself (1 Corinthians 2:14ff); a "re-programmed" and "re-sensitized" conscience with a new perspective on the concept of "sin" (Galatians 5:16–21); an indwelling of God through his Holy Spirit, accompanied by new or changed abilities (Romans 12, 1 Corinthians 12); a new set of moral and ethical capabilities (Galatians 5:22–23); a deep and abiding sense of "peace," distinguishable from earthly equivalents (John 14:27); and an inner awareness and confidence that one is indeed a newly adopted child of God (Romans 8:16) and a possessor of eternal life (John 10:27–30).

Conversion to Islam results in none of these things; indeed, it is difficult to hold that conversion to the Muslim faith involves anything other than the jettisoning of allegiance to one set of religious beliefs and practices and the adoption of a new set. The Qur'an speaks of no "new birth," no inner awareness of God's presence, no spiritual indwelling or empowerment for holy living, and no sense of assurance of eternal life in the presence of God.

Muslims would hasten to assure new or potential converts that there *are* advantages to conversion, such as belonging to a worldwide fellowship unified doctrinally by the Shahada and ritually by the daily prayers, the giving of alms, the keeping of the Ramadan fast, and the making of pilgrimage to Mecca. But all of these practices are essentially external and institutional, as opposed to the internal and personal changes effected in Christians by their faith.

An important question is: if conversion to Islam is made on the basis of an external and institutional decision, will the basis for such a decision be sufficient to keep converts "in the fold?" Are there enough "benefits" to hold their allegiance, even when nothing analogous to a "new birth" occurs? If not, then it can be expected that a convert's sojourn in Islam might be short-lived, lasting only until such time as another religious alternative—evincing a greater number of "benefits"—is encountered.

Muslims may increase their fervency, heighten their involvement in American society, sharpen their "marketing" skills, and improve their public relations image, but they cannot create an inner spiritual dimension *ex nihilo*. It is for this reason that they will ultimately fail.

## The Future of Islam in America: Issues Facing the Church

While conversion to Islam is ultimately meaningless, this does not mean that Muslims will not succeed in convincing some persons to convert. Indeed, not only will they continue to win people to Islam, but they will most likely become increasingly adept in their proselytization. Unless the Church at large takes steps to deal with two fundamental issues, defections will continue, and may conceivably increase.

The first issue is one of theology. In recent years, Christians of all kinds have changed their view of the nature of the Bible, and as a consequence have altered their convictions regarding many of the subjects about which the Bible speaks. Freed from a view of the Bible as the sole source of revelation from God to humankind about Himself and his activity in human history, men and women alike have adopted alternative views of God and issues pertaining to salvation.

God, for instance, is presently seen as consisting entirely of "love" and "justice" to the exclusion of his other biblically revealed attributes. The conclusion drawn is that He is *so* loving and *so* just that He could never condemn and punish the billions of persons—including Muslims—who "through no fault of their own" have been born into non-Christian religious systems and have died without knowledge of the good news of Jesus Christ.

The "softness" of such a view leads inevitably to a weakening of the Bible's clear message that men and women without Christ are lost in sin, are unrighteous before God, and will be eternally punished in a "lake of fire." Biblical faith is no longer seen as the sole avenue through which a person may attain righteousness. Some teach that God accepts the devout adherents of a variety of religious paths—including Islam—while others are not so bold but still hold that God's love and justice will make a way for many outside the Christian faith to be saved. Precisely how this will occur is not specified; an appeal is simply made to God's love and justice.

The above is one of the greatest—if not the greatest—of the issues facing the Church in the coming decades. *Exclusivism*—the conviction that only those who have deliberately acknowledged Jesus as Lord and been born again of the Holy Spirit will be considered righteous in the sight of God—has become a "politically incorrect" concept, even among Christians who consider themselves "conservative." *Inclusivism*—the idea that there are many paths to righteousness before God, only one of which is the Christian path—has become the vogue at the present time.

As implied previously, this is a double-edged issue. First and foremost, the Church must come to terms with the nature of the Bible. If it is maintained to be the only inerrant, verbally-inspired revelation of God to humans, then the issue is fairly easily resolved, for the Bible is clear regarding the exclusivity of the Christian faith. Jesus declared, "I am the Way, the Truth, and the Life; no one comes to the Father except through me" (John 14:6). The Apostle Peter proclaimed that "salvation is found in no one else, for there is no other name under heaven given to men by which we must be saved" (Acts 4:12).

The Apostle John stated that "no one who denies the Son has the Father" (1 John 2:23). And the Apostle Paul considered *all* competing religious constructs—both in Old Testament and New Testament times—to be at best "foolishness" and at worst "the doctrines of demons" (Acts 14:15; Romans 1:21–23; 1 Corinthians 10:20; 1 Timothy 4:1).

Islam falls under all of these categories because of the sub-biblical position it assigns to Jesus. Muslims—even the most devout—are not righteous before God, because they deny that Jesus is a member of the Godhead, is the incarnation of God in human flesh, and atoned for the sins of humankind through his crucifixion. The adherents of Islam are lost and will suffer eternal punishment unless they are reached with the Christian gospel, turn from Islam, and acknowledge Jesus as their Lord.

Consequently, the members of the Church must:

• return to and teach convincingly the inerrancy of the Christian Scriptures and the authority that these Scriptures have over the believer's life;

• return to the exclusivist teachings of the Bible with regard to the non-Christian religions;

• see each Muslim as a lost human being facing eternal punishment;

• communicate to all that salvation is only attained through acknowledgment that Jesus is Lord of one's life.

For those Christians who have maintained their commitment to the Bible's exclusivistic teachings, there is another issue to be faced. It has been shown previously that biblical Christianity is, in principle, superior in every way to the Islamic faith. There is no alleged "benefit" in Islam that does not exist in a more complete sense in Christianity, and there are many benefits conferred by Christianity's new birth that have no equivalents in Islam.

But these facts are not apparent in the lives of most who call themselves Christians today. Measured from the standpoint of a moral and ethical lifestyle, it often appears that it is not Christians, but rather Muslims, who have "the edge." The majority of Christians do not meet certain "standards of righteousness" held up by Muslims (as well as others) and do not exhibit the "benefits" listed above. Thus the motivation for a Muslim to consider Christianity as an alternative faith system is either extremely low or non-existent.

Christians exhibit a shocking ignorance of the teachings of their Scriptures. Few memorize individual verses or passages, much less the entire New Testament, whereas many Muslims memorize the entire Qur'an. Christians pray perhaps only once per day (during their "quiet time"—assuming, of course, that a daily devotional time is a part of their lifestyle), while Muslims around the world pray the five daily prayers. Few Christians fast for any length of time, while Muslims fast for a full month each year. Few Christians pursue notably moral lifestyles, while Muslims live strict lives.

When a Muslim views a Christian, he sees a person who wears his Christianity as a casual garment, useful for show on certain occasions but tossed aside when not needed. He sees Christians as captives of a materialistic culture that has co-opted Christianity by marketing Christian music, books, clothing, and other assorted paraphernalia. He sees Christians involved in promiscuous, extra-marital sexual relations, homosexual relations, and divorce rates indistinguishable from those of secular society. He sees Christians as soft, uncommitted, and quite at home with the surrounding culture.

Not all Christians are this way, of course. But truly devoted ones are few and scattered, and Muslims in general have little contact with them. This must change, and drastically so. The members of the Church must:

• place increased emphasis upon and accountability concerning Bible study, Scripture memory, prayer at regular intervals, fasting, and other such spiritual disciplines;

• heed the Bible's commands regarding withdrawal from or excommunication of persons who claim to be Christians but who do not live in accordance with biblical precepts. They should simply not associate themselves with those who willfully pursue lifestyles of adultery, fornication, gluttony, laziness, gambling, deceitfulness, greed, false teaching, and so forth;

• devise creative means of arranging contacts between Muslims and men and women who live truly biblical lifestyles. In other words, send the "best" to the front lines, so that the stereotype of Christians held by Muslims may be transformed. This suggestion would involve sending such Christians to Muslim conferences, having them visit mosques and Islamic Centers, involving them in university ministries with outreach to Muslim students, and the like.

At present, however, Christians still have a window of opportunity to forestall a Muslim advance. This goal will not be attained by emphasizing the stereotypical images of Muslims, most of which are demonstrably false and degrading. Nor can it be reached by creating new stereotypes, which will likely turn out to be equally misleading. Rather, Christians must become "comparative religionists" in their approach to Islam. They must strive to understand both the religion and its adherents in enough depth to be able to point out characteristics which, seen from a humanistic point of view, may be considered admirable, and those which, from the standpoint of biblical theology, must be completely rejected. Indeed, perhaps the term "comparative religionist" should be abandoned for a title such as "contrastive religionist." For from the standpoint of the gospel, it is the *contrasts* between the competing faith systems that are far more important than any alleged similarities.

Christians must position themselves as chess pieces, participants in the greatest match of all time. They will need to position carefully their kings, queens, bishops, knights, and others, but at the same time, the importance of the pawns must not be underestimated. Each piece has its own place and its own moves, and a good player makes the most of each piece. So it must be with the Church, for while the ultimate outcome of the match has already been decided, Christians are yet deeply in the midst of the game, and they must be careful to guard their own pieces while moving to defeat their opponent.

## Endnotes

[1]   Yvonne Haddad is undoubtedly the foremost researcher on Islam in America. Her books includes *The Muslims of America* (Oxford University Press, 1991); *Islamic Values in the United States* (with Adair Lummis) (Oxford University Press, 1987); *Muslim Communities in North America* (with Jane Smith) (SUNY Press, 1994); and *Mission to America* (with Jane Smith) (University Press of Florida, 1993).

[2]   A "para-mosque organization" is the Islamic equivalent of a "parachurch" organization; in other words, an agency which has grown up parallel with a mosque structure and which performs a specialized religious function, but which is not usually directly connected with a mosque.

[3]   There are some exceptions to this general observation. Muslims did indeed "clump" together in places like Dearborn, Michigan, and in certain parts of Southern California.

[4]   Lang is the author of *Struggling to Surrender* (Beltsville, MD: Amana Publications, 1994) and *Even Angels Ask* (Beltsville, MD: Amana Publications, 1997).

[5]   See, for instance, Leon Podles, *The Church Impotent* (Dallas, TX: Spence Publishing Co., 1999).

[6]   See Larry Poston, *Islamic Da'Wah in the West: Muslim Missionary Activity and the Dynamics of Conversion to Islam* (New York: Oxford University Press, 1992).

[7]   One such organization is CAIR, the Council on American-Islamic Relations.

[8]   This situation is much like that of Old Testament Israel. During this phase of God's redemption plan, men and women were required to express faith in God by becoming Jews in order to be accounted righteous.

# CHAPTER 2

# Islam's Agenda in North America: Patterns of Islamization

*A. AbDat-Isa*

## Introduction

Islam has an agenda not only for North America, but also for the world at large. This agenda contains hopes for seeing the entire world submit to the religion of Islam. The Muslim agenda for North America is to see it become a part of the historical pattern of world Islamization that has been going on since the beginning of their religion. They would like Islam to spread and take control of North America in the same way it has taken over other countries of the world.

Some of the things Muslims do to try to spread Islam in America are intentional, thought-out actions and strategies that they have spent much time and effort developing and implementing.

However, there are other things Muslims do that they do not think about at all. These matters either flow naturally out of aspects inherent in Islam, or they are acts Muslims have engaged in for centuries, resulting in the growth of Islam around the world. These items are a part of their "subconscious" agenda, not any "intentional" effort to spread Islam. In this chapter, we are dealing more with these "unintentional" efforts.

As we look at the history of the Islamization of the world, we can see a number of patterns. Many of these examples are either happening or just starting to happen in North America and the Western world.

If we examine these patterns of how other countries have been Islamized, we can then strategize about how the Christian church can counter these factors. We can look at history and work to see that history does not repeat itself on the North American continent.

The discussion will begin with the phases that Islam went through in its various patterns around the world. First was the Islamization of the Middle East and North Africa. Next was the Islamization of the rest of Africa and Asia. Then we will look at how the Western world is currently being Islamized.

In conclusion we will examine another factor—how Christians have tended to respond to Islam and its advances. Then I will suggest new methods of response that may help us strategize and develop better ways to address the Muslim presence and their attempts to Islamize the world.

## Patterns in Islamization
## Phase One: The Middle East and North Africa

The Middle East and North Africa were the first parts of the world to be Islamized. However, they were also the first parts of the world to be Christianized. Most of the seven churches of the book of Revelation were located in what is now modern Turkey. The homelands of many of the most influential early Christian theologians were under Muslim control within a generation after the death of Muhammad.

A number of factors help explain why these once Christian lands so quickly became Muslim.

### Jihad

The most apparent reason the Middle East and North Africa became Muslim so quickly is war-like conquest. Conquered peoples do not usually have much choice concerning what religious practices they will outwardly observe when faced with possible death.

However, before the fall of Communism, Martin Goldsmith points out that Islam had succeeded where Communism had failed. When Communism persecuted and killed Christians, this only caused the Church to grow (Goldsmith 1983). The history of the early Church also shows that persecution and death only spurred the Church on to better health.

So war and conquest can account for why nominally Christian populations may have converted to Islam. But this cannot be the reason why virtually no Christian presence whatsoever was left in North Africa (the homeland of Saint Augustine and of Tertullian, the theologian who coined the term *trinity)* or the Saudi peninsula (which was known to have had twelve Christian tribes at the time of Muhammad). Persecution and death seem to strengthen Christianity, while Islam totally eliminated Christianity in all but a few places.

Current trends among Christian minorities in these areas show that they are dwindling year by year—some to the point of non-existence (Blincoe 1998:xiv, 183). Some of this can be attributed to emigration, but some can also be attributed to conversion to Islam. There are still forces at work in an attempt to Islamize such minorities centuries after the last conquest ended.

Therefore, I conclude that the sword may have influenced some of the conquered peoples to submit to Islam, but Christianity was not totally eliminated from the area for this reason. Other issues must be looked at to determine the true reasons why there is no Christian presence remaining in all but a few areas of the Middle East and North Africa.

## Political Appeal

While much of the Middle East and North Africa was Christian at one point, history shows that the invading Muslim armies were actually preferred over the existing oppressive political rulers who claimed to be Christian. The Muslims offered a better political climate, so the population welcomed them and saw them as rescuing people from oppression.

Thus Islam had a political appeal that put the Muslims in good standing with those who were conquered. Their rule was seen positively and the Christian rulers were seen negatively. This, of course, made Islam more acceptable than Christianity, and therefore easier to convert to.

## Financial Appeal

Not only were there political benefits, but there were also financial benefits to accepting the Muslim conquerors into Christian lands.

The promise of substantial economic benefits (i.e., a 2 percent *jizya* paid to the Muslims as opposed to a 16 percent tax paid to the Byzantines)...brought enormous numbers of people into the Islamic fold with relative ease (Poston n.d.: n.p.).

Goldsmith reports that one reason Islam was so successful in comparison to Communism was that instead of persecuting Christians, Muslims merely made them pay an extra tax if they wanted to remain Christian. Hitting them in the pocketbook was more effective than persecution and revealed what really counted to many Christians (Goldsmith 1983).

Even in modern times a financial advantage remains in certain instances for an Orthodox Christian who converts to Islam in some

Middle Eastern countries. For example, in Egypt Christians are many times very poor. To marry, a man must have enough money for a house, the wedding, and support of a family. Muslims may sometimes offer a daughter as a bride and the finances to cover these expenses to poor Christian men desiring to marry, but only on the condition that they convert to Islam first. Or Muslims may offer Christians a much needed job if they convert (Boulos 1997).

## Social Appeal

The *dhimmi* status of Christians in the Muslim dominated lands of the Middle East and North Africa not only hit Christians financially, but also socially. They were required to wear special clothes that were ill fitting, to keep their church buildings lower than mosques, and other factors showing that they were obviously of a lower social status (Goldsmith 1983).

Again using modern-day Egypt as an example, a Christian who converts to Islam may be offered a job promotion or some such other benefit that will raise their social status (Boulos 1997). A Muslim open to Christianity once told me that to become a Christian in his country meant being a second-class citizen (Abdul-Raymond 1983).

## Intellectual Appeal

Another aspect that Goldsmith believes made Islam successful in spreading so easily in the once-Christian areas is that every Muslim is an amateur theologian (1983). I personally like to describe it by saying that the average Muslim can chew you up and spit you back out again! They definitely have an ability to intellectually challenge Christian beliefs.

A Christian well versed in the Bible and Christian beliefs can be very challenged in a theological discussion with a Muslim. Christians not well grounded in their faith can be easily convinced by the Muslim intellectual arguments that Islam really does make a lot of sense after all.

I know this from personal experience. I grew up in a Christian home that emphasized Bible memory and understanding very early on. I cannot consciously remember a time when I did *not* know John 3:16. My grandfather was a pastor in a strongly fundamentalistic denomination that taught the Bible to even the youngest of Sunday school children. My father accepted Christ while in the Air Force and had been part of the Navigators after being discipled by them. My mother worked at helping us children memorize Scripture every morning at breakfast before any of us could even read, and continued this daily memorization effort well into my junior high years. On my own I had read the Bible all the way through numerous times by the time I reached my early twenties. In addition I had read a number of books relating to theology and apologetics, especially concerning Islam.

My family and church did an excellent job at teaching me the Bible. In fact, I just obtained an M.A. in Theology from the largest independent seminary in the U.S. But I can *honestly* say that with the exception of one class and a better grasp of Greek and Hebrew (which I had already studied at a secular university), I did not learn a single thing in any of my biblical studies courses that I did not already know.

So, growing up, I had a better than average education in the Bible. Or at least I thought so until I had my first major theological discussion with a Muslim and almost converted to Islam.

The intellectual arguments presented to me made so much sense that I was quite convinced in my mind to become a Muslim. However, somewhere deep inside I realized that I knew Jesus was very, *very* real to me, and I knew that to convert to Islam would be to turn my back on him. And this was something I could not bring myself to do, no matter how intellectually compelling Islam appeared to be. This relationship with Jesus was the *only* thing that prevented me from becoming a Muslim.

It took three years of reading through the Bible for me to find the answers to the intellectual arguments that had been presented to me that day. I had never been warned about the particular arguments encountered by me that day in any of my readings regarding how to respond to Muslim arguments against Christianity. It took effort and searching for me to understand why the arguments that almost convinced me to convert to Islam did not make so much sense after all.

So, imagine the reaction of the average Christian who typically is not nearly as grounded in the Bible as I was. As amateur theologians, Muslims are already equipped to convince most of the Christians of the world how much Islam makes sense.

## Moral Appeal

A final reason Goldsmith gives as to why Islam has been so successful is that the works orientation causes Muslims to live what they believe. On the other hand, the grace theology of Christianity makes it easy for Christians to be lax in living out their faith (1983). People living what they believe seem to be better able to influence the world toward believing likewise.

For instance, I once met an international student in full *hijab* who almost immediately upon meeting me said, "I used to be a Christian." When I asked her why she had become a Muslim, she replied, "I saw they were living what they believed and I wasn't. I felt it was better to be in a religion where people lived what they believed."

### Cultural Appeal

Another reason Christianity did not survive in most of the Middle East and North Africa is related to cultural issues. If we look at the North Africa of Augustine and Tertullian, Christianity was the religion of the Roman rulers, not the Berbers or Carthaginians. Christianity never became indigenized (Gilliland 1991), so when the Romans were gone there was no foundation in the culture to keep Christianity around when Islam pushed it out. It had merely been an invader/ ruling class religion that never trickled down to the masses or the heart of the culture.

But if we look at the Copts, the Armenians, and other Orthodox Christian groups in the Middle East, Christianity was indigenized (Gilliland 1991). It was integrated into the culture well enough that Islam could not easily expel it. Christianity and cultural identity became one and the same for the Armenians, who are intensely proud of their long Christian heritage; the ancient Coptic language is still used in Coptic liturgy.

So a remnant of the followers of Christ survived the Islamic invasions because Christianity had become a religion of the heart language and the core culture of the society. When the rulers changed, faith in Christ did not totally disappear as it had in the homeland of the man who first tried his hand at an understandable explanation of the Trinity—a concept that Muslims still argue about with us.

## Patterns in Islamization
## Phase Two: Africa and Asia

The Arab armies conquered just so much and then rested from their campaigns. But this did not stop the spread of Islam. It continued on into the rest of Africa and Asia. Some of the previous reasons given for the spread of Islam into the Middle East and North Africa are valid for this region as well (every Muslim an amateur theologian, Muslims tending to live what they believe, and so forth). However, new patterns of spreading Islam also developed. In this section we will look at the factors that contributed to the spread of Islam beyond the lands conquered by war.

## Business and Trade

Muslims are quick to point out that *jihad* and force were never used in spreading Islam to sub-Saharan Africa and Asia. Numerous times I have heard mention of Sufi traders who spread Islam to Malaysia and Indonesia. However, trade was a major force in spreading Islam to more areas than just Malaysia and Indonesia.

Arab traders took traditional trade routes across the Sahara into the interior of West and East Africa and used shipping routes along the coast of East Africa and South Asia. They set up trading posts in Timbuktu and other major African cities that later became centers for Islamic learning (Gilliland 1991). Business opportunities took Muslims into both Africa and Asia, and along with their trade they brought their religion.

## Intermarriage

The Arab traders did not just arrive, trade, and leave. They moved into these areas, married local women, started families, and became a part of the local society. They not only spread Islam to their customers, but also increased the Islamic presence through intermarriage and biological growth.

Even today in parts of West Africa a Muslim will sometimes marry a Christian woman expressly with the intention of either using the marriage to try to get her to convert to Islam, or of having children with her so that her children cannot be Christian, but must be Muslim. Sometimes—unless she is willing to convert to Islam—the Muslim husband will divorce her, take away her children to insure that they will be raised as Muslims, and then marry the woman he really wants to have as a wife (Kantiok 1997).

## Immigration and Migrations

Another factor making the spread of Islam into sub-Saharan Africa successful had to do with the movements of populations from one place to another. For example, in West Africa Islam succeeded in penetrating the interior, while Christian missionary work remained on the coast and never reached the interior until after the beginning of the Colonial era. On the other hand, Christianity successfully penetrated the interior of East Africa with relative ease (Gilliland 1991).

The main reason for all this was that in West Africa the migrations of people were toward the coast and away from the interior. Islam came from the north into the interior and went along with the migratory movements. Christianity was going against the flow of where people were moving. Therefore, it was never successful at getting into the interior (Gilliland 1991).

However, in East Africa, the migratory flow was toward the interior and away from the coast. Both Christianity and Islam were attempting to move in the same direction as this flow of people, so both were able to penetrate the interior (Gilliland 1991).

Movements of people also contributed to Islam reaching into other parts of the world. Most notable is the Indian Diaspora, brought about by the British moving cheap labor from India to other colonies. Large numbers of Indian Muslims ended up in Malaysia, South Africa, and various Caribbean countries. One of the best known Indian Muslims living in another homeland is Ahmed Deedat of South Africa.

### Syncretism

Although not a cause, syncretism contributed to the ease of the spread of Islam into Africa (Gilliland 1991) and Asia. Christian missionaries have tended to require purity and orthodoxy of Christian belief and practice among new converts. Muslims newly moved into an area to live and do business are not as likely to be concerned if the local folk practices merge and blend with Islam, as long as the most important aspects of Islam are adhered to. As a result, Islam is comfortable with syncretism in a way that Christianity is not. This factor enables Islam to enter a culture and meld with non-orthodox practices in a way that Christianity is not willing to do (Gilliland 1991).

Additionally, the accommodation to syncretism allows for folk practices that give people a sense of power against what they see to be a very real spirit world. When Western Christianity (influenced by rationalism) enters the scene and does not provide answers to issues such as fear of spirits, healing from curses, or even healing from certain "incurable" diseases, Islam is seen as having answers that Christianity does not have. This syncretism can give people a sense that Islam has spiritual power while Christianity does not.

### Islamic Schools

Islam influenced the entire remainder of the world in its first few centuries of existence through its interest in education. For example, Qur'an schools were started to teach Arabic and the Qur'an. In many parts of the world this was the only formal education available. Those who went through the Qur'an schools and learned to read and write Arabic were the only literate people in their societies, especially in Africa.

This tendency to start schools led to major centers of Islamic learning in parts of Africa. Some of these—along with other Islamic learning centers in the world—eventually became the world's first universities. In fact, the first universities in Europe emerged from schools in Muslim-dominated Spain.

So Muslim traders brought Islam, which in turn brought Qur'an schools. As these schools became major centers of Islamic learning, they helped spread Islam further into Africa and other parts of the world.

### Cultural Influence

Muslim Arab traders influenced the cultures of the countries into which they went. Their spreading of Islam especially influenced the local languages. For example, Hausa, Malay, and Indonesian have numerous Arabic terms. Trade along the coast of East Africa resulted in the language of Swahili being born as a trade language when Bantu and Arabic blended into a new linguistic entity. The Urdu language developed when the nouns from Arabic, Turkish, and Persian blended with the verb structure of Hindi.

When a culture is strongly influenced by Islam, it is much easier for a person in that culture to see Islam positively. Viewing Islam as a part of one's culture and as a natural part of one's heart language makes a person more likely to convert to Islam.

### Ethnic Identity

Cultural influence developed into Islam becoming an ethnic identity for some peoples. For example, in parts of West Africa, to be African is to be Muslim (Gilliland 1991). In Malaysia Malays are automatically considered to be Muslim no matter what their true beliefs may be.

Once Islam was able to establish itself within a particular ethnic group, the ethnic identity issue later hindered attempts to evangelize and bring people to Christ. To become Christian was not merely seen as leaving Islam, but as turning one's back on the whole ethnic identity and culture. To be Tiv was to be Muslim (Gilliland 1991), and to be anything but Muslim was to consider oneself no longer Tiv.

## Politics

Part of the ethnic identity may possibly have come first as a result of politics. In Africa, at times when a tribal chief became Muslim, the rest of the tribe was expected to convert along with him (Gilliland 1991). In the cases where this was not the expectation, the mere fact that the political leader was a Muslim had a big influence on whether individual tribe members decided to convert or not.

However, Muslims also see involvement in politics as a means to spread Islamic control and direct the state toward Islamization. In some countries they have become so successful at gaining political control that the non-Muslims no longer feel their own involvement in the political process will do any good. For example, a Chinese Malaysian once told me that many non-Malays do not bother to vote because everyone knows the non-Malay political candidates will not win anyway (Yung 1993). Modern-day Nigeria is another example of Muslims attempting to gain control of the political process. Until recently, when a non-Muslim won the presidential elections, Muslims were able to maintain control of the government. This was largely because they had managed to consistently vote Muslims into power and keep a Muslim president in power for a number of years earlier.

### Attempts to Establish an Islamic State

Involvement in politics is a step toward attempting to set up an Islamic nation. Nigeria is an example of a place where Muslims have used the political process to try to establish an Islamic state. However, they have not been yet been successful.

On the other hand, Malaysia has successfully instituted an Islamic state, in spite of the fact that Muslims are less than sixty percent of the population. An overwhelming majority of those in political power are Muslims, and the government has successfully declared the nation an Islamic country.

### Attempts to Implement *Shari'a*

After setting up an Islamic state, the next stage of Islamization in a country is to implement *shari'a* law. Again, Malaysia is a prime example of this. Shari'a has already been in effect for Muslims for some time. In the last several years there have been attempts also to apply shari'a to non-Muslims (Woodberry and Gilliland n.d., n.p.).

## Patterns in Islamization
## Phase Three: Europe and North America

Europe has been the next part of the world to head toward Islamization. However, many of the same patterns in Europe are also beginning to happen in North America. The Muslim presence may not loom as large, but in reality North America is only a step behind Europe in the Islamization process. Therefore, we need to look at the patterns of Islamization occurring in this region, especially in light of the patterns that have previously occurred in other parts of the world.

### Jihad

Other than the exception of occasional terrorist-related incidences, there has not been the kind of violence or force perpetrated in the name of Islam that could lead anyone to believe outright that *jihad* is being waged by Muslims on the Western world. So, on the surface, one could say that this pattern has not exhibited itself in Europe or North America.

However, the Western mind sometimes does not realize that *jihad*, popularly translated as "holy war," really has another meaning. Most Muslims will say that jihad actually means "exertion," especially in the name of Islam. So jihad can include not only war or violence, but also any form of exertion that could influence people to become Muslim. This could include writing literature, theological debates, or even a mother's efforts to bear and raise children as devout Muslims (MISG 1982).

So, using this meaning, it is quite easy to see any effort to convince Westerners to convert to Islam as jihad. Therefore, we may conclude that the pattern of jihad is very much in play in Europe and North America at this time, even though it is not in a form we would normally recognize as such.

### Political Appeal

The pattern of political appeal is most evident among African American Muslims. One of the first things I always notice when I look at a photo of the very symbol of the Civil Rights Movement—Martin Luther King, Jr.—is the group of men in the background who are obviously Muslims by their dress. Just as Islam came to the oppressed in Byzantium and offered a better political deal, it has appealed to those wanting freedoms and political power that a corrupt system has not allowed them to have in the past.

### Financial Appeal

I know from personal experience that the pattern of financial appeal is alive and well in North America. Again, if Jesus were not as real as He is to me, I could have converted to Islam over this issue.

I very clearly remember a time in my life when I had no job, no income, and no means of support other than God alone. On the one hand, my African American Muslim friends were offering me—a White person—genuine concern and numerous offers of financial help if I ever needed anything. On the other hand, I spent Easter dinner totally alone in my room eating leftovers because no one in the church invited me over, even though they knew I had no family in the area. As soon as I got a job and managed to catch up on my rent my landlord—a retired evangelical pastor—evicted me.

I am not the only one the Church has treated in such a way. I have spent the last several years interacting with women who are married to or dating Muslims. One woman I know actually did convert to Islam because her church kicked her out for dating the guy, but at the same time the Muslims accepted her and gave her a much-needed job.

### Social Appeal

Social appeal is also an existing pattern in the Western world. Muslims are definitely involved in some of the social causes that appeal to many of the Boomer and Buster generation who are disillusioned with the world. Although this is not a major force in our society, it is still a way in which Muslims can get good "PR" that makes Islam appealing to many people.

These social involvements are also sometimes a means by which Muslims try to spread Islamic viewpoints. I once heard an associate of Ahmed Deedat speak to a Muslim audience on ways to influence Americans for Islam. One of his suggestions was to get involved with social causes that Christians were also interested in as a means of establishing good contact with Christian believers in order to influence them (Bakus 1985).

### Intellectual Appeal

Especially among students, the intellectual appeal pattern is in full play. Numerous debates and other Islamic presentations are going on at universities across the country throughout the year. The centuries-old art form of debate (Stacey 1997) is still a Muslim favorite, and there has been no decrease in the percentage of Muslims who are amateur theologians. The intellectual route has been so successful that it is highly unlikely that Muslims will quit using it any time soon.

## Moral Appeal

The moral appeal of Islam can be very attractive to some people in our society who feel there has been no moral direction in their lives, or to those who feel distressed about the lack of morals in our society. I have met a number of women who have converted to Islam and as a result have felt liberated by what many Westerners see as a very restrictive moral code on women. They especially feel that covering gives them a freedom and sense of security that they never had before becoming Muslim. The modesty appeals to them once they see its benefits.

## Cultural Appeal

Again, African American Islam is the area where the cultural appeal of Islam is the most notable. For many it is a cultural identity issue, not a religious issue. Jesus is seen as the god of the Whites, Muhammad is for the African Americans. As Warith Uddin Muhammed once said, "In Christianity when you die who is at the pearly gates? Peter—a White man!" (1986).

However, if we look at the patterns of Islamization in North Africa, we see that the Church was never indigenized. I see also that Christianity is not being indigenized for the younger generations of the unchurched in this country.

The current worship patterns of most North American churches are culturally from before World War II. Few culturally relevant or appealing churches exist for the younger generation. Christianity has not been indigenized for them, even though it was for their grandparents. Due to the cultural revolution that happened in this country in the sixties, we have a totally new generation of unchurched people turned off by the cultural patterns of the traditional church service.

For example, my brother is a Baby Buster. He grew up in the church, even went on summer short-term mission trips while in high school. Since I am the one who led him to the Lord, I know that at least at one point he had an authentic relationship with God.

However, he has not been to church in years. He appears to have no interest whatsoever in spiritual things. As far as I can tell there is no difference between him and any other non-Christian his age that I might meet, with the exception that he does still have good moral standards.

At age 28 he came to visit me. I was determined to take him to church. So, I took him to a church that focuses its whole outreach on Baby Busters. The average age of the congregation is 28, the same age he was at the time. The church very strongly focuses on presenting the gospel in a way that is culturally appealing to that generation. I will always remember the comment he made when we were walking to the car after the church service: "I wouldn't mind going to church if it was like that!"

I have a very real concern that Islam will become more and more appealing to the future generations of this country. If the Church does not somehow make sure that future generations also feel that they do not mind going to church, Christianity will lose its indigeneity in this continent and set people up to accept other alternatives.

Christianity is no longer a natural part of this culture as much as it was forty years ago, and if the Church does not do something to remedy that, spiritual hunger will cause the younger generations to go after other religions to fill the void Christianity cannot fill.

### Business and Trade

More and more one can see businesses, especially if one lives in a large metropolitan area, where there are Muslim names on the signs. An increasing number of doctors from other countries are also taking up residence and setting up practices here. Europe especially has large areas where people might think they were in the Middle East since all the stores are owned by Muslims. The pattern of business and trade is definitely at work in the Western world.

### Immigration and Migrations

Many immigrants are coming to North America. The two most noticeable groups are international students and refugees. In the last few years an increasing number of refugees has entered from Muslim countries. This number has included Iranians trying to escape the turmoil of the Iranian revolution, refugees fleeing from the wars in Afghanistan, Kurds coming out of Iraq and Saddam Hussein's op-pression against them, and most recently the Kosovars. Many Mus-lims from other nations are entering this country to become perma-nent legal residents, and they will only increase the number of Mus-lims in North America.

## Intermarriage

Intermarriage between Muslim men and non-Muslim women is definitely going on in the West. I have spent the last few years interacting with a number of non-Muslim women who are married to or dating Muslims. I have had contact in some form or another with at least one hundred women romantically involved (or not so romantically involved, but who are stuck living with the guy anyway) with a Muslim man. Romance plays a big factor in the conversion of Caucasian American women to Islam. A majority of the White women who convert to Islam do so because of the influence of a boyfriend or husband.

## Syncretism

I have seen Islam's ability to deal with syncretism firsthand. A White American friend of mine has a Jewish background, but is non-practicing and very New Age in her mentality. She is fascinated with Islam. Although she has not yet converted to Islam, she says this is a religion she would not mind adhering to. She sees no contradiction between her New Age beliefs and the beliefs of Islam.

I also know a young Muslim high school girl who immigrated from the Middle East to Canada about three years ago. She is very devout in her beliefs and practice. At fifteen years of age she was telling me how she prayed because she wanted to, not because her parents made her. But at times when I e-mail her she sounds more New Age than most North Americans who have lived here all their lives. At times she even argues for New Age points of view totally contradictory to orthodox Islam.

Finally, another woman I know was very much into mysticism. Sufi Islam seemed to appeal to her in a way that orthodox evangelical Christianity never could. After much searching, she converted to Islam. She felt right at home with its mysticism that never contradicted anything else she already believed.

## Islamic Schools

Islamic schools are in abundance in Europe and North America. These are not just Qur'anic schools like the ones in Africa and Middle East, but are full-fledged Western style schools covering a full range of subjects, just as any private school would do. Since England has no separation of Church and State laws, it opened its first public/state-funded Islamic school last year (Internet 1998).

## Cultural Influence

Islam has had massive cultural influence among the African American community. But subtle cultural influences affect other parts of European and North American society. Suffering through algebra—a Muslim invention—is something almost every high school child has experienced. The Muslim invention of the zero even today affects modern technology since the zero is essential to the binary code on which computer systems are based. Universities were a Muslim invention. And if it were not for the Muslims preserving the ancient Greek and Roman sciences, we might not have the medical abilities we have today, or the ability to travel in space. Even though it is not immediately obvious, the Western world would not be culturally what it is today without the Muslim influence.

## Ethnic Identity

The ethnic identity pattern is again most prevalent among the African American Muslims. However, a not-very-well-publicized movement also tries to get Hispanics to convert to Islam, based on their Andalusian heritage when the Muslims controlled Spain. Muslims have attempted to play off of this Arab influence in the Spanish culture, and I have met a number of Hispanic converts to Islam in this country. A large number of Muslims are also present in Mexico and several other Latin American countries.

## Politics

Muslims are quite active in politics in Europe. The British Parliament has Muslim members, and there are aspirations to establish Muslim courts in certain parts of England. Muslim voters have quite a bit of political clout and have great hopes of England's political system eventually becoming Muslim (Internet 1998).

Although not yet as active in politics in North America, Muslims do have hopes for increasing their political activity. They have been running for Congress, and the U. S. armed forces now has a Muslim chaplain. I see only an increase in political activity from this time forward.

## Attempts to Establish an Islamic State or Implement *Shari'a*

These factors have not yet exhibited themselves in any noticeable way in Europe or North America, although at least one European country has declared Islam its second official religion after Catholicism. However, since all the other patterns are definitely in play, it would not surprise me to see a European country someday declare itself Muslim. At the least, the Muslims of England are hoping it will happen there soon.

## Historical Patterns of Christian Response

The first historical encounters between Muslims and Christians show that Christians did not fully understand Islam. The Christian attitude was that Islam was just a Christian cult. Therefore they treated the Muslims the same way they did any other cult—intellectual attack, apologetics, polemics (Gilliland 1990).

From the beginning the stage was set for Christians to attack Muslims, tell them where they were wrong, and develop negative attitudes toward them. Is it any wonder the Muslims began to use polemics, debates, and attack in return? They were only doing what they had learned to do so well from the Christian community.

The picture didn't improve much over the next several centuries. And then it worsened. Instead of mere verbal attacks, Christians became physical and spent the next several centuries conducting Crusader wars in an attempt to kill a large number of Muslims and curb Muslim control.

Even after the Crusades were over, it was still a long time before Christians started to realize that Muslims were human beings whom God loved and wanted to redeem. Centuries passed before some Christians quit treating Muslims like an enemy who needed to be attacked (Gilliland 1990).

Although the Crusades have been over for centuries, Muslims have not forgotten them. Many Christians trying to minister to Muslims will say that the Crusades were wrong, but their attitudes and actions toward Muslims seem to indicate that they still have a "Crusader mentality" against them. Their method of trying to bring Muslims to Christ is to attack, tear down, and attempt to destroy whatever they can in the Muslim belief system as a means to convince Muslims to convert to Christianity.

Even though these Christians mean well, and may truly love Muslims and want to see them come to Christ, they are still communicating a message that comes across negatively. Muslims see the negative style of the message and therefore see the message itself as negative. They do not see it as a positive, hopeful message communicated in love.

## Suggested New Patterns of Christian Response

The first way Christians should respond to Muslims is in Christ-like love. Of all the cases that I personally have studied where Muslims became Christians, quite a number saw the love in Christianity that did not exist in Islam. In essence, the Christians they saw were living out what they believed and demonstrating the message of love so central to the gospel.

We must incarnationally demonstrate that God is love by doing as I Corinthians 13 exhorts. We must remember that love is not rude, self-seeking, easily angered, and does not keep a record of wrongs (vs. 5). Love always protects (vs. 7). Are our actions toward Muslims protective of them instead of being in attack mode? We are to "follow the way of love" (1 Cor. 14:la) in our dealings with Muslims. We are exhorted to let all peoples know we are his disciples by our love.

Coming across to Muslims in attack mode does not seem to fit the description of love in I Corinthians 13. One of the best instructors I ever had in teaching interaction with Muslims once said, "If you win an argument with an Arab, you've lost" (Lawlor 1983). According to communications theory we must seek to understand and know the other person for the best and most effective communication (Kraft 1991). But we cannot understand if we are always seeking to attack.

Jesus did not defend himself. He never answered the Sanhedrin when they attacked him before Pilate. He spoke to Pilate, whom he amazed because he refused to get drawn into the attack mode. If Jesus did not think he needed to defend himself, shouldn't we follow his example?

# CHAPTER 3

# Islam and the African American Community

*Dr. Carl Ellis*

To understand the spread of Islam in the African American community, we need to go back about 150–200 years. The doctrines of groups like the Nation of Islam have often been looked at in a vacuum. But when seen in historical context, these doctrines begin to make sense.

First, let's look at some current statistics. In Canada, about two-thirds of Muslims are overseas born while one-third are Canadian born. In the U.S., the overseas born/American born ratio is about 56 to 44 percent. The greater proportion of native-born Muslims in the United States is mostly due to the response of the African Americans. Without African American Muslims, the demographics of U.S. Muslims would likely be about the same as in Canada.

When we look at the ethnic diversity of the U. S. Islamic community, the largest group is African American—42 percent. South Asians comprise the next largest section—24 percent. Arabs number about 12 percent and after them, the Africans—6.2 percent, Iranians—3.6 percent, Turks—2.4 percent, Southeast Asians—2.0 percent, Whites—1.6 percent, and other—5.6 percent (*USA Today* 1994).

A newer study by the Council on American-Islamic Relations, showing their own view of ethnic diversity with different classifications, reports that the largest group is South Central Asians—33 percent. African Americans comprise the next largest sector—30 percent. Arabs number about 25 percent and after them, the Africans—3.4 percent, Southeast Asians—2 percent, Europeans—2 percent, and others—nearly 5 percent (Bagby, Perl, and Froehle 2001).

In terms of U.S. born *converts* to Islam, according to the first study, about 85 percent are African American and 13 percent White.

The second study, by the American-Islamic Council, reports 64 percent African American and 27 percent White. In any case, the White segment is now growing faster than African Americans. American citizens are responding to Islam increasingly across ethnic and racial lines, but African Americans had a head start.

When African American Islam is mentioned, Louis Farrakhan and the Nation of Islam usually comes to mind. However, there are about 2.6 million African American Muslims. Only 18 or 20 thousand belong to Farrakhan's Nation of Islam. This is less than one percent.

Essentially, there are two kinds of African American Muslims, "mainline" Muslims (like those in Saudi Arabia) and Black nationalist oriented Muslims (of which Farrakhan's group is one). Among these Black nationalist oriented groups are at least 6 Nations of Islam (each with its own leader), the Nubian Islamic Hebrews, and two Moorish groups—the Moorish Science Temple Divine Movement of North America and the Moorish Temple of Science. Technically, Black nationalist oriented groups are not really Islamic. Many of their teachings are diametrically opposed to basic Muslim doctrine.

At most, the total number of Black Nationalist oriented Muslims is two hundred thousand—less than 10 percent of all African American Muslims. However, between 70 and 90 percent of African American mainline Muslims started their journey to Islam through one of the Black Nationalist oriented groups. If they became Muslim before 1970, then the percentage is closer to 90—after 1980, it is closer to 70 percent. Therefore while most African American Muslims are not in one of the Black Nationalist groups, many of them were converted to Islam through one of those organizations. After three to five years many realize they cannot build their lives on the doctrines of those groups, so they convert to orthodox Islam.

To better understand how Islam made its impact on the African American community, we need to look at some African American church history.

Theology develops among a people when they interact with biblical truth and try to make sense of their situation. In the antebellum South, the slaves developed a theology of suffering. In a traditional African American church you can still hear this theology expressed in the oral tradition. The slaves in the South would never have come up with a triumphant theology like that which came out of Europe. The theology of suffering was couched in the Exodus paradigm. The slaves identified with the children of Israel in bondage and saw God's hand at work in their hopes for deliverance. This theology addressed basic themes of salvation by grace. It also dealt with core cultural issues faced by slaves. These issues were survival, refuge, and resistance to oppression. Whenever the church is able to tap into the core cultural concerns of a people group, there will be a significant response to the gospel.

In the North where slavery had died out, African Americans began to develop a theology of empowerment. The question in the North was, "How do we overcome marginalization?" This Northern theology was couched in the exilic paradigm.

Freed slaves began to sense a special calling to bring the gospel of Christ to the "African Diaspora" (people of African descent living in the South, in Canada, the Caribbean, South America, and beyond). This was Pan-Africanism—originally a Christian concept.

Afrocentrism was also originally a Christian concept—an application of Romans 12:2. The larger culture was defining the race as Negroes, but Northern theologians were declaring, "No, we're not Negroes. We are what God created us to be—African." That is why so many of the early churches had 'African' in their names. At that time they were dealing with issues such as dignity, African identity, and the divine significance of the African American experience. They preached Christ and Him crucified and salvation by grace. But how did it work out in the community? How did they practically apply their faith? An example of this was the Free African Society, founded in Philadelphia in 1787.

Among its goals were:

Fostering economic development

Installing sound economic principles in its members

Providing strong fatherly oversight for fatherless children, especially boys

Supporting and aiding the sick and the widows

The Free African Society was a Christian organization seeking to implement the principles of the kingdom of God in the community. This was in essence what the Nation of Islam came to be known for 250 years later. But in 1787, Christians were doing this.

The abolition of slavery in the Post Civil War Reconstruction set the stage for astounding progress by African Americans. The need for the theology of suffering was declining. Slavery was over. The exodus paradigm was being realized and we were on our way to the promised land.

Thus the Southern church adopted the Northern church's developing theology of empowerment. Because of this, self-help societies modeled after the Free African Society proliferated throughout the South. By 1870 the indigenous African American church was experiencing explosive growth. Why? Because core cultural issues were being addressed theologically. The growth of the African American church between 1870 and 1910 was one of the most dramatic examples of church growth in the history of the church. But this is not taught in our evangelical seminaries.

Three great traumas between 1875 and 1900 radically changed the picture. First, the Post-Civil War reconstruction of the South ended. After the 1876 presidential election of Rutherford B. Hayes, federal troops who had been protecting slaves from increasing White hostility were withdrawn from the South. When this happened, White supremacy was reestablished within five years by way of terrorism, political disenfranchisement, the Black codes (laws of racial segregation) and exploitative economic relationships (including the sharecropper system).

Trauma number two involved the Industrial Revolution of the North. The former slaves who had all the trade skills would have been the ideal labor force for the Industrial Revolution, but this was not to be. The industrialists encouraged massive European immigration as the key to their need for a labor force. As a result of this immigration, "White-only" trade unions developed. African Americans were thus excluded from the skilled labor force within one generation. To make matters worse, the "melting pot" concept developed, which exacerbated the exclusion of African Americans from mainstream American life.

The third major trauma involved events in Africa. The African American church was heavily involved in missions in Africa. However, the European colonialists were also there. At the Congress of Berlin (1878) and the Conference of Berlin (1884–85), the colonialists carved up sub-Saharan Africa and consolidated their hold over it. The colonial authorities then began a systematic program of barring entry to new African American missionaries and expelling the ones already there. The missions activity of the African American church was decimated.

These traumas had devastating results. The church was caught off guard. Concern for survival became the overwhelming issue again and the developing theology of empowerment was being abandoned. As a result, the church reverted to the theology of suffering that had been developed during slavery. A theology vacuum developed in terms of empowerment. By 1910 the explosive growth of the church had ended. This was a great reversal in the development of the African American church.

What does all this have to do with Islam? The church was no longer addressing empowerment concerns. Therefore issues like dignity, African identity, and the divine significance of the African

American experience were not being theologically addressed by the church.

Several attempts were made to fill this "vacuum." By far the most successful of these were several Black Nationalist oriented Islamic sects.

In 1913 a young man named Timothy Drew (called Noble Drew Ali) started a group in Newark, New Jersey, called the Moorish Science Temple Divine Movement of North America. Of the sixteen major Islamic sects in the African American community, eleven of them can directly or indirectly trace their roots back to this Moorish Science Temple Divine Movement. Noble Drew Ali claimed to be a prophet after the order of Jesus, Muhammad, Buddha, and Confucius. His eclectic mixture of Eastern thinking and classical Islam was specifically designed for African Americans (Haddad and Smith 1993).

Drew Ali addressed the matter of empowerment—particularly in terms of dignity, identity, and divine significance. He taught that "Individuals need a national identity before they can have a God or a religion." This points to the issue of identity.

Any new people group has a struggle with identity. This is especially true if that people group is a subdominant culture. Colored South Africans have the same struggle. The Koreans had the same problem. The church in Korea was a major force in helping the Koreans understand what being Korean was all about. Have you ever wondered why the church grew so fast among Koreans? The core cultural issue of identity was being addressed by the church.

Drew Ali also taught that God is tied to a nation. The original nation of the Black man was Morocco. That's why Black people are called Moors. The original god of the Black man was Allah, and the original religion of the Black man was "Muslimism."

For a person looking for identity, these claims were naturally going to be attractive. Drew Ali also asserted that North America was originally a part of Africa. Therefore, it rightly belongs to the Black man. He also claimed that Allah had ordained him to be his prophet to the dark people of America. We are somebody because God has sent us a special prophet. According to Noble Drew Ali, salvation was found by discovering one's true identity—by refusing to be called Negro, Black, or Colored.

Next came W. D. Fard. He claimed to be the reincarnation of Noble Drew Ali and a wealthy man from the tribe of Quraish—the tribe of Muhammad (the 'prophet of Islam'). He claimed to be the Mehdi—the guided one of the end times. He also claimed to be the leader of the Nation of Islam, and later Allah himself. He was here to tell the world that the White man was the devil. According to Fard, Black people of the U.S. had been deprived of their heritage by Whites, who had kidnapped and enslaved their African ancestors and continue to oppress the Black race today (Poston and Ellis 2000, 111).

In 1930, Fard arrived in Detroit selling silks. He claimed to have the remedies for the social and economic problems facing Americans of African descent. Fard saw his mission as gaining freedom, justice, and equality for the Black man. Dignity and divine significance were being addressed here. Some of these claims may sound silly. But if understood in the context of the core cultural issues that were raging in the African American community at that time, they begin to make more sense.

Next came Elijah Muhammad (Poston and Ellis 2000, 113–118). He became Fard's right-hand man and eventually Fard's successor. The essence of his message was: 1) Christianity is a tool in the hands of White slavemasters to control the minds of Black people, and 2) White people are devils, the embodiment of evil. This may be a harebrained theory, but it explained the bad behavior of Whites against Blacks.

From the beginning, racial solidarity was a primary motivation behind African American Islam. Elijah Muhammad asserted that the only hope for the Black man was in separation and self-reliance. His five-point program included:

1. Racial pride and unity
2. Moral discipline
3. Economic development
4. Territorial separation
5. Pooling resources to build Black business

Of course, Elijah Muhammad tried to explain the origin of the Black man and the origin of White racism. So he came up with a mythological explanation of how White folks got here. According to him, Black people originally lived on the moon and were called moon men. The moon blew up. Those who survived came to occupy the holy city of Mecca. The survivors of the great catastrophe lived in the city of Mecca in peace and harmony.

A mad scientist named Yakub rebelled against Allah. He was exiled to the Island of Patmos along with his 59,999 followers and began producing a hybrid race of humans without pigmentation. Blacks had two germs—one Black and one Brown. So Yakub only allowed Browns to marry Browns and Blacks to marry Blacks. Then he killed the Black babies, so the race would get lighter. Likewise, the Browns had two germs: Brown and Red. So they killed the Brown babies and let the Red babies live. The rest is easy to figure out. The Red man had two germs: Red and Yellow. Then finally came Yellow and White. However, the Whites were morally the weakest and the most susceptible to evil influence. Thus Yakub created a group of sub-humans lacking in humanity.

The Nubian Islamic Hebrews was founded by Dwight York (Isa Abdullah) in the mid-1960s. They had their own twist on the Ham myth. According to this myth, Ham looked at his drunk and naked father, Noah. As a result, Noah cursed Canaan and turned his skin white. The Canaanites became the outcasts. But some Blacks intermarried with the Canaanites anyway. Out of those unions came the Chinese, the Japanese, the Sicilians, and so on. This group has evolved through the years and continues in a state of flux today.

The Five-Percent Nation of Islam (separated from Elijah Muhammad's Nation of Islam in 1964) started under Clarence 13X. Originally, Clarence 13X was in Mosque Number 7 in New York when he started teaching strange doctrines, including the belief that Black people were Allah. Malcolm X, who was the minister of that temple, expelled him. He then started the Five-Percent Nation of Islam—supposedly consisting of a chosen five percent of humanity who live a "righteous Islamic" life. This movement is still in existence. At the time, many expressed the desire to be "real Muslims." As a result, the Islamic Party of North America started—one of the major orthodox groups.

Warith Deen Muhammad (then called Wallace D.), son of Elijah Muhammad, had left the Nation of Islam along with Malcolm X. But after the assassination of Malcolm, Warith returned to the Nation in 1969. His father restored him to the ministry in 1974. In 1975, Elijah Muhammad died of congestive heart failure. The following day the Nation of Islam pronounced Warith Deen the new leader. Under his leadership, the organization was transformed into an orthodox community of American Sunni Muslims. Several reactionary factions resisted the changes in favor of the doctrines of Elijah Muhammad.

Silas Muhammad broke with Warith Muhammad and started the Lost, Found Nation of Islam in 1976. Silas Muhammad fully restored the doctrines of Elijah Muhammad. Encouraged by the success of Silas Muhammad, Louis Farrakhan broke with Warith Muhammad and started the Original Nation of Islam. Caliph Emanuel Muhammad broke with Warith Muhammad and started a Nation of Islam in 1978.

Then John Muhammad broke with Warith Muhammad and started yet another Nation of Islam in 1978. Kalid Abdul Muhammad, Louis Farrakhan's right-hand man, made inflammatory statements about Jews in 1994. His speech was so controversial that Farrakhan expelled him. As a result he started the New Black Muslim Movement. This splintering continues today.

These Black nationalist oriented Muslims are a small minority of African American Muslims. But most African Americans Muslims got their start in one of these groups because they addressed core cultural issues and attempted to answer significant questions. After a while they realized that the Black nationalist creeds were based on fairy tales. As a result, they converted to orthodox Islam.

Other groups have sprung up. The Al-Hanif, Hanafi, Madh-Hob Center, Islam Faith, United States of America, American Mussulmans (The Hanafis), and the Islamic Party of North America are all orthodox. The Tijaniyyahs are Sufis. The World Community of Al-Islam in the West became the American Muslim Mission and decentralized in 1985. The Naqshabandiyyahs are a Sufi group, organized in 1986. These organizations have limited membership and are primarily localized. Aminah McCloud's book, *African American Islam* (1995), gives a brief description of some of these groups.

A fellow named Solomon was supposedly picked up by a space ship and escorted throughout the whole universe. In his grand tour he came to know that he was Allah. So he emerged from obscurity in the mid-1990s as "Solomon, Allah in Person" and started the United Nation of Islam in 1997.

These are just a few of the groups I have been able to identify. The American Muslim Mission is the largest by far. That organization represents about 2 million Muslims—maybe more. The rest of the 600,000 or so are scattered between the other groups. We must remember that the doctrines of these groups were put together to address basic cultural issues.

The African American church is running rings around the nation of Islam in terms of community involvement. This is quite remarkable. In every city there are Christian churches involved in feeding lunch to the homeless and meeting community needs. The problem is, they have yet to significantly address core cultural issues. They are at least beginning to wrestle with such matters, while the Black Nationalist oriented Muslims continue to address many of these cultural issues. Churches need to get back to the core issues of dignity, identity, and divine significance and undergird them with sound theology.

# Muslim Women in North America

---

*Dr. Janet Metzger*

A. P. Beaver (1968) demonstrates how American women in the 1800s—denied the privilege of preaching or teaching men in their own country—actively propagated the gospel overseas. These women supported each other financially, developed mission boards and sending agencies, and built the orphanages, hospitals, and schools that nurtured Third World nationals and leaders, even in Muslim countries. (N.B.: the ministry of the African American woman in mission has had a different history.)

By the 1920s these ventures had been co-opted by Evangelical men in America, leaving women without formal leadership structures. As a consequence, in ministry to Muslims in North America, the voicelessness of the missionary woman mirrors the hiddenness of the Muslim woman. Richard Bailey describes the contemporary situation:

> The average woman worker in North America in the ministry of women/marriage/children is a white female, age 50, that has a 50 percent chance of being married or single. If married, her male spouse is usually not involved in any similar type of ministry. She is very well educated, having a master's degree. While her Muslim ministry has a 50 percent chance of being full or part-time, she will probably be too poorly focused in that ministry to be very effective in the ministry of women/marriage/children. She may, for example, also be involved in campus ministry, administration of workers, and teaching English as a second language. She spends about 50 percent of her Muslim ministry time in indirect and about 50 percent in direct ministry. Her indirect ministry is most likely to teach or train other workers. Her direct minis-

try is most likely to be friendship evangelism. She has about 10 years experience in ministry to women/marriage/children, though she has been active in Muslim ministry in some capacity for twice that many years [personal communication, 1999].

This seems to paint a bleak picture. In fact, given this kind of understanding of the situation, it is obvious why women are not seen as involved in mission or seen as leaders. However, give this picture a different frame and a marvelous portrait emerges: Despite institutional and personal obstacles, women in North America have persevered in ministry to Muslims in North America. These women are Kingdom professionals, tentmakers in their own countries, using all the strategies available for creative access to an unreached people group, strategies that include rocking babies and serving tea as well as grant writing and teaching. This is a picture of active and strong leadership.

In 1999 this leadership was recognized both internationally and domestically. In the spring, Frontiers hosted the first consultation for women in ministry to Muslims to which international workers (excluding Canada and the U.S.) were invited. In October, another group hosted its consultation for Muslim-ministry workers in North America. A woman was on the Steering Committee, and the session on women was one of the six main sessions, co-equal to the strategy sessions about men's ministries.

The initial request from the conference was that the session contain a strategic, missiological, or theological paper on women's ministries. However given the lack of resources, time, and even knowledge of who the women were or what we as women were doing, this kind of philosophical presentation was not possible. The purposes of this session, therefore, were to introduce women to each other, and to introduce to the broader community the breadth and value of women's ministries to Muslims in North America.

Because finances and time were short for many women, only about a fourth of those women contacted for this session could attend. Nevertheless, excluding art and Internet research, this session highlighted what is being done by Christian women working among Muslim women in North America, and the challenges they face.

This symposium session had three major divisions: 1) People groups, 2) Ministries, and 3) Special Needs. Each speaker had 3–5 minutes to address the following topics (in this order): 1) name, 2) agency and title or position, 3) what I do, 4) the people group I work with or my ministry area, 5) the basic things I do in my ministry, 6) areas of growth,  7) three issues that must be addressed or areas of need, 8) ways in which we can help others, and 9) ways in which others could help us. The speakers' presentations were followed by a discussion session. For security reasons, women's names and agency names have been withheld.

As Dotsey Welliver notes,

The field of ministry to Muslim women has often been difficult, without enough information and resources to adequately meet the needs. Ministry workers are looking for new understanding, fresh vision, and more adequate tools for service. [In the] three main topics...addressed below: people groups (specifically Arabs, Kurds, Somalis, and South Asians), ministries for Muslim women (such as hospitality, ESL, refugee services, and so on) and special needs (including African-American women, wives of Muslims, and missionary women), many of the issues examined are issues that mission agencies face at the most grass roots level (personal communication, May 2001).

## People Groups

### Arabs

My ministry involves an Arab-American Friendship Center. We are working with the people from Iran, Lebanon, Egypt, Syria, Jordan, Yemen, Bahrain—in fact, about whatever you want, you can find there. Our ministry involves building friendships and meeting women's needs; such as Teaching English as a Second Language (TESL) or helping them prepare for citizenship class. As we are teaching, we are living a Christlike life before them. That's how we witness to them. In helping with English, even using "certain" and "uncertain" was a way to witness. The teacher said I could not explain the plan of salvation to them, so I asked the ladies, "Are you certain or uncertain that when you die you are going to heaven?" They replied, "No, we are not certain." So I asked the teacher, "Are you certain?" And she stated, "Yes I am." Then they asked, "Why? How can you know?" Thus we were able to share with them.

In teaching citizenship, what does history have to do with Christianity? In class, we were talking about who can become the President of the United States. I happened to say, "You need to be born in America." A lady looked at me and asked, "Can I go back to my mother's womb and be born again?" I replied, "No, ma'am, only in Christianity does that happen." With surprise, she exclaimed, "What?" And we were able to share with them the plan of salvation.

We provide three things for them: the separation they need of the men from the women, the transportation, and the nursery for their children. I was driving the van once before we got a driver, and one lady said, "You and your teachers are really nice. It's the other bad Christians who cause problems." Then she went on, "These bad Christians say that Jesus Christ is the Son of God. Aren't they wrong?" I replied, "You know, if they tell you that Jesus Christ is the Son of God because God Almighty came down, married Mary, and begot Jesus, they are wrong. But if they're telling you that Jesus Christ is the Son of God because He is the Word of God become flesh, you'd better believe them." We do preach the gospel right on the spot. We share with them when they ask us why.

### Kurds

I've been in the Washington D.C. area for almost two years working with the Kurds there. Altogether I've been working with Kurds for seven years. I started in 1992 after the Gulf War. While abroad, I lived with a Kurdish family and did a bit of English teaching there, but my main job was language and culture learning. Because of that, I learned Kurdish. As a result, I have had many doors and hearts open to me. I'm still learning the language and culture, and it has really helped in opening doors for me. I'm the only missionary working with Kurds in the Washington D.C. area. One of the needs that I have is for more teammates, especially for at least one man to come and work among the men there.

I have had seven interns over the last two years—people who come for two months or so at a time. That's been of real help to me. Three or four of them have been men, and they've delved into the men's world that I have not had much part in, so I've really appreciated their help. My interns learn some Kurdish and learn about the culture. That's their main job. I find it a lot of work to have interns. I have to do a lot of calling and recruiting and working with them on the telephone and through e-mail before they actually come. When they do come I have to orient them and introduce them to Kurds one-on-one. But I'm happy to tell you, all seven of my interns are either already into, or are planning to go into missions full-time. I consider that a real ministry.

A concern I have is not only for teammates, but also just for some Kurds to come to Christ. There are no Kurdish believers in the Washington D.C. area that I know of, and about 3,000 Kurds live there. The Kurds have a fantastic network. They are constantly on the telephone

with people in Kurdistan, Holland, Germany, and Sweden, networking with their family and friends. This network could become such a
positive thing, should some of them become believers. It could also
be negative, but I think the Lord could use it for his glory. Pray not
only that Kurds will come to know Christ, but also that they will
come in family groups and in community groups, so that when they
become believers they will not be exiled from their community.

### Somali (Refugees)

My husband and I have been working as missionaries for over 35
years: First in Somalia, then in Ethiopia for a short time, and then in
Kenya. When we came home, we settled in Saskatchewan. We were
studying at a Bible college when our director came out to see us and
invited us to come to Toronto to start a ministry among the Somalis.
They were coming in by the thousands because of the brutal civil war
in their country.

We moved there in October of 1991. We immediately met Somalis near where we lived and began to make friends with them. Because we speak their language, that opens some doors. We find they
are so open to friendship. We introduce people from the church, or
other friends to them, and they accept them because they're our
friends. Many of the women that we work with are single moms. The
husband may have been killed in war, or he may have stayed in the
homeland and sent his wife and children to what he considered a safe
place. Others are divorced. They have many problems, so we just try
to help them in many different ways. Sometimes I just visit and listen
to their problems. At other times there will be opportunities to pray
for them in their home.

We also have programs for them in our church. We've had classes
for the women on parenting, living in a multicultural city, training up
your children in Canada, and disciplining them. Discipline is a big
issue, because they're afraid of Children's Aid. They think if they
discipline their children, Children's Aid will come and take them
away. In Somalia they had their own way of disciplining them, and
that was to hit them with a stick or to slap them, and sometimes it left
marks. But if they leave marks on their child in Canada and it is
reported to the teacher, immediately Children's Aid will come. They
are really afraid of that. We try to teach them other ways to discipline.

We also have socials for the women in the church. We often try to
have something from the Word of God to give them. We've shown
the Jesus video. We showed a part of it in one meeting, and afterward

several of the women took it home and watched it. So we just continue to build relationships with them. We tutor in schools, because the children have sometimes missed several years of school, and they struggle with English.

One of the needs that we have is for more people to help us make friends with the Somalis. When they meet a real Christian, that begins to break down some of the barriers that they come with—sometimes they think that anything Western is Christian. We discipled one close friend who is a Christian for two or three years, and that's what she thought. She said she thought everything on television was Christian until she met us. So they come with a lot of barriers that make it difficult to win them. Prayer support helps. One friend has a prayer team praying for us when we have a social time for the women.

## South Asians

I am working at a South Asian Friendship Center. The people I work with are Muslims from India and Pakistan. My position is ESL Director, but deep within my heart, the reason I am ESL Director is so I can reach the hearts of the women. I do that by connecting them with teachers, and also teaching some myself.

My ultimate goal is to find out where they are hurting. I teach the volunteers as well about how to detect the hurts or abuse the Muslim women might be going through. From my experience, maybe 90 percent of the women that we come across either have been abused or they know someone who is being abused. My heart really goes out to these women. I want to help them, and eventually let them know that the source of comfort is Jesus Christ only.

During the school year we have plenty of volunteers, but during the summer we don't have as many because the volunteers from various schools go home. I am praying that God will send more workers, so we can continue the ministry during the summer as well, because that's when these women have a bit more time and they can come to us. I try to be a good listener. I talk, but I am also a good listener, and that's when they open their heart.

As our ministry grows among the abused women, eventually we are going to need Christian homes to provide shelters to these women while we are helping them. Some will not need to leave their homes, but others will. [For example,] at the present time I am teaching one young girl who is 21 years old. After five weeks she just hung around me and said, "I don't want to leave you alone. I don't think you should be left alone." I replied, "Why? I can do some work. You can go home now." She answered, "No, I don't think you should be left alone." Finally she sat down and said, "I don't know what to call you: Auntie, Friend, just a person?" She came up with these different terms that expressed different relationships in Urdu. I assured her, "You don't have to be so concerned. Just call me whatever you are comfortable with." Then she said, "I do not have anybody to help me here. I live with my family, but I am hurting. I feel I'm being used by my own parents, by my own brother." She wants to go to school. She needs to learn to drive. But her family situation is holding her back. I will continue working with her to see what I can do to help.

## Ministries

### Couples Ministry

Behind every religion stand the women. If you want strong Muslim youth, it's the mothers who are with them 24 hours a day. The women are there holding things together.

We minister as a couple. This really works out well in the Muslim community because of the segregation. The women tend to go in one direction and the men go another. I get a chance to form strong relationships with the women, and my husband with the men. We've gotten many opportunities to share the gospel.

On our first mission trip, when we went to Iraq among the Kurds, we did not realize how big a witness our relationship would be. Sometimes in Western terms we think of a couple showing a public display of affection, and that's how we know they love each other. But of course, in Iraq we didn't touch each other in public. We just didn't realize that the love the Lord has given us for each other would show through so much. The comments from Muslim women are sometimes unbelievable. They will say things like, "We've never seen a marriage like this." And they'll say, "How can I find a husband like yours?" I reply, "Well, you need to become a believer because you need to get a believing husband." Then I tell them that the Bible commands husbands to love their wives, and exhorts wives to reverence their husbands. It's been a great witness of the love of Christ, and it's exciting to be able to minister as a couple.

We feel strongly about evangelism. That's our main focus, and we do this through strong relationships, spending time together, hospitality, and providing social help. We had a Muslim Kurdish man live with us for a year in our little two-bedroom apartment. In the process, we learned a lot about Kurdish culture.

An issue that I think is tough to deal with and I haven't quite known how to handle—a couple of women have come to me about being abused in their homes. I've heard of some ministries trying to help out and it ends up backfiring on them.

## Friendship and Hospitality

I have the privilege of having served in India, Pakistan, Indonesia, and Wheaton, Illinois. Yes, there are Muslims in Wheaton. I want to tell you the story of a young man named John (pseudonym). John is from Egypt. A friend brought John to our house about ten years ago. He wanted my husband to take John to a conference for Muslim background believers because John had accepted the Lord a while before.

John was brought up in Alexandria, Egypt. When he was little he was taken to the Madrissa to learn the Qur'an and he is practically a Hafiz (someone who has memorized the Qur'an). He can recite almost the whole Qur'an. When he was small, if he made a mistake in recitation he would be beaten on the bottom of the feet. When he got older he used to travel around the Mediterranean. He was a bit of a wanderer so he just worked here and there.

One time when he went back to Alexandria he impregnated a girl who was related to him, and he had to escape. So he fled to the United States. He was not a good Muslim. In fact, he was basically nothing. He went to a bar and met an American girl sitting on a barstool and proposed to her. She had come under the influence of Youth for Christ during her high school years, so she replied, "I couldn't marry you because you'd have to become a Christian." He retorted, "Well, that's no problem."

They did get married and she took him to the church where she had attended before. They had a baby, and John gradually grew in the faith. For about two years he didn't accept a lot of what the preacher was saying, but gradually he did start to grow. However, the way he treated his wife was not very nice. We know that one time he beat her, and another time she just said, "I've had it! Get out! I can't stand this anymore." He called us and stated, "I have no place to go." So we said, "Come on, live with us."

He came and lived with us for six months. During the time he was there he was able to see a Christian marriage modeled. Also my husband took him aside and said, "Hey, you shouldn't beat your wife, no matter what she does or doesn't do." After six months John did go back to his wife, and they have been together since then, although their marriage has certainly had its ups and downs. We praise the Lord that John is gradually growing.

I feel John will have a big place among Muslim background believers, bringing his own countrymen to Christ. He has a tremendous ability to communicate. He can get the attention of a Muslim by just pointing out one verse in the Qur'an. We trust that some day he can go to Bible school and become better equipped.

## ESL and Church Planting

The people group I help reach are Muslims from South Asia. They may be Pakistanis, Muslim Indians, Bangladeshis, Sri Lankan, or whoever else comes along. ESL is one of our strongest, most effective programs. I make a lot of contacts through ESL. I go out into the market places and connect with new people. It's the easiest way of getting to know people and bring them in. By doing this, we earn the right to be heard.

The students feel comfortable on our premises because it's not a regular classroom set-up. They can talk, sometimes one-on-one, and sometimes in a group. We don't have any problem getting volunteers in the churches we work with. By doing this we share the love of Jesus.

There was one Pakistani Muslim lady who saw all the work our volunteers do in our ESL program. I am the only Pakistani. All the other ladies are Americans. But when the Pakistani lady saw all these people offering their services free of charge, providing transportation and so forth, she made a profound comment. It's not biblical, but it still has an effect on people when I tell them. She commented that surely Americans deserve to be leaders of the world, just by seeing all the work they do. And it wasn't just me. She was speaking of the Americans.

I am from Pakistan and I've lived in the Middle East for 10 years. From my experience I must tell you that there are three things I have observed being an outsider living in North America for five years now. 1) Americans are truly hard-working people, 2) they are honest, and 3) the heart that they have to serve others is something I haven't seen anywhere else.

Another aspect our organization is involved in is church planting. In four years three churches have been established at three different locations. The church in Toronto is an ethnic church with a Pakistani and Indian congregation, and there's another one in Michigan. Then we also have a White church. This is important for the assimilation of people coming from different ethnic backgrounds. In the English church these ethnic people can worship in English.

## Women's Ministries

I am the Director of Children and Youth at a South Asian Friendship Center. I also have the privilege of being involved with women's ministry and administration of the bookstore.

In addressing the issue of women's ministries, I want to look at two questions briefly. The first one is "What is ministry?" I believe that ministry is sharing the gospel by word and by deed. Typically women minister more to women and children, but we also need to remember that women can have a great influence over men and families. Historically women's ministry has been in three basic areas: education, medicine, and evangelism. In modern missions their involvement also includes work in the area of church planting.

The second question is "What can women do in ministry?" I'm just going to list what women have done and continue to do at our center. This is not an exhaustive list, but will touch on a lot of things that we are involved in.

First of all, we have ministry through hospitality. At the friendship center we reach out through ladies luncheons once a month. Then there's ESL, which involves a lot of phone contact. We've learned that to have contact and good relationships, we need to give personal invitations to them. That means making several phone calls a day, just to keep the relationships going. We also have monthly family events for mothers and children. We meet practical and spiritual needs through relationships and conversation, just meeting them where they're at. We have also used drama. Women's Aglow came and presented "The King," with the Father God as King. And we conduct ministry with children. We have a Kids' Club weekly and also a homework center.

In addition, we provide transportation to medical clinics. We have developed a clinic at the center as well, with a woman doctor visiting women in their homes, because often women's medical needs are neglected.

We have a fellowship and worship service on Sunday evenings that arose out of women expressing curiosity about Christianity and also wanting to come for prayer. So we have a significant ministry in terms of intercessory prayer.

We help meet their felt needs in terms of employment opportunities as well, giving them referrals when it comes to immigration and citizenship. And sometimes we provide shelter for them or refer them to a shelter when they come from an abused background.

One need involves learning how to better connect our Muslim friends' husbands with Christian men on our team. This is important because ministry to Muslims must have a holistic approach with men and women working together to reach families.

## Refugee Services and International Human Rights

I am the director of a refugee service. I've been working for the past eleven years specifically helping refugees as they arrive in our city. I have settled more than 2,000 refugees, the majority being Muslim. I've also been involved, not only locally, but also nationally in refuge-related committees, and internationally, representing Canadian churches at UN HCR meetings in Geneva several times.

It's important to understand the two types of refugees who are arriving in North America. There is a lot of confusion. Many people think they are all sponsored refugees and that there are groups, either the government or churches, that help sponsor them. However, more than 75,000 refugee claimants, or asylum seekers as they're called in the States, arrive each year who have no sponsors whatsoever. They arrive and there is no one to welcome them. They may sleep on the street or at homeless people's shelters with drug addicts and alcoholics. This is a terrible welcome to a "Christian" country.

Over the years, as I've worked with these types of refugees, I have gained a great burden for them. Out of that burden, I have developed a vision to have a Christian reception home in Toronto. After years of intercession and prayer, we were able to open a refugee home about a year and a half ago in Toronto for these homeless refugees.

I must confess that even I was rather amazed at the response of the refugees staying in our home. They have been so open to Christianity. Many of them are from strong Muslim backgrounds, and they have literally been asking to come to church or to go to Bible Study. I couldn't quite figure out why. Being at this meeting has helped me to understand perhaps one of the reasons. We have talked a lot about the effectiveness of caring, loving communities, and our refugee home is in many ways the ideal of that. We have a wonderful Christian man who lives there overnight. The Christian staff and probably about 50 volunteers from local churches are there helping these refugees find apartments, register for school, and prepare for all the other steps they must take. It's a bit like pieces of salt. I call people for help and tell them, "You're like a piece of salt." Everyone working together can be incredible salt and light.

I would also like to share my vision for what churches in North America can be doing, in light of the world refugee situation.

Right now the world contains more than 20 million refugees. Unfortunately xenophobia (fear of other races) is growing. Countries of the world are becoming more and more closed to refugees. In Europe, even as we meet, there's a meeting of all the European national leaders regarding asylum seekers. They are trying to think of ways they can close their doors to refugees flowing into Europe. North America shows frightening signs as well. If Europe is shutting its doors, the implications for America are significant. More refugees could be coming here if they can't go to Europe. The ministry potential is incredible! The refugees are such a vulnerable group, particularly refugee claimants, because no one is speaking up for them, no one is trying to protect them. If Christians can stand in the gap, look out for their rights, help them with their practical needs, and provide them with a safe place to be, the potential is amazing.

I would like to mention at least a few areas of involvement. One is airport reception. Refugees are arriving all around North America. I know thousands pass through John F. Kennedy Airport in New York because many of them end up in Toronto. I have a dream for some kind of refugee reception program at the airport.

Another plan would be reception houses throughout North America. There are some now in Buffalo and Detroit, and there's a coalition that sends them to Toronto. A lot of refugees prefer to come to Canada because Canada happens to have the more humane refugee system.

Advocacy would be yet another need, and networking still another.

### Prayer

My ministry organization started with four women around a kitchen table. Today we work in 140 countries around the world. We have a call from God for a prayer focus in our ministry. It's not something we just thought up on our own. And we're finding our way as we go along. We have instituted what we call swift teams. These are teams of five to six women, no more than can get in one car. They live in close proximity, they can be mobilized quickly, they research what is going on in their area, and they do what we call drive-by praying. They go right to the source. Since we were invited to this meeting in July or August, our swift team for this area has been praying for this conference. They have been driving by the campus, praying for these meetings. They do this for us wherever they are and whatever our needs are.

We also have what I call our war council. They are our strategic prayer force. These are women across the United States and Canada with whom I can get in touch immediately when I need to fire out immediate, urgent prayer needs. They pray through until the end. But we're relatively new in this business. We would like to link up and ask how we can help. How can we all work together?

## Special Needs

### Introduction

The next group involves women dealing with special needs. One woman speaks about wives of Muslims; one woman talks about [other] missionary women; a third person on the agenda gives us some resources.

First, I want to present a brief statement from someone who could not be here, a woman with a Ph.D. from Fuller Theological Seminary in missions. Her specialty was the contextualization of the church to work with African Americans who were prone to convert to Islam. She works with the African American multi-religious community, and her ministry is Christian-Muslim relations. She teaches seminarians about Islam and Muslims. She helped plan the first national dialogue on African American Christians and Muslims that took place in the year 2000.

She also plans local dialogues between Muslims and Christians. She teaches seminars and workshops for pastors and church leaders about religious diversity, especially the challenge of Islam, and participates in global research projects about Christian theological education in Muslim society.

She mentions three issues that must be addressed. First is education concerning and contrasting the various Islamic and proto-Islamic faith communities in urban centers from the perspective of theology. Second, the need is to increase Christian knowledge of the Qur'an and its message. And third, educational collaboration should be promoted with Ghanian African Christians in an effort to historically identify the role of Islamic Christianity in the African Slave Trade. This is necessary knowledge a) for refuting Islamic claims of its moral/ethical superiority in the U.S.A. (because of alleged non-involvement in the slave trade), and b) for helping to bring about reconciliation. She could help others develop an authentic Christian theology of religious pluralism, and help bring about an increased awareness and need among denominational and mission organization and staff for strategic recruiting and training of more African American workers among Muslims locally, nationally and globally.

## Wives of Muslims

I started my own ministry at one point, but later on I joined my work with an international Arab ministry because they had so much to offer. I needed the support and guidance that they could give me on reaching out to American women married to Muslims.

We have many internationals in Orlando. They come to work for Disney. They come to UCF to go to college. Many of the men marry American women for a host of reasons. I myself married a Muslim. I called myself a Christian, but I realized after about five years into our marriage that I was a pew sitter and I needed to do something about that. So I started working for Campus Crusade for Christ, and this helped me decide that I have an opportunity to make a difference in other women's lives. In my marriage, I did not have the usual problems, but through all the people we knew who were married to American women, I saw many women who were victims of abuse, neglect, convenience marriages, and so on. The Lord kept prompting me, "What are you going to do for these women?" I had no clue. How does one get started?

Finally, I decided to put an ad in the newspaper. It was simple: "American women married to Muslims, looking to start a support group. For fun, fellowship, and prayer." That was basically it, with my name and phone number. The Lord blessed this effort. The calls just kept coming and coming. There were more people interested than I ever imagined. And the ministry keeps growing.

The women come to the group for about a year, then usually leave. They make decisions about their lives, whether they want to divorce their husbands because of abuse, or whatever. I encourage them to love their husbands, and to be more godly women. Many of them were like me—nominal Christians. I encourage them to get into the Word of God. Many have rededicated their lives to Christ. Many who had converted to Islam are now back into Christianity. All of this happened just because I followed the Lord's prompting. He asked me to do something so I did. I was scared, thinking, what if the Muslims come after me! But I did it, and the Lord has blessed my efforts.

There are many women who need your help. Where do they belong in the church? Where do people like me belong? How are you reaching out to them? Often there isn't a place for us, even though we are a couple. We have needs, but who is helping us? I encourage you men. You need to look for opportunities, not only to help women like me, but also to educate Muslim men on what being a Christian means. They are totally confused. They have no clue about what being a Christian really means. But it's about being a follower of Jesus Christ. The term Christianity has many negative connotations when you talk to a Muslim, so just talk about being a follower of Christ, and what it means to you.

I am looking for other women who would like to have a similar ministry. I want this to spread across America. We have many large cities with large Muslim populations, and the time is now.

## Missionary Women

I have been asked to talk about some of the issues related to missionary women and some of the things they go through. This does not come from a feminist agenda. Perhaps it's a good thing that I'm not a feminist, because in a Muslim environment, the men can get quite chauvinistic. It's also a good thing because (and I don't know why), but often there's something about Muslim ministry that seems to attract Christian men who are into "macho-ism."

I was at Urbana one time, and a fellow was speaking who has written a number of books that have been very influential on how to witness to Muslims. During a question and answer time, someone sitting right in front of me asked this guy a question, "Where is a place for single women in ministry to Muslims?" And he just flatly told her, "Go find another field." His whole attitude was, if you're a woman and you are single, you have no business trying to reach out to Muslims. Fortunately for the questioner, a woman came to her afterwards and said, "Don't listen to him."

Algeria had a strong contingent of single women. And if you look over the history of missions, there have been a lot of women, single and married, out there. More women than men have been involved in the history of the modern missions movement. A Muslim-ministry scholar once told me, "I think God's secret weapon is a woman." One reason he said that is because of the Muslim attitude toward women. Muslim men may think, "It's just a woman. Therefore, she's not dangerous. She can't do too much." So I have been able to do a lot of things because they just ignore me and let me do it.

The other thing that was helpful is that someone once said to me, "In a sex-segregated society, who is going to lead the women?"

Females are essential in ministering to Muslims. When you stop to think about it, half the Muslim population of the world is women. The only way we're going to reach them is with other women. Men obviously can't do this. But Muslim women still have a profound influence on their society, even though they appear to be oppressed.

One time I asked the scholar mentioned above, "How do I deal with the attitudes of men who are against me as a woman?" His advice was, "Be unstoppable." So if there are any women who need encouragement, just remember, "Keep going. Be unstoppable. Don't let anybody talk you into thinking that you can't do Muslim ministry just because you're a woman."

### Resources

I work some in the training department of my organization— some with women's ministries, and I'm also on a church planting team working among Kurds in our area. I help with ESL, we build friendships, we sponsor events, including camping in the mountains with Arabs. It is quite an experience. But what I'm talking about specifically tonight is available resources. For a long time, there were no resources for women working among Muslim women. But now, there are some wonderful resources out there.

There was a consultation on women ministering to Muslim women, and I had the privilege of helping with resources. About 35–40 women were there from all over the world. Out of that we do have a compendium coming out that includes all the presentations, all the panels, all the papers that were presented.

As well, some wonderful books are coming out. Books are being published to help females understand all the different things that they need to know in order to minister to women. Bible studies are published concerning hospitality, spiritual growth, nearly everything. There's an extensive bibliography including books by authors who are Muslim and secular, as well as Christian. It's specifically about working with Muslim women. Then, consider websites. This is a resource you cannot do without. A woman in Canada has put together an extensive list (it runs 10–12 pages when you print it out) where she has gleaned every possible website that would relate to Muslim women. She has put this all together in categories. Abuse? It's there. Muslim children? There. Wearing the covering? It's all there, categorized.

One of the next projects we're working on is to put together something we're hoping will be in CD ROM form. This will be a church planting manual for church planting among Muslim women. We have Bible studies that have been written for Muslim-Background-Believer women. And the Southern Baptists have published *God and Women*, a chronological Bible story that looks at the Bible from a woman's point of view about the issues that most concern her. Let's share our resources.

## Discussion Session

[*Editorial Note:* Originally, after 6–8 minutes of open discussion we were going to form breakout groups to discuss specific topics. The original comments from the floor, however, touched such a profound chord that we decided to remain together as a group and discuss what we had heard. Because of the situation Muslim women sometimes find themselves in, they may see Christian workers as outside their community and therefore safe to talk with. The following discussion is not a statement about relationships all Muslim men have with their wives, but these are the hurting ones who have come for help.]

### Abuse in Muslim Marriages

*Question:* [What is the percentage of abuse in Muslim marriages?]

*Response:* A good ratio that I've seen is about two out of ten. When you compare it with American men abusing their wives, perhaps it's similar, but I find it is harder for the women to get out of the Muslim marriages when the abuse is so bad. They may go to a crisis shelter and get help but then they wonder, "What am I going to have to give up in order to get out of an abusive marriage?" So sometimes they go back and it starts all over again. If you want an average just in the Central Florida area, I would say two out of ten but more than physical abuse is neglect and verbal abuse. I knew a lady who tried to commit suicide twice just because of verbal abuse from her husband. He was not even hitting her, but the verbal abuse was that bad. Words hurt and everyone needs to be aware that the matter includes more than just hitting. There are deep emotional scars from which many of these women never fully recover.

### Ministry to Western Women Married to Muslims

*Question:* How do men see your ministry? Do they think the Westerners are helping the American women to divorce because the husband is from a Muslim background?

*Response:* I try very hard to make sure the men know that I'm here to help their women understand their culture, how to love their husbands, how to encourage them in a country where they are foreign. I do not tell them to divorce unless it is absolutely critical. I tell them there is a major price to pay and ask if they are willing to pay it. Don't even mention the word divorce unless they are already prepared. If they get that on their minds and the controlling gets even tighter than it was before, soon they are in prison in their own home.

*Question:* I'm in a situation where I investigated the relationship—a Muslim-Lebanese man married to an American woman, for 10 years now. I've been following them since before they got married. I advised her not to marry him, but she went ahead anyway. Now she comes to my office crying and I actually found that she is at fault more than he. She has a lot of insecurities. He is very kind to her, very nice, and he doesn't want to divorce her. At first he was not abusive; he only became a bit abusive later. What do you do with those situations? Do you confront the Christian woman and challenge her to get her act together spiritually?

*Response:* Very much so. I work with them one on one and the first goal is to help them be more godly women. If what they are doing is not within the Word and what the Lord tells us to do, I have to approach them. I can't just let it go because they are ruining their marriage. She may really love the man but because of the insecurities, begins to act up rather than getting help. She needs help, he needs help, and they need to learn to work together and cope.

## Christian Women Marrying Muslim Men—or Multiple Wives

*Question:* There's another very complex side to this whole issue of Christian women marrying Muslims. There are Muslims who are married in their own countries. Then they come to this country and marry women over here as well. I know several. What is a person to do in such cases?

*Response:* I'm not sure of percentages. I know that it does happen. In most of the cases that I know about, the wife here doesn't even find out about the other wife until years down the road. Sometimes she doesn't ever find out that he's already got another wife. I don't know that the percentages of abuse are higher but there are the cultural differences that add to the stress of the marriage.

There is a lot of fear sometimes. First of all, it seems like women who are more insecure do tend to marry these guys because it's sometimes easier to get one of these fellows than an American man. I know American women living in the Gulf who are married to Arabs there and they are very much abused. They are truly terrified to try to get out of the marriages because they know they will lose their children. They know they cannot leave the country without leaving the children behind. They are especially fearful of leaving daughters behind to grow up in a Muslim country.

*Response:* In addition, there are relatives to deal with. If the man is abusive, sometimes the relatives are also abusive. I know one woman who wouldn't convert to Islam so the sister-in-law came after her with a pair of scissors, missed, hit the maid, and the maid had to have more than 100 stitches. You have such issues as the family trying to force them to convert to Islam and the woman not being accepted by the relatives. Somebody also asked about percentages of abuse. I am not sure of the difference between American marriages versus marriages of Muslims, but a general statistic for the United States overall is that at least 1 in 4 women in the U. S. have been sexually abused. When you think about it, if one out of every four women you run into on a daily basis could have been abused as a child, that profoundly affects their ability to relate to people.

*Response:* At the two secular agencies I worked with for several years, I would say that at least one out of every four or five women had husbands back in Pakistan or India. The men were married there, left their wives, came here and married a Muslim or American woman to get a visa. Basically the women were abused emotionally and after the man got the visa, he left that woman and went back to the woman he was married to and brought her back to America. That does happen. Sometimes you can deal with it. You can let the men know that they can be reported, but the men really cover their path well. They plan ahead when they get their visa from Pakistan or India, and they declare themselves single. It can be an immensely complicated situation. They marry here and sometimes they have children with these women. Then they may claim the children but leave the wives.

*Response:* Let's not be that pessimistic. I have met a number of women who have led their husbands to Jesus—formerly strong Muslims who went back to their own country to witness to family at great cost, so don't be too pessimistic. God is sovereign; He can save those men and the Christian women.

*Response:* We are talking about two subjects here. We are speaking about abused women and then we are talking about a ministry mentioned earlier. I think that ministry is a supportive system for these women who are in need. I knew a few marriages in Denver, Colorado, where they lived in hell because their cultural understanding is different. That is a different subject. But to answer the person here who said that Muslim people sometimes get married in their home country and then come here and marry. Sometimes they bring their second and third wives into the house right here in America. I'm working with two or three cases and the American woman doesn't just marry the Arabic man because he's not going to divorce her. I see about 75 percent divorce, if not more.

## American Church and Cultural Sensitivity

*Question:* If Muslim men come to the church and they see the American church culture of hugging, are we just teaching that culture to them? What is your experience? If we don't hug them and then go the opposite way and hug some other man or woman, will they wonder, "Why don't you hug me?"

*Response:* Since we've been working with Muslims, especially when there are Muslim men around, I don't hug any men anymore. My whole mindset has changed. In fact, I don't even extend my hand to any of the Muslim men. I let them extend their hand first to shake hands. One time I did extend my hand to a man who had shaken my hand many times, but I guess he had just washed his hands to pray. When I held out my hand and he drew back, I was humiliated. It seems like a safe rule. I do think that we should be sensitive about such matters when we bring Muslims into our church. I know we can't change everyone, but we can begin to educate them.

*Response:* When I meet men from different ethnic groups, Muslim or Hindu even, I do not give them a hug. Actually in front of them, I do not give hugs to American friends either because it represents something different to them, and [so it] doesn't work. It gives a wrong impression.

*Response:* We were in a church in Ohio and our pastor made it very clear from the beginning that he will not allow any man to hug a woman or any woman to hug a man. That was maybe fifteen years ago, and I remember thinking maybe that was a bit extreme. Now that I'm more mature, I think maybe he was right. There is so much temptation. I was naïve and a friend told me, "You don't know what goes on in the man's mind. You think it's nothing, but we don't necessarily think it's nothing." You who are pastors here, I don't know if this advice is helpful to you. Maybe you think it is extreme, but in this permissive society in America, it may be time for the church to stand up and make a difference, to say that we stand for righteousness and we don't want to give even the appearance of evil.

That will help Muslims who come into our church.

*Response:* At the same time it's a holy case when I see my friends hugging each other, saying hello, feeling a part of God's family in a holy way. I think it's not wrong.

### Christian Men Marrying a Muslim Woman

*Question:* Are any of you aware of a Christian man marrying a Muslim woman and if so, what are the challenges of that marriage?

*Response:* There's a Pakistani couple we meet with. She is from a Muslim background. He is from a Christian background. She understood when she married him that she was becoming a Christian. Her parents were both dead and she was the oldest child. Of course, she had uncles and others that didn't approve. So the couple ran off and got married, and both families were furious. The Lord has used this for good though, and now they are following the Lord.

*Response:* I had a man call me and say he is married to a Muslim woman and he is a Christian. Basically he faces the same difficulties that the women face being married to the Muslim men. It's a little bit different in that he is the man and the head of the household. However, when they began to have children, things really started to get ugly. To me, I don't see any difference unless in love you are constantly talking about what a difference Christ makes. Christ is the only one who can change the hearts of husbands whether they are Muslim or not. He is the only one, and if we can't model this, how can we expect them to want to be like us. Be prepared to model it and show it even in the worst situations.

*Response:* One of my Muslim friends who had accepted the Lord ended up marrying a Muslim. She was still a secret Christian. He did not know that she was a Christian, but he could detect that there was something about her that did not accept the Muslim faith fully. He was abusive, not beating her but closing her off from the whole society.

### Marriages of Convenience
### Complicated by Family Arranged Marriages

*Question:* We have heard questions about the Muslim man who is married back home and comes to the States and marries an American girl. There is another situation where we find that a single Muslim man gets married to an American woman. After he has obtained his green card and paper, his family finds him a bride back home and he needs to go back and get married to her. The wife here later finds out he is leaving, not to see his family back home but to get married to a lady his family has assigned to him. How can you deal with this situation?

*Response:* It does happen. With the people I work with, it is so blatant that our immigration officials are sometimes just downright nasty to any foreigners who come. They are so sick of it, they are making the laws tighter. How do you deal with a brokenhearted woman who is left because he brings in the new wife, kicks out the old one, and tells her she has served her purpose? It's sad, but from my experience in working with them the American spouses are sometimes just there to provide a service—a marriage of convenience and a green card. I know that sounds terrible because we're talking about loving them, but really, only Jesus can change their heart. I don't know how to solve it, but many people are being hurt on a daily basis and it's not stopping.

*Response:* Prevention is one of the things that I'm involved in. One of the things we really have to watch out for is a woman who is just charmed off her feet by this great-looking guy who is nicer than any American. Maybe he treats her like a queen and he's much better looking than any guy she's ever seen. When these guys show up, often they seem like Prince Charming in person—the romantic accents and the exoticness. If you tell her not to do this, she will just say, "Yeah, right." Or she may say that all her friends are telling her that he will abuse her or it will be just like the movie, "Not Without My Daughter," but is this really real?

One of the things we have had to watch out for on the Internet is that the majority of the women who are dating Muslims are not Christians or are nominal ones. But most of them who are married are Christians. Usually they married the guy when they were backslidden or before they became a Christian.

Now when the kids come along a lot of times he gets more religious. But she also gets more religious. Suddenly she comes back to Christ or finds Christ to begin with. At the beginning, when a new girl would come online saying, "Oh, I'm dating Prince Charming Mohammed down here" the married women would quickly urge, "Don't do it!" "Run the other way!" However it would only turn these girls off and they would reply "You're just being Muslim bashers." So we've really had to train them to be careful and not tell the bad news right away but gain trust first. Then maybe in ongoing conversation online (it's a bit like a chat line), they can talk about their problems. "He lectured to the kids for an entire hour on Islam last night." As they talk about the daily things that happen to them, some of these girls finally start thinking, "Wait a minute." We've had a few girls who have become Christians as a result. A few others have broken up with their boyfriends.

*Response:* Regarding this prevention that someone commented about, I would like to suggest something. When I was in Pakistan, I used to come across a lot of men who had been to America for studying and then went back to their country. I would ask them how they found it. They would say, "We had such a good time." "We had fun there." "American girls are so easily available." That was such a painful expression for me to hear. I felt very bad because we in the East are very sensitive about these things. We teach our girls to be sensitive about these matters. So when we see American girls so easily available, it really hurts us. One thing that is so important is for American girls to be trained not to be that open in their relationships and not to be so available to these men.

### Abortion in the Muslim Community

*Question:* When we ministered in England, I had Muslim ladies come to me and ask me if I knew a doctor who could give their friend an abortion because their religion didn't allow it and they didn't know any doctors. It got so bad in the hospital in our area with the Muslim ladies that they [the medical workers] would quit telling them what sex the baby was because if they told them it was a girl, they would have an abortion. Then for those who did get pregnant outside of marriage and decided to keep the baby, there was a need for safe homes. Is this an issue in North America at all and do you deal with this?

*Response:* Yes, in San Diego we have some translation we are trying to do for the pregnancy care center right now. We just took them Jesus videos. Some of the Kurdish women are there often, but not understanding what they are providing. And they are having abortions, so the issue has been raised. They [the center] basically contacted us. We're trying to connect them with resources to get material translated about why you shouldn't have an abortion. The same thing we do in America for these pregnancy centers, we are trying to translate so it can be given to the other ladies as well.

*Response:* I see a trend and I wanted to let you know. People who have daughters need to train them up and give them self-esteem and self-worth. I realize that it comes from Jesus, but they are teenagers still struggling with independence. I can tell you that my self-esteem when I married my husband was very low. I am finding that with many women I come in contact with, this is a major problem. So if you have daughters, hold them tight and tell them how much you love them and how beautiful they are, so they feel like they are worth something. Then they won't just give themselves to anyone. Mothers and grandmothers, we need mentors. We have lost the mentoring and that's why we are marrying outside our culture. We're marrying Muslim, Hindu, whoever—it doesn't matter. The point is we have lost something somewhere along the way and we really need to mentor our young women. I implore you to get involved. If you don't have a daughter, find one in the church and adopt her.

## Conclusion

These sessions show that women's ministries to Muslims parallel men's ministries; for example, women engage in hospitality and sharing the Gospel. Women's ministries also diverge from men's ministries, as found in the tone of the discussion. The way these presenters focused so intensely on relationships prompted deep discussion from the audience (not all transcribed) and raised questions such as the following: 1) What is the relationship between time spent in ministry with time spent with my family? 2) How can we minister to women who are abused? 3) How can we minister to Muslim Background Believer (MBB) men in the churches, who are perceived as being abusers because of their cultural and religious background? 4) How do we find brides for MBB men? 5) How do we keep young Christian women from marrying Muslim men and converting to Islam?

As the discussion unfolded it became apparent that even if men and women are working in different worlds, these worlds do interlock; and men's and women's expertise is needed mutually across borders in order to solve problems. For example, we can solve the issue of MBB marriages and family needs if, and only if, men and women are working together.

This arena of mutual need in mission is theologically important. Not only does it underscore the need for reconciliation (cf. Hansen and Powers, 1997), humility, submission, and patience, but it also demonstrates that the church can grow only when both men and women are able to use their gifts to the fullest. The issue of women in leadership, therefore is a primary strategy issue in missions to Muslims in North America.

I would like to discuss in greater detail, however, two issues that missionary women raised while preparing for this session—hijab and vulnerability. These issues are, for women, theological, missiological, and strategic issues that are actually lived.

In the Muslim world women are marked socially, spiritually, politically, and theologically by their age and by the way they dress. Missionary women in the U.S., therefore, wore—depending on the ministry context—hijab; shalwar kameez; a long skirt and long-sleeved blouse without jewelry; bermudas and a tank top with make-up and jewelry. Regardless of what was worn, all the women noted that this was an issue of obedience to Christ, an issue of servanthood, an issue even of humility: am I willing to lay aside my own desires (and even the dictates of fashion) for the sake of the Gospel? The issue is complicated and not self-evident, for what is appropriate dress in one situation may carry inappropriate personal or political overtones in a different situation. It is an issue that calls for discernment and prudence. These women were willing to make the hard choices. Several mentioned, however, that it was difficult to recruit younger women into the ministry simply because the issue of dress was a stumbling block.

Missionary women must deal not only with the issue of dress, but they must deal also with the issue of being female in the very masculine Muslim (and evangelical) world. Even very competent women that I have interviewed or that spoke on the panel (married or single, leading at a local or at a national level) could perceive themselves to be vulnerable: not protected where they needed protection; not supported financially or emotionally where such support would have been appreciated; verbally and sexually abused; isolated; with little or no institutional voice; their ministries buffeted by personal and financial challenges, often fruitful, but ephemeral, and unnoted.

For example, who today remembers the work of Carol Glasser and her Task Force for the Evangelization of Muslim Women, Zwemer Institute for Muslim Studies, 1979-82? Another example: women involved in hospitality ministries said, "I am not really in ministry; talk to xxx." Yet these are the women who prepare the way for the Gospel to be heard—and who DO preach the Gospel. These women have ministries that are in many ways equivalent to campus ministries. And yet out of this hiddenness and vulnerability emerge women of strong character and rich ministries.

Based on the stories shared in the panel and in the preparation for the panel, if we were to develop a theology, missiology, or strategy for women working with women in the Muslim communities of North America, I would probably start in some unusual places.

In addition to the mission strategy mentioned above of reconciliation of men and women in leadership and ministry, I would develop a strong theology/missiology/strategy of hospitality (MBB Esther [pseudonym] talked about God as host and the deep value of this for Muslims). I would discuss a theology/missiology/strategy of hiddenness and of small things (salt, yeast, widow's mites). I would consider a theology/missiology/strategy of domesticity (Sarah, Shiphrah, Puah, Miriam, Ruth, Mary, Dorcas). I would begin even to develop a theology of women's leadership and prophethood and holistic ministry (Sarah, Esther, Ruth, Mary Mother of Jesus, Mary Magdalene, Dorcas, Lydia). We would need to learn to cherish the humble, the vulnerable, the hidden, and the fleeting (Philip and the eunuch). We would need to learn to celebrate the goals, theologies, and strategies of the practical details of friendship and daily life. In order to model for Muslim women a good balance between private and public, domestic and institutional (Love, 2000), we need to celebrate women accomplishing the goals and strategies in both settings, the home and the church, the self-supported ministry and the fully-supported.

Helping women to find their voice theologically would affirm their ministries. Recognition of the work that women do would also strengthen their ministries. Financial support and the development of institutional leadership positions would be marvelous. By whatever Godly means, however, it is vital to strengthen and encourage women in their ministries, just as it is necessary to strengthen and encourage men. But women are the only ones who can reach women; women are essential for reaching half of the Muslim population and for reaching the younger generation—it is the mother who first trains the sons and the daughters. As women in partnership with men develop ways of reaching the Muslim woman (as well as the Muslim man) may we model the Kingdom of God here on earth as well as proclaim it boldly.

# CHAPTER 5

# Muslim Background Believers (MBBS) in North America

In the past, research efforts concerning Muslim Background Believers (MBB) in North America have been sparse. What has made this task difficult is the number of MBBs in various churches who have no contact with other MBBs. Neither the MBBs themselves nor the North American church considers them different than others who accept Christ. Fortunately, an increasing amount of research is now being attempted, although much more needs to be done in both quantity and quality. Presented below are some research efforts reported by various groups and individuals concerning a number of different ethnic groups.

## South Asian Muslim Background Believers

*Dr. Samuel Naaman*

Only a few times have people gathered together for an historic event to assess, discuss, and envision the future of Muslim ministry in North America. The time is now crucial as we look toward the next millennium.

Students of the history of missions will recall that the end of the last century was the beginning of a new era in world missions. SVM (Student Volunteer Mission) and other Christian mission organizations formed, and Western Christians took on the task of reaching the world. I praise God for this since many of us from South Asia are here because of their hard labor. Writing about believers with a South Asian Muslim background is my passion and burden because I grew up in such a home in Pakistan. I express my deep gratitude to all the brothers and sisters who opened their hearts and shared their thoughts with me on this topic.

First, we are going to look at first-generation Muslim Background Believers (MBBs). Then we will move on to the second generation, and after that, examine the role that the church in North America can play in reaching South Asians MBBs. A concluding section includes some personal observations.

## First Generation MBBs

This group has been in North America for many years. They include people who speak Urdu (the language of Indian/Pakistani Muslims). Few in this group heard the Gospel in their home countries or were able to read the Bible in their own languages. Some of them came here as refugees; others as immigrants. Some have children. Their impression of this country is quite negative. They mention that even the church has given them a cold shoulder. They miss the warmth and friendship they had in their home countries. Individualism, secularism, and materialism are evident in the lives of these people here, and they are often caught up in making money.

Some of them have been "used" by the local churches and organizations as a token of their labor in reaching Muslims. Many have been hurt as they have felt betrayed by the Western missionaries who used them for their own purposes. They have tried to fit in the local church, but have not been able to stay there. They have become isolated and at times it is hard for another missionary to approach them and bring them out of their shell.

Some who are married are busy with their family lives, but those who are single have found it difficult to adjust to this culture. Expectations on their part are at times too high for the church or the missionaries to fulfill; thus a cold relationship continues with no end in sight.

The tragedy is that some of these former Muslims are not even accepted or welcomed by the Christians from their home countries. This is not too surprising as history presents a very clear picture of how the national church has failed to accept Muslims who have received Christ and also fails to welcome them into the fellowship. Most of the people in this group are members of some mainline denominations with not much active participation. Some also attend the local South Asian worship services. However, many of these services are functioning to cater to other social needs of the society. Some have very little interest or burden to reach other Muslims. A number of missionaries do serve the MBBs faithfully, and our prayers should support them. They try to meet Muslims where they are and encourage them on an individual basis. The first generation MBBs seem to be closed to considering more options for fellowship. They tend to keep things to themselves.

## Second Generation MBBs

This group includes people who have come to know the Lord in North America. They feel very much part of the local church. They feel comfortable worshiping in English and taking part in the other activities of the churches. Many are eager to share their faith with other Muslims and want to learn more about Islam. They too share about the hurt and pain they have sometimes received from people who wanted to "use" them to present their ministries, but after that goal was accomplished, failed to encourage them on a consistent basis. This group has a lot of energy and enthusiasm, but little direction. Some of them are confused as to where the right place is for them to fit in.

It is interesting to see that many, though they were part of the local church, still felt empty and clung to the few South Asian workers. In some cities evangelical pastors have discipled them and this has been helpful.

This group also goes through identity crises. They are South Asians in their outlook, but have been raised in Western culture with Western values. At times it is difficult for them to mix with first-generation believers. Loneliness, rejection from their families, a cold attitude from the local Christians, and uncertainty about future life (including finding a Christian mate) are some of the main issues. Some are graduate students and some common workers.

## The Local North American Church

The local church in North America is beginning to function as a corporation. Many different approaches are tested to reach the seeker. "Seeker sensitive" services have become one of the trends of present-day Western Christianity. The local church on the whole is so busy keeping its members occupied and happy that it appears the church has little time for Muslims. I say this with caution because there are individuals in many churches who have a heart to reach Muslims and they do that outside the church through different groups.

I do not want to be overly critical about the North American church, but at times I wonder what is going on in the minds of local pastors and the people in the pews. Is it the whole aspect of "acceptance of diversity" that has hindered their efforts? Is it a fear of Muslims? The media certainly does not help in this matter. Is it complacency or the thought that all religions point people to the right path?

The fact of the matter is that the present church in its witness is not very open to reaching Muslims. They might like to support someone who wants to work among Muslims overseas, but when approached to participate in reaching them in North America, they show a cold response. Missionaries sometimes struggle to raise support if they want to reach Muslims in North America, but the story is a bit different if they are going overseas. Many believers still have not accepted the reality that North America is a mission field, and God is bringing people here for a special purpose.

The North American church and many of its pastors are not prepared to accept the challenge to reach Muslims. However, seminars and training courses are available if they want to be equipped for Muslim ministry.

## Conclusion

We could spend more time lamenting some of the above issues but that will not help our purpose. Here are some thoughts that may help those who are burdened to reach South Asian Muslims.

1. To reach South Asians, we need to have a "team approach." This is not a "lone ranger" game. Greg Livingstone in his book, *Planting Churches in Muslim Cities* (1993), has highlighted the importance of a team approach in reaching Muslims overseas, but the basic principles can be adopted in this country too. We are blessed by an excellent team of North Americans and South Asians in Chicago at the South Asian Friendship Center. People are attracted to this ministry because it portrays a community. Muslims want to join a Christian "Ummah"; they do not want to live in isolation. A big vacuum develops when they leave their family and culture to accept Christ. If it is not filled immediately, they revert and are difficult to reach again.

A team approach is crucial to have a significant impact on Muslims. This team may also cross denominational barriers in order to reach Muslims. We need to have a Kingdom perspective if we want to reach the masses. Denominational distinctives will always be with us, but we who are called to reach Muslims must put some of those aside and focus on the Kingdom of God as our priority. When people come to the Lord they want to be part of the Christian family. Let us not confuse them with our divisions and denominational preferences. Have our own denominational preferences hindered the Gospel proclamation? If so, let us confess and move on to have victory in Jesus' name. The South Asian Friendship Center in Chicago is a classic model for having a multiracial and interdenominational team.

2. In reaching Muslims we have to confront the issue of racism. It is sad that people who claim to be Bible-believing Christians still struggle with this sin. It surfaces in our conversations, but we need to repent and accept people of all races into our fellowship.

3. People who have accepted the Lord need a "safe home." Some may need jobs and shelter in a time of crucial need. Western churches become cautious when they encounter such situations. Often there is no place to send these people. It is sad that the very people who are champions of "friendship ministry" in some of the big suburban churches in Chicagoland have nothing to offer for situations like this. It appears at times that we use the South Asians just to calm and soothe our guilty conscience. We invite them once a year for a Thanksgiving dinner or a cookout in summer. Our friendship ministry is then accomplished. We take a lot of pictures that become part of our prayer letters. But if someone needs more than that, we get confused and overwhelmed. At times laws may restrict us as we try to help someone in need, but at other times there is simply no excuse for not opening our homes to them. We need to address this problem as a body.

4. We need to accept the reality that the local church with all its good intentions is not equipped to reach Muslims. We can argue and debate, but that does not accomplish much. Instead of lamenting and counting the failures of the North American church and its role in Muslim evangelism, we need to identify, champion, train, and encourage individuals who have a heart for Muslim work. Many who feel inadequate because they fear that they do not know much about Muslim evangelism become willing, with encouragement, to learn and move out of their comfort zones to reach the Muslims.

During the last few years at Moody teaching courses in Islam, I have met many students who have a heart to reach Muslims but are scared because they do not know how. Often, all it takes is to give them confidence, pray with them, and assure them that God will and can use us, broken as we may be, to reach Muslims. In my experience the younger generation is ready to respond to the challenge of Islam and is willing to pay the price. We may need to admit and accept the fact that their ways will be different from ours. Are we willing to love them and build them up to be new pioneers in Muslim evangelism? It can be hard to pass the torch to this new generation as they may do and approach things differently. But if we do not invest in them, putting aside our own prejudices about their lack of commitment, we will lose them. We need to invest our lives in them and give them the confidence that they can be effective change agents, able to revolutionize the world in reaching Muslims.

5.  We need to be sensitive to the needs of new MBBs. This is absolutely crucial. Time and again I come across people who have been saved but who have had no proper follow-up. Therefore they become bitter, lukewarm Christians. The new believer watches other Christians closely. If the Gospel has not made much difference, they are labeled as hypocrites. This follow-up has to be done on a long-term basis. Giving the Gospel is not enough. Are we willing to pay the price of being consistent in our relationship and friendship with the new believer? Friendships in the West appear to be very seasonal at times. Are we willing to be friends for life?

6.  The cost of leaving Islam is often not communicated to a South Asian new believer. It is important for us to tell them the price they will pay in accepting Christ. At times we feel that persecution in the West is not as intense, but many times I see the same things happening to Asians who accept Christ here.

7.  For Western change agents, the issue of "time and space" is a real barrier. Western workers are accustomed to events happening on schedule. They may become frustrated when it requires a longer period of time to get results. In the West, people are also accustomed to having personal private space, and they guard it jealously. The South Asian does not have this understanding of private space and may expect the home to be open to them at all times. New missionaries will have to tackle such issues.

8.  Individualism and independence are valued in the West but are contrary to the concept of family and interdependence, which are highly praised values in the East. Can we put aside our Western values to the point that we can adopt New Testament church values and become an apostolic group of believers strongly dedicated to Muslim evangelism?

9.  We need to train many more women workers if we want to reach South Asian families. The separation between sexes is common among traditional Muslims. So we need trained women workers, maybe even more than men.

10. Second-generation Muslims are more open to reason and to exploring truth. We need to invite them into our homes and fellowships since they want to feel part of society. The younger generation is the key to reaching students in our high schools and colleges.

11. Counting results is always a point of tension. We need to communicate to workers how important it is to be patient. I sometimes ask the question, "If a Muslim shares about Islam and extends to us the invitation to become Muslims, would we usually accept it the first time around?" Or, "Do you want your child to go to a Muslim kids club or program?" If the answer to the above questions is "no," this will help us learn to be patient in letting the Holy Spirit take his time to convict them. Only then will they accept the truth.

12. We need more networking among people who are working among South Asian Muslims. This kind of sharing will help as we shape new strategies and share our struggles, joys, successes, and failures.

It is never my intention to criticize any specific group or ministry. Rather my fervent prayer is that we will learn from each other and become better equipped to share the Good News of the Gospel with Muslims. May God help us all to do that.

## Iranian MBBs

### Abe Ghaffari

In a survey by Iranian Christians International, the average age of those who responded to the questionnaire was 44 years. The average age of the Muslim background believers who had accepted Jesus Christ was 26. Unfortunately, only males responded to the questionnaire, likely because the questionnaire was in English only. It was the responsibility of the people who sent the questionnaires to the specific ethnic groups to translate it, and this task was not accomplished.

At least fifty percent of the conversions involved the Christian church or a direct Christian witness. It is also important to note that 50 percent said there were personal factors or crises involved in their experience. One of the main attributes they stated about their changed lives in Jesus Christ was the peace they now have. Time and time again in looking through these converts' responses, some similar statement was found: "Now I have peace." Some also said that now they had hope, while others said that they were now experiencing genuine, true Christian love.

Eighty-three percent indicated that they had received help or fellowship from the local church. Many remembered that the church had prayed for them. Sixty-six percent stated that they were currently part of a local church. One respondent indicated that his local Iranian church was having some problems so he was in between churches at that time. There is not always a rosy picture in the churches.

Concerning the needs to which they felt the local church should direct its attention—they deeply desire sound teaching. They need to know the difference between law and grace. One respondent wanted to know how he could effectively witness to Muslims. Another felt that the church had not been involved in his life since conversion. As to whether the Iranian Muslim MBB has a passion for other Muslims, there is little doubt. They want to see other Muslims come to a saving knowledge of Jesus Christ. A full one hundred percent said they had a desire to reach and evangelize other Muslims.

In an article printed in *Religion Today*, October 7, 1999, I stated: "There are currently 35 Iranian churches in the United States. The Iranian church is growing but it's falling way short of its potential. We need to encourage and mobilize Iranian Christians to evangelize more effectively."

## International Student MBBs

### *David Philip*

This survey was among Muslim background believers who had specifically come to Christ while students in North America. This is a very focused group. In the end, we came up with fourteen names of those who have come to Christ while university students in North America. Contact was actually made with twelve, and of the twelve nine responded. Two of them I met with personally. The others I corresponded with by e-mail.

The nine ranged in age from 21 to 68, but most were in their 20s or early 30s. The group consisted of two females and seven males. In terms of national background, five were from Turkey and one each from Kuwait, Lebanon, Afghanistan, and Sudan. We cannot necessarily conclude by these small numbers that God is working in some special way among Turks. Perhaps the Turks simply responded because my background involved Turkey. Concerning careers, several are still students, but their number also includes an engineer, a translator for the U.S. military, a retired government official from Afghanistan, a social worker, and one who is a full-time Christian missionary.

With the small group involved in this survey. we cannot draw any hard conclusions, but we can at least examine some of the responses.

*Question 1—How and when did you meet Christians?*

For most of this group, their first exposure to Christians was during the 1990s, although one was a student at Iowa State in the early 60s who returned to a long career in Afghanistan and is now a U.S. citizen living in America. They met Christians by being invited to

Christian activities on campus or simply met individual Christians there or went to church.

*Question 2—What are the factors that led you to trust Christ as Lord and Savior?*

Most of the respondents indicated that it was the influence of Christians and/or studying the Bible with them that made the difference. Personal contact with believers, observing their lives, and then working through the Scriptures with them answered their questions. One mentioned a personal crisis in his life. Another mentioned that he had become dissatisfied with Islam in his country before he came to the United States. So in addition to his studies, he had purposely come to the U.S. to seek out Christians to answer questions that his Muslim scholars would not answer back home. One of the first things he did was to obtain a Bible and then search for Christians. One respondent indicated that he had read the Bible completely on his own without any contact with Christians and trusted Christ without outside influences.

*Question 3—How has Christ changed your life and do you feel satisfied?*

A wide variety of responses were given as to how Christ changed their lives. Some of those factors were that they matured emotionally; they gained confidence; Christ took away their fears; they feel love now instead of hate; they are no longer worried about the future; and Christ took away desires for partying, drugs, alcohol, and immoral relationships. Another interviewee indicated that life has completely changed and he now feels peace—a factor often mentioned by converts in the above survey.

In terms of satisfaction, eight out of nine indicated satisfaction but of those, one said, "I've suffered much." He had been in prison, his grandson was murdered before his eyes, and he was cut off from his family. Another one said that she had given up a lot of dreams she had when she came to the United States as an international student. She abandoned many of her former goals and had lost loved ones as a result of her decision. But nearly in the same breath she stated, "I have absolutely no regrets. If I were to die tonight, I'd be the happiest person in the world." Another respondent talked about how much he had suffered, but again, had absolutely no regret about the decision he had made. One respondent pointed out that he was not satisfied because of what he described as "his inability to carry out the decision to walk with Christ."

*Question 4—Did you receive any help or fellowship from a local church?*

Three reported no—just individual Christians had helped. The other six replied yes, but it was interesting that the help received was no more than any other average new American Christian might receive. The help that came their way was not anything special or different from what they saw happening with other converts in the church. They received teaching and friendship. But one person responded that she received lots of help from the church—emotional, spiritual, financial, and prayer support. It is interesting to note that this person is now a full-time Christian worker.

*Question 5—Are you part of a local church?*

Five of the nine said that they were very active; two attend but with no active involvement; and two said they do not attend.

*Question 6—Do you have any needs that are not being met by the local church or individual Christians?*

The answers fell into two categories. One might be called spiritual needs. They mentioned that they felt needs for greater discipleship, a prayer partner, or some kind of support group, particularly those who were cut off from their families. They yearned to have someone who was closer to them than what they were now experiencing.

Other needs might be characterized as practical, such as help in finding a job. One was very worried about providing for extended family that he is trying to bring to the United States. Two mentioned that they feel a need for help finding a wife who comes from their kind of background. The question is, "What can I do to find a partner who would really complement me and my background?" One other comment concerned experiencing loneliness, but that situation partly involved a recent move.

*Question 7—Do you have the desire to share Christ with other Muslims?*

The Iranian response mentioned above was similar to the response that we received. Seven of the nine very clearly answered yes; they had the desire to share Christ. However, they were quick to add some "buts"—they experienced some very real concerns. One said, "I'd like to, but it would be a lot easier if it wasn't with members of my immediate family." Another added, "Yes, but I don't know enough yet to do that." Another answer was, "Yes, but I am afraid of the consequences." And another has definite health limitations. One person is asking the Lord if that is something the Lord wants him to do because he is very aware of the persecution that will come if he does so. One respondent has not yet told anyone of his decision because he is so concerned about the reaction of the Muslim community.

## Conclusions

There are obviously individuals who have come to Christ from this background, but the numbers are very small. Maybe there are more out there that we don't know about, or some who are just afraid to give out that information. Perhaps they didn't want to communicate with someone they didn't know by means of the Internet, and we can understand that.

Because the response is not that great among Muslims, unless there is a very strong call it is easy right now to tend to work among other nationalities who are more responsive. The other factor to consider, for those of us in a campus situation, is that generally the Muslim community is not that big, and doesn't seem to justify a full-time position working only among Muslim students. What happens is that one ends up spending more time with other nationalities. Is that right or wrong? I don't know. That's just the reality of the situation.

In terms of individual Christians, God is using believers who are taking the initiative with Muslim students. Their lives are attractive to the Muslims, and personally they are able to share the gospel. Concerning the North American church and Muslim international students, what I hear is that the North American church is friendly and willing to teach, but that's about the highest level of commitment they are going to give to Muslim background believers. My feedback is that in general, they don't really understand the needs of a Muslim background believer. It's not so much intentional as it is just ignorance. The church in the Middle East or India, living side by side with the Muslim culture, tends to understand the needs of someone coming out of that background. But the North American church just cannot comprehend the situation that the Muslim background believer faces.

Finally, the Muslim converts that I talked to are willing to share their faith, but they still have very real concerns and dangers, even living here in North America. I felt encouraged as I interacted with them.

## African American MBBs

### Wilford Darden

I am the president and founder of a ministry that primarily deals with sharing Christ with those involved in the Nation of Islam. To really get a grasp of what it takes to share Christ with that group, we first need to consider some of the problems.

We primarily target two types of men. If you can move the men, the women will usually follow. We target the men because of the identity issue. The first type are men who have been influenced stereotypically by the Nation of Islam. This means they are caught up in the rhetoric and philosophy, but they are not actually members attending a mosque. The percentage is high and often imported into the local African American churches. It is quite easy to find someone in an African American church who is a sympathizer to the Nation of Islam. So when we go in and say this group needs to be saved, this causes tremendous psychological persecution toward us.

The second type are those who are actually members of the Fruit of Islam. In order to become a member of the Fruit of Islam you have to change your name and attend the mosques. It is a totally different issue to bring them to Christ because doing so could cost them their lives. The Nation of Islam is not exactly Muslim but cultic. This means you don't necessarily think for yourself. You think according to the stereotypical teaching of the leader.

So whatever Louis Farrakhan has to say is not really challenged by the young Muslim. In fact, when Farrakhan comes to town and we take groups out to share Christ with them, when Farrakhan starts to speak, young Muslims stand around the building like security guards. While others are having an identity crisis or are trying to find something to belong to, these guys stand there militant and unified.

Here's one of the strategies we use. While they are standing there, we go over and say, "Let me ask you this question." The sergeant over them will sometimes tell us we can't talk to them. We just reply, "You can't tell me that. I can talk to anybody I want. Perhaps they can't talk to me, but I can talk to them. So if you don't mind, and I don't mean you any harm, you need to patrol over that way somewhere. I need to talk to this brother."

Then there's often a certain look on the guy's face, so I say, "Listen, you remember Jim Jones? Jim Jones took 900 people into this place called Guyana and all of them had to drink poison. Let me ask you, if Farrakhan says go to Guyana, do you go?" Then I can watch a big lump come in this fellow's throat, and he's looking around as though he wants to ask someone, "Are we supposed to go there?"

At that point we can see that there are actually some things they haven't really thought through. So sometimes we'll say, "Listen, we're leaving information around. If you really want to know if Farrakhan is going to Guyana, call us and we'll let you know because you'll probably be the last to know." This is effective. Sometimes they will call.

However, here's the challenge. If they come out of the Nation of Islam, where do we take them from there? As we share Christ on the street corners, here's something that has really challenged me. This is what one man said when I was talking to him about coming to Christ. He asked, "Come to Christ and do what? Join a local church and sing in the choir? Be called to preach? We aren't attracted to that." He went on to say, "In the Nation, we're involved in helping our people. What are you all involved in?" It's a good challenge to the church. In order to lead these men to Christ, we have to get them involved in some type of ministry to people.

## Conclusion

In one questionnaire, an Arab convert stated, "Being raised in a Muslim home, I knew the teachings of Islam. My dad is a Haji. An uncle and a brother-in-law are both Imams at local mosques. So for one year of my adult life I chose to be a true practicing Muslim. But I continued to feel empty. I knew I was going to hell."

The same person also emphasized, "Let your friend ask questions and you answer. Win Muslims to Christ by letting them see the hope that lies within you. Let your Muslim friends ask questions and allow the Holy Spirit to lead them into all understanding. Have patience and persevere."

That MBB, as with so many others mentioned from the many different groups touched on in this chapter, began her search for Christ because of a relationship with a Christian. Her sister's friend gave her a Bible to read. She read every day for ten months, and then went to church with her friend. Although there were a few exceptions, in every group, contact with a Christian was the main avenue for finding Christ. Christians need to be looking for Muslims at their work and in their neighborhoods and forming friendships with them. It may be the first step toward seeing that person won to Christ.

Another theme running throughout the various groups of converts was a search for peace. The present unrest in Muslim lands makes this search for peace even deeper. These Muslims greatly desire peace in their hearts and lives, and indicated that they found it in a personal relationship with Jesus Christ. When visiting with Muslim contacts, and when sharing our own experiences, we can stress the peace we find when Christ brings our life into his kingdom and grants healing through forgiveness of sins.

Another repeated topic was the ineffectiveness of argument, as a general rule. Christians need to be as informed as possible when dealing with Muslims, but with many of them, forming a friendship with a Christian and watching a Christlike life will be convincing points. Christians should not be afraid of establishing friendships with Muslims but rather seek them out and let them see a daily walk for Christ. Though campus ministry groups might overlook Muslims because of more responsiveness by other groups, they can link groups seeking to minister to Muslims. In most populous areas with a significant Muslim population, some type of Muslim outreach can be found. These are key groups or individuals to give counsel on relating and witnessing to Muslims.

The local church played a role in the lives of those surveyed. The amount of time and interest the church invested in the life of the MBB had an effect on the person. Though many of the needs are similar to other converts, there were special needs that came from their background, such as loss of family. The local church became the new surrogate family. This was expressed with a desire for closer relationships. The need of finding a mate was also expressed and is a concern that requires a broader networking with other MBBs.

In most of the surveys, the respondents indicated a strong desire to share their newfound Christian faith with their Muslim brothers and sisters. But many did not know how. Just because they come from a Muslim background does not mean they know how to witness to their own people. Some may need training in this area. Many indicated very real threats and consequences because of their conversion, and persecution for witnessing. The local church needs to be aware that some MBBs need special care due to their circumstances. The church should take time to listen and provide assistance as MBBs work through some of these faith-related issues.

When a decision does not seem to be immediately forthcoming, loving patience and perseverance are important points. Costly decisions are usually not made overnight. Sometimes it takes years of loving witness to overcome the costs of a decision for Christ. Continue to be a friend, offer practical help where possible, and answer questions as they arise.

Muslim ministry in North America is not without its difficulties, and may seem to show very slow progress. We must remember that Islam's history in North America is relatively recent. However, the church is beginning to recognize this new element of society and to respond to this religious group. Though infant in its beginnings, there is a willing heart, a growing amount of information, and prayer. With God's help it is possible to help Muslims find the peace they are seeking in Jesus Christ.

Section 2

# A Way of Presenting the Gospel to Muslims

# CHAPTER 6

# Christ the Victor

*Roy Oksnevad*

## Introduction

Three great monotheistic religions exist in the world today; Judaism, Christianity, and Islam. All three speak against idolatry, affirming that God is One while calling people to a higher moral standard. All three teach that people should be submitted to God and follow his word.

In recent years, Westerners have been meeting Muslims up close as they have been emigrating en masse to the West. As Christians in the West seek to share Christ with Muslims, they are confronted with a religious belief they have not encountered before. Can the Christian message be shared without causing so much misunderstanding? Is there something the Western Church is failing to understand as it tries to share with its new Muslim neighbors? If Christians will take into consideration fundamental differences as they present the gospel, they will be more effective in sharing the Christian message with new Muslim neighbors and friends.

### Conflict

For the Christian, the heart of the gospel is to share the wonderful message of Christ's gift of salvation through his birth, death, and resurrection. The first conflict arises over the nature of Jesus. All too often, while attempting to share the reason for Christ's birth, Christians present the theological concept of the Incarnation (God becoming a human being). This raises the "hackles" of the average Muslim, who proclaims God's Oneness in every prayer five times a day. The hallmark of Islam is the Oneness of God. Though Christianity also teaches that God is One, Islam is particularly sensitive to what they consider a Christian heresy, the Trinity. Muslims are unwilling to accept the Christian affirmation that God is One and are told that Christians believe in three gods.

The conflict continues over the nature of Jesus because Muslims see Jesus as a great miracle-working prophet, not the second person of the Trinity. Muslims are taught that the role of the prophet is to call people to repentance and that some prophets were given God's word for a specific people and time. They are taught that Jesus was given the Gospel for the Christians, but He is not the Savior of the world. They are told that Muhammad is the last and greatest prophet so Jesus cannot have a position greater than Muhammad.

Another major area of conflict concerns Islam's understanding of justice. When Christians share that Christ died to save us from our sins, the Muslim calls this reasoning unjust, for everyone must die for his or her own sins; there can be no substitute. Muslims have a clearly defined understanding of God's justice, which does not accept substitution in a sacrificial system, particularly the Christian definition of atoning sacrifice.

As Christians share the gospel, they should keep in mind that when they impose the biblical understanding on these subjects, the Muslim will be offended. It is not unreasonable for Muslims to refuse to try to understand the Christian position, considering the things they have been taught. Any attempt by the Christian to use the Scriptures to redefine the Muslim's understanding of the person of Christ and his work gets a standard response, basically stating that the Scriptures as recorded in the Bible are corrupt. The last revelation as found in the Qur'an is the latest word on the subject and is not corrupt.

## Purpose

Rather than unending dialogue over such issues as those mentioned above, I have gone back to the gospels and church history to discover ways the early church presented the message of Christ's work on the cross. It is my intent that the liberating message of Christ's work on the cross be proclaimed without continual rejections and assumptions by Muslims.

## Various Approaches

Various approaches have been used to reach Muslims. First, there is the apologetic approach. Here the Christian attempts to answer each objection with a truthful and reasonable answer found either from Scripture or from historical evidence. For this approach to be effective, the person needs to be knowledgeable about Christian doctrine and apologetics (answers to objections) as well as Islamic sources and arguments. Authors N. Geisler and A. Saleeb have written an excellent book entitled, *Answering Islam: The Crescent in the Light of the Cross* (1993).

The second approach is called the Bridge. In this approach, the person tries to find some aspect in the other's religion from which they can build a bridge to a similar concept in their own religious perspective and give it meaning. An example would be using the Muslims' annually celebrated feast of *al-Adha* (at which a sheep or ram is sacrificed) and trying to use it to explain Jesus as the sacrificial lamb.

In the third approach the basic assumption is that God's Word is truth and all we need to do is share the Word. It is understood that the Holy Spirit will take the words of Scripture and the word of witness and convict the person of sin, righteousness, and judgment.

Another approach takes into consideration some of the cultural ways of passing on information. Story telling is one such vehicle. Some have retold the parables with the perspective of introducing one aspect of the Kingdom of God to the listener as Christ did, in a culturally relevant manner. Martin Goldsmith, in his book *Islam and Christian Witness* (1983), gives excellent examples of this cultural method.

Yet another approach uses common evangelistic tools with modifications for the Muslim audience. Campus Crusade for Christ, Lebanon, has done this with their time-tested tool, *The Four Spiritual Laws.* They changed the order of the points and added a defense for the Scriptures to address the common objection Muslims have about the corruption of the Bible.

A method I have found helpful is "Christ the Victor." This approach looks at the Islamic worldview, which sees the universe inhabited by a myriad of spiritual beings, some good and some evil; the whole concept of Satan, jinn, and angels is used to determine key issues to address. The concept of using Christ the Victor speaks to the Near Eastern worldview of the great battle of Satan against mankind.

This came together when I was in Belgium and shared it with an Algerian in a coffee bar. At the end, he said, "This is the first time I have heard the Gospel," although others had witnessed to him before. And he accepted Christ.

## Biblical Foundations for Presenting Christ to Muslims

I try to follow two themes in presenting Christ to Muslims. Both themes are found in Johannine literature and were themes of the gospel in the early church Fathers. First is the theme of life, and secondly, Christ the Victor.

### Life

In Revelation 20:12–15 entrance into heaven is based upon whether an individual's name is found in the Lamb's book of life. In Gen. 2:9 there was the tree of life, and in Revelation 22:2 there is the tree of life. In John 10:10 Jesus says, "I have come that they may have life, and have it to the full" (NIV). I John 5:12 states, "He who has the Son has life; he who does not have the Son of God does not have life."

This theme of life is found in the early church Father, Irenaeus.

> … For what purpose did Christ come down from heaven? Answer: "That He might destroy sin, overcome death, and give life to man." By the side of this pregnant saying we will set another, chosen from among many similar passages, which develops the dramatic idea in fuller detail: "Man had been created by God that he might have life. If now, having lost life, and having been harmed by the serpent, he were not to return to life, but were to be wholly abandoned to death, then God would have been defeated, and the malice of the serpent would have overcome God's will…through the Second Man He [God] bound the strong one, and spoiled his goods, and annihilated death, bringing life to man who had become subject to death" (Aulen 1937, 35).

### Christ the Victor

The second theme is Christ the Victor. The Bible is pregnant with the theme of a cosmic battle fought for God's creation. It tells us that a foundational reason Christ came was "to destroy the works of the devil" (I John 3:8) and to "destroy the one who has the power of death, that is, the devil" (Heb. 2:14). Satan had to be defeated. For a fuller development of this concept, Gustaf Aulen's book *Christus Victor: An Historical Study of the Three Maine Types of the Idea of the Atonement* (1937) is an excellent resource.

> In the first of these passages Irenaeus speaks of sin and death as the enemies of mankind; in the second there emerges by the side of or behind death the figure of the devil…The work of Christ is first and foremost a victory over the powers

which hold mankind in bondage: sin, death, and the devil...the victory of Christ creates a new situation, bringing their rule to an end, and setting men free from their domination (Aulen 1937, 35).

The strength of the Christus Victor approach is that it doesn't assume the deity of Christ to understand the purpose of Christ. It doesn't require Muslims to understand a new judicial system that requires substitution. Christ the Victor stresses the sovereignty of God and the victorious aspect of God (familiar Islamic concepts), and broadens the scope of Christ's work to include the devil and death, as well as sin. It is not my intent to change the gospel or to unduly criticize other attempts in presenting the gospel, but rather to give another tool and perspective to be considered when introducing Muslim friends to Christ.

## A Critique of Popular Western Premises

In viewing the popular evangelistic material presently being passed around in Christian circles, much of it seems to begin with a Western orientation or worldview. These methods then seek to find symbols or cultural events in the Islamic world that might explain Western theology. However, these presentations are used in a way foreign to Muslim thinking.

Islamic symbols and cultural events are often reinterpreted to reflect Western priorities and theological points of view over against Islamic priorities and theological sensitivities. For example, should the presenter use the "Id Al-Adha" bridge approach, Islam rejects outright substitutional sacrifice. The explanation given by Muslims of this festival and story is generosity, not substitution. On a theoretical basis, it seems that we make certain theological assumptions (it is obvious that God provided an acceptable sacrifice) and needlessly spend much of our time trying to convince the audience to accept these assumptions.

We should remember that the aim of the Qur'an is man and his behavior, not God. Islamic teaching centers on 1) everything except God is contingent upon God, 2) that God is the all-merciful God, and 3) a proper relationship between God and man is a relationship of the served and the servant. Trying to convince Muslims of certain Christian theological priorities may be a needless hindrance in presenting Christ.

## Where to Start

Common ground is an important place to begin. When Christians begin with God as they share Christ with Muslims, they immediately enter into the Islamic theological worldview where Muslims have clear definitions of God. Christians may have to shift common ground away from a theological starting point, toward how human beings experience life.

I would suggest that instead of starting the gospel presentation from God's perspective, we use instead the perspective of how man experiences life on earth. All too often Christians end up arguing about the God perspective in their presentations and rarely get on with the message of God's salvation found in Christ. Basing a gospel presentation on how God enters into daily life to help face life's challenges, to live life to its full, and to have a living hope avoids speaking about philosophy, ideology, or religion. The way all people face life and the quality of their life may be the best common ground.

## Fellowship with God

*Christian starting point.* Most gospel presentations begin with the theological assumption that an intimate relationship exists between God and man. However, this relationship was broken when man disobeyed God by eating of the fruit in the Garden of Eden. Both God and man are trying to reestablish or restore this relationship. Man has been unable to do so, yet God promised to do so and has done so through Christ.

*Islamic perspective.* Fellowship with God is not possible. To bring God down to an interactive level with mankind is considered disrespectful. God is to remain distant and unapproachable. God does not need man nor is He like man. Therefore, a relationship is not expected, sought, or taught. (An exception to this is popular Sufi Islam. In Sufism, God is presented as being close and an intimate relationship with him is sought.)

*Alternative starting point.* Since so many of the assumed Biblical perspectives have another meaning in Islam, I think it best to start with the creation story in Genesis, not with fellowship between God and man. Since Islam so strongly guards its understanding of Allah or God, this issue can be sidestepped until another time.

I begin with God as the creator of mankind (accepted in Islamic teaching). Mankind was created 100 percent good—full and complete. God makes everything perfect and human beings are the crowning work of God's creation. Muslims will not disagree with this description. It is better to avoid using the phrase "created in God's image" for fear of needlessly entering into defending what "image" means and does not mean. (Muslims who love to debate might take this opening to argue that God is wholly other, and mankind is not the image of Allah, for God has no form.) In beginning with a positive image of man, we avoid the Islamic argument that they have a better image of man, which does not include a sin nature.

## The Fall

*Christian perspective.* Following the theme of fellowship with God in Western presentations, Christians often proceed to a discussion of the breaking of this fellowship with God, called the Fall. They may state that now man is separated from God. God is presented as seeking to re-establish this intimate fellowship with man through the promise of a Messiah Jesus. Christ is presented as the bridge between God and man so again God and man can have fellowship.

*Islamic perspective.* Muslims believe that Adam's sin did not affect all mankind. Adam asked for forgiveness and Allah, who is forgiving and merciful, forgave Adam's sin. Each person is born sinless. From a Muslim perspective, man's duty is to reverence, honor, obey, and respect God. Any familiarity between God and man is disrespectful.

*Alternative view.* How then should we present the Fall? Both Islam and Christianity have a concept of temptation and a Fall where mankind is no longer in paradise but sent to earth (or the Christian version where mankind was banished from the garden). Rather than pushing Christian theology on the significance of the Fall, we can explain that since the time of Adam, the human race has suffered from the effects of sin. Murder, rebellion, wars, lying, cheating, coveting, misplaced sexual desires, abuse of power, greed—the list goes on and on of the unworthy deeds mankind commits, no matter the religion, race, or nation. This is neither the will nor desire of God for mankind.

By presenting the fact that persons are unable to achieve balance by themselves, the biblical concept of original sin is introduced. When the various remedies for sin are presented, such as knowledge, discipline, religion, or law, it becomes clear that none of these has the power to produce balance or control the evil in human lives.

## The Concept of Sin

*Christian assumptions.* Within the Christian understanding of mankind, after the Fall all human beings are born into sin. Man after the Fall is not born neutral, but born powerless to do good. Thus the Christian usually seeks to convince non-Christians that they are sinners—born in original sin. Christians quote Romans 3:10–23, which declares there is no one righteous who seeks God, or does good. Therefore, mankind is in need of a Savior to forgive sins.

*Islamic perspective.* Islam usually presents mankind as essentially good, although the teaching is not always clear and at times, mankind may be bent toward corruption. According to Islam, the problem of sin is basically ignorance of God's law (shari'a) and the Qur'an. It is taught that what people become is due to a collection of influences; heredity, environment, destiny, and jinn. Added to this is an understanding that God is merciful and forgiving. Allah will overlook sin if persons truly repent and do some good to counterbalance the bad. Sin is relegated to a weakness of mankind. There is no need for atonement. The Qur'anic teaching on forgiveness can be found in Surah 3:18:

> Say: "If ye do love Allah, Follow me: Allah will love you and forgive you your sins: For Allah is Oft-Forgiving, Most Merciful..."

*Caution.* For the Christian, sin separates mankind from God. All were born sinners and therefore separated from God. The Christian view of sin seems rather unpalatable to the post-modern person as well as to Muslims. Muslims could easily pride themselves that their understanding of mankind is positive and filled with hope in comparison with the Christian understanding of human nature.

The Muslim is taught that Allah will judge good and bad deeds. Inherent in their concept of sin is found the motivation to strive for a holy life. According to their logic, if all the person's sins are forgiven, past, present, and future, then the motivation for striving to live a good life is removed. By saying that Christ forgives sin, we do not want to leave the impression that we have removed motivation for holy living, or that Christians can do any sort of vice or sin with no consequences from God.

*Alternative.* Most Muslims speak of themselves as not being good Muslims. All human beings, if they are honest, will share how they struggle with sin. Getting people to acknowledge that sin reigns uncontrollably in them is the first step in understanding Jesus' death. Regardless of one's theological or philosophical understanding of this phenomenon, it is an undisputed fact that human beings are sinners.

Christianity recognizes that human nature has a bent toward sin, such as greed and selfishness. Generally speaking it takes effort and concentration to achieve a good deed. At the same time, no one has to make very much effort in order to act selfishly—hurting someone, avoiding responsibility, or even doing something evil. Man disobeyed God and something foreign (bad or evil) entered into mankind. But this bad is not God's plan for mankind. At the same time, the good that might be in humans becomes latent or dead. Some examples are:

1) Relationship with spouse: We understand how we are to act around our spouses, to love them and to do good to them. Yet the good we try to do often comes out wrong, or we just fail to do the good we know we should do.

2) Parent/child relationships: The same goes for parent/child relationships. It seems that effort must be applied to doing good, to being sensitive and understanding, or the bad side just comes out naturally.

3) Children: Parents know we do not need to teach children to be bad. They act badly, get into trouble, and turn mean so easily. In contrast, we must regularly correct them and teach them to do good. Even then, the good sometimes seems forced.

### Doctrine of the Atonement

*Christian assumption.* Western Christians assume that Christ's work on the cross can best be explained in the concept of the atonement. This perspective has been popular since the time of the great theologian Anselm in the eleventh century AD. There is ample biblical support for the substitutionary atonement throughout the Old Testament, as shown in the sacrificial system. Many Western Christians are taught that a person cannot come to faith in Christ without first understanding the atonement, explained as the penal substitutionary atonement.

*Islamic perspective.* The words "substitutionary atonement" put most Muslims on guard. They are quick to quote, "No one can die in the place of another." They are taught that one of the lies of the Christians is what they say Jesus came to do—die on the cross for our sins. Consider what is repeated in the prayers of Muslims five times daily. Throughout their daily prayer the uniqueness of God is espoused and the slave/master relationship is affirmed. Muslims cast themselves upon the mercy of God and his guidance. No concept of substitution is mentioned.

*Caution.* The doctrine of the atonement evokes several concepts for the Muslim that the Christian must unravel. First is the concept of justice. Muslims view the atonement as not fitting into their understanding of Allah's justice. In Islam, each person must die for his or her own sins. Second, sacrifice in Islamic tradition and teaching, particularly as understood by the average Muslim that Westerners meet, has only the significance of generosity and duty.

To legitimize the concept of substitution, Christians may use the annual feast of *al-Adha* and try to create a redemptive analogy of Christ. For Muslims worldwide the festival is a generous time of year. Part of the meat from the killing of the lamb is distributed among the poor and needy for food, and the remainder is used to feed the household and is shared with relatives and friends. The more informed Muslims are instructed that the word "sacrifice" used in this context does not have the usual meaning of atonement for sin or an attempt to appease an angry deity. It signifies the remembrance of the willingness of Abraham to sacrifice his own desires and attachments in submission to God.

*Alternative.* To avoid the misconceptions found in the Islamic worldview of the atonement, we should ask ourselves whether it is possible to explain the essence of Christianity, which is the death, burial, and resurrection of Jesus Christ, without looking at it from the substitutionary sacrifice point of view. It is true that any person coming to Christ will at some point need to come to understand the cross of Christ from this perspective. Yet, again I ask, at the initial stage of explaining the gospel, is this the time to introduce this concept? Gregory Boyd in his book, *God at War: The Bible and Spiritual Conflict* (1997, 240), states

> The New Testament speaks about the significance of the cross in a variety of ways: it was an atoning sacrifice for our sin (Heb. 10:10–14); it satisfied God's justice (Rom. 3:25); it provided an example for believers (Phil. 2:5–11; I Pet. 2:21); and it conquered Satan (John 12:31; Col. 2:14–15; 1 John 3:8)…

> Since at least the time of Anselm in the eleventh century AD and especially since the Reformation in the sixteenth century, the tendency of the Western church has been to focus almost all its attention on…the atonement, usually to the neglect of the cosmic dimension that is central to the New Testament.

> From the perspective of the New Testament…the significance of Christ's death and resurrection is rooted in something more fundamental and broad that God was aiming at:

to defeat once and for all his cosmic archenemy, Satan, along with the other evil powers under his dominion.

Presenting Christ as victor over Satan is a way to open doors without getting the usual Islamic objections. Christ the Victor is a powerful concept not foreign to the Muslim's worldview. Our goal from this angle is to present Jesus as the One who is more powerful than evil. I John 3:8 is our reference point:

> He who does what is sinful is of the devil, because the devil has been sinning from the beginning. The reason the Son of God appeared was to destroy the devil's work (NIV).

Presenting the death, burial, and resurrection of Jesus as a purposeful act designed to overcome evil takes away the shame so often associated with this fact in Jesus' life. His death and resurrection becomes linked to a celestial battle to overcome evil.

Jesus made it clear that no one would take his life from him. His purpose was to die and rise again. Thus the words of Jesus spoken in John 10:17–18:

> The reason my Father loves me is that I lay down my life—only to take it up again. No one takes it from me, but I lay it down of my own accord. I have authority to lay it down and authority to take it up again. This command I received from my Father (NIV).

*Illustration.* There was once a man who boasted that he was stronger than the prison and all the prison guards. Hearing of these boasts, the prison guards went to capture the man. But the man disappeared. Was he stronger than the prison guards or not? (Some at this point may say "yes" or "we can't tell." In Muslim belief, of course, when enemies came to capture Jesus and crucify him, God beamed him up to heaven).

A second man boasted that he was stronger than the prison and the prison guards. When the guards came for him, he came out and met them. They captured him, beat him severely, bound him and then took him past all the prison cells to the farthest dungeon and locked him in, leaving guards at the door. The superintendent of the prison then sat in his office with his buddies laughing at the man. But they did not laugh long. Soon they heard sounds from within the prison. The man had torn off his chains, pushed open the door, thrown the guards aside, and then proceeded to open all the doors of the cells one by one, calling, "Anyone who wants to leave this prison, follow me!"

Some of the prisoners were afraid. If they joined this man now and he was recaptured, they along with him would suffer even worse torture than before. But others said, "Look, they've already done to him the worst they can do and he has shown himself stronger. I'm following him out!" Those who followed him closely followed all the way out, finding as they did so that he shared with them his power to open cell doors and defeat the guards on the way. Eventually they followed him all the way to his kingdom of righteousness.

## Love

*Christian assumption.* Christians see God's love for mankind as the hallmark of the Christian message. John 3:16 becomes a key verse. The Apostle John is considered by theologians to be the Apostle of Love. This is borne out by the fact that the word love in its various forms is used 117 times in the Johannine writings.

*Islamic perspective:* What is important for one person or culture may not necessarily be important in another culture. For Muslims, God's superiority, sovereignty, and authority over mankind and man's necessity of submission to the will of God are their hallmarks.

*Caution.* While love may not be as clear in Islam as it is in the New Testament, nevertheless it is found in the Qur'an. (See Surah 2:195; 2:222; 3:3 1; 3:76; 3:132–135; 3:146; 3:159; 5:13; 5:42; 5:54; 9:4; 9:108; 1 1:90; 49:13; 60:8; 61:4; 85:14). Granted, Allah's love is usually conditional, based upon obedience. So some may argue that Islamic society suffers from a lack of understanding of biblical love.

However, if intimate, accessible, open relationships are not expected in marriage or family relations, but other aspects equally as noble such as respect, submission, and honor are sought after, then why would Muslims respond to the Western definition of love? It is possible that the loving God of the Western Christian may not have the appeal often thought.

## Presenting Christ: An Alternative Approach

Muslims will respond positively to love genuinely expressed. And Christians are to love people into the Kingdom of God. However, the Muslim is taught that Allah is the master, and mankind is his slave. In such a relationship love would be considered out of place. The master is not on the same level with the slave. So God is not on the same plane with mankind.

*Alternative.* I believe the hidden spiritual world, the Muslim's relationship to this unseen world, and issues of destiny are greater felt needs for Muslims than love. Though Western Christians downplay the unseen world, many Muslims are greatly interested. When Christ is presented as victorious over the unseen world of jinn and demons, a Muslim audience may be more eager to listen. The Bible has much to say about the unseen world if Western Christians will only look.

### Changing the Moral Behavior and Living for God

*Christian perspective.* The Christian holds that it is impossible for the unregenerate man to live for God outside a personal relationship with Jesus Christ. Therefore, to become a Christian the unregenerate person must accept Jesus into his or her life. The person will then be born again and will have eternal life.

*Islamic perspective.* Muslims hold that the reason why people are not Muslims is that they are ignorant of Allah's law. When persons hear and understand Islam, they will recognize that this is what they really are. They will submit to Allah and say the Shahadah (the Islamic Creed). Saying the Shahadah three times in the presence of a Muslim makes you a Muslim.

Allah requires five things of Muslims, called the pillars of Islam. They are the Shahadah (Islamic Creed), the Salat (prayer five times a day), the Saum (fasting during the month of Ramadan), the Zakat (alms giving), and the Hajj (a pilgrimage to Mecca once in a lifetime). Many Muslims will admit that they are not "good" Muslims and fall short of living a truly submitted life. Yet, Muslims contend that Islam is a superior religion since it encompasses every aspect of life. It influences government, education, media, religion, and private life. Islam controls and forbids vices originating in the West such as pornography, alcohol, and the low moral standards propagated through the media. Muslims are proud of their religion and speak openly about Allah and the great heritage they have.

*Alternative.* Seeking to get Muslims to accept Jesus as the way to live for God can often be misunderstood as Christians seeking to make Muslims simply change their religion. To avoid a battle of one religion against another, we might instead deal with the arguments some Muslims use to show Islam's rightness.

Four reasons are generally given for achieving a life pleasing to God. The four are knowledge, discipline, religion, and law. To promote understanding I use the various arguments I have heard from Muslims and ask questions. A key question is: How can one revive the inner good? What can the person do to gain control of the bad?

People may suggest various ways to accomplish this:

1) Knowledge—If we instruct people more, their behavior will change accordingly. But are the most knowledgeable people in the world the best people? Can knowledge by itself give life to the good in us?

2) Discipline—If we are more disciplined in our lives, concerning our thoughts, habits, exercise, etc., then our lives will improve and we will do more good. But are the most disciplined people in the world the best people? Can discipline by itself give life to the good in us?

3) Religion—If we go to church, mosque, temple, or adopt a new religious perspective, then we will become better. Are the most religious people in the world the best people? Does religion by itself always bring alive the good in us?

4) Law—If we have legislation to regulate our moral behavior, then we will be better citizens. There are two types of law, civil law and moral law. But are societies with the most law necessarily the best places to live? Too much civil law may cause society to result in martial law or military lockdown, which is oppressive. With too much rigid moral law, society can end up with a totalitarian/dictatorial form in which sometimes thought becomes a crime. Can law by itself give life to the good in us? Is not law's purpose rather to contain the bad?

*Points to stress.* If a seeker wants to get off on a side issue, the person should be challenged throughout with the fact that *the good in us must be revived (reborn)* before we can truly live. When the various remedies for sin are presented, such as knowledge, discipline, religion, or law, it becomes clear that none of these has the power to produce balance or to control the evil in human lives. However, the Christian is promised the indwelling power of the Holy Spirit to become alive to good, although final perfection does not happen until the resurrection from the dead.

## The Nature of Good and Evil

In many world religions, as well as the popular New Age movement, the world is explained dualistically, meaning that this world is involved in a cosmic conflict between good and evil. Neither side is more powerful. The challenge of life according to this worldview is to identify both evil and evil influences and rid oneself of these negative forces. Harmony is sought through neutralizing negative forces and achieving balance between body, mind, and spirit.

*Christian perspective.* In the Christian worldview, there is also an element of good versus evil and the achieving of balance. The major difference is the recognition that we as human beings are incapable of achieving balance or of ever combating evil victoriously solely by ourselves. It is God himself who takes on this battle for us through Christ.

*Islamic perspective.* Islam sometimes allows for man being a blend of good and evil, ignorance and knowledge, power and impotence. Sufi Muslims have held the view that Satan is really "in" man, or is identical with the negative self of man. But Islam mostly teaches that the basic nature of man is good. It is important to get as much good (*baraka*) as possible into life. Every good deed is multiplied tenfold while an evil deed is counted as one evil deed.

> He that doeth good shall have ten times as much to his credit: he that doeth evil shall only be recompensed according to his evil...(Surah 6:160).

*Caution.* Islam teaches that this life is a test to see what we will do. When confronted with the temptation of evil the Muslim is to choose good. All too often the Christian will deny that good works has anything to do with knowing God. Ephesians 2:8–9 are often quoted to prove that we are not saved by works, but by grace through faith.

However, deeds are important in Christianity. They are in fact the fruit of a holy life. According to Matthew 28 what we have done to the least of the brothers we have done for Christ. Since the Islamic worldview does not have a concept of a savior, the system of accumulating good deeds becomes important. We will need to start with this worldview and help the Muslim understand that God is calling us to the purpose for which He made us, which is good works. However, our good works fall short of God's perfect standard.

*Alternative.* Using the Islamic worldview that the purpose of life is accumulating more good deeds, we might agree with them that if God has created people only as a test to see what they will do, it seems logical that we would be judged according to our deeds on earth. But God has created us with a purpose. We were created before the foundation of this world for good works (Eph. 2:10).

To illustrate the point I look for a glass or use the cup of tea from which I am drinking. The glass was once filled to the top with God's purpose for us—the good works He created us to do. There are three ways we take away from the glass. First, when we do a bad work we remove liquid. Secondly, when we miss an opportunity to do a good work, we take out a measure. Thirdly, for a good work that is not wholly good, or perhaps self-serving (I am kind to my spouse because I want to ask for something later), we take some of the liquid out. God intended us to be wholly good.

What happens when we surprise ourselves and do a really good deed with no ulterior motive behind it? When we do good, the best good possible, we take nothing out of the glass because then we are simply doing what God has purposed for us to be and do from the beginning.

How can we add to the glass and fill it up again? It is impossible to add liquid to the glass by doing good works, for this is our purpose. All we can do is draw from the glass and end up short of the mark God has set for us.

*Points to stress.* We have a struggle with evil in our lives. The good is there but we are powerless to live it out. We try many things to revive the good in us. Yet we fail to live the good life. I am not saying that a person is incapable of doing any good act. We can do good acts, but the good acts are often forced or artificial. And the good we do can come out wrong or be misinterpreted.

### The Centrality of Power

*Christian perspective.* The teaching of power is shunned in Christianity. The meek, not the strong, inherit the earth (Matt. 5:5). Jesus taught that whoever would be the greatest in the Kingdom of God must be a slave of all (Mark 10:42–45). The humility of Jesus in giving up the right of equality with God and being humble even to death is praised in Phil. 2.

*Islamic perspective.* In the Muslim understanding, God is on the side of those who win. This is illustrated in the rise of Muhammad to power as the priest-king in Saudi Arabia. The quick expansion of the Islamic kingdom during the time of the four Rightly Guided Caliphs and afterward until 732 AD seems further proof for the rightness of Islam. The superiority of Islamic culture in its glory years while the Western world slipped into darkness shows again the greatness of Islam. As the significance of the Islamic Empire waned and Egypt was invaded by Napoleon in 1798, the Islamic world went through much soul searching. Nasr (1994) explains:

> From the Islamic point of view, the success that the Muslims had had in the world during their history had been a sign and consequence of both the truth of Islam and their firm allegiance to that truth, for as Allah asserts in the Qur'an, "If Allah helps you, none can overcome you" (3:160).

The theme of victory or power permeates Islamic teaching. Among Muslims the cross is perceived as a sign of weakness, and it is shameful for any prophet of God to suffer defeat. God would not allow his prophets to suffer humiliation. It may help to point out that the Qur'an recognizes that the prophets were mistreated and sometimes even killed (Surah 3:183–184). It should not come as a surprise to the Muslim that infidels will seek to destroy a prophet who exposes the people's sins.

*Alternative.* The gospel should be presented in such a fashion that the Muslim understands that we are honoring Jesus by presenting Christ the Victor over Iblis (the devil) or al-Shaytan (Satan), the jinn (evil spirits), and death (the last enemy). This celestial battle between God and Satan is a major theme in the Scriptures. From the promise of God to crush the head of Satan in Genesis 3:14–15 until the dethronement and casting of Satan into the lake of burning sulfur in Revelation 20: 7–10, the Scriptures are pregnant with the spiritual battle. The death, burial, and resurrection of Christ are trumpeted as victory over sin and death. I Corinthians 15:54ff says, "...Death has been swallowed up in victory...But thanks be to God! He gives us the victory through our Lord Jesus Christ."

Since power is such a central theme in Islam, in the beginning we can focus on Jesus as conqueror of Satan and evil. Jesus was with his disciples three years before they came to the realization that He was the Son of God. The disciples made this proclamation only after they saw Jesus' power to forgive sins, his power over nature, and power to heal people.

After Muslims have come to understand Jesus as Conqueror over Satan, they will be more open to understanding Jesus as Son of God. However, I sometimes challenge Muslims with this question, "Can a prophet take on Satan and beat him? If not, then who is Jesus Christ?" This question prompts the Muslim to think about who Jesus really is, and leaves the discussion open for the next meeting.

## The Christian Life

### Three Necessary Elements

A confusing concept for Muslims is what the Christian life is all about. They may think Christians are presenting a perfect life through Christ. At that point I introduce three elements needed to live the Christian life: the Bible, the Holy Spirit, and the Church.

The world in which we live is not neutral. It pressures people to compromise. For example, at work perhaps coworkers do not want anyone to tell the boss that they are cheating on their time, taking little things home for their personal use, or lying on a report. They may want us to remain silent. And when we are tired or lose our focus, we sometimes surrender to the bad.

We also have an enemy who is like a roaring lion seeking for someone to devour. This enemy is Satan. His desire is to entangle us in his web of deception, anger, or bitterness. Satan's grip is so strong that once we are entangled in his deception, deliverance is only possible from someone more powerful than he.

However, God has not left us to fend for ourselves. Not only does God revive the good in us through Jesus, but He has also more than adequately provided for us to live this new life continually.

*The Bible.* The Bible is the Christian's guideline for living. Scripture not only contains God's law, which is the believer's delight and desire to follow, but also God's perspective on life and this world. The Bible is the Word of God and with it one is able to understand the will of God. Jesus used the Bible to combat Satan, and believers can do the same.

*The Holy Spirit.* The Holy Spirit is God's Spirit living in all those who have received new life. The Spirit informs the person who is alive in Christ as to what thoughts and actions are contrary to God's way. When the person who is alive in Christ listens to the inner voice of the Holy Spirit, he or she will be guided in making right decisions and following the will of God.

*The Church.* The church is the community of God's people. This community of believers serves several purposes. The church models the new life in Christ. The church gives examples of people who follow the Holy Spirit, even in situations where there might be a high price to pay for obedience. The church provides encouragement and direction to live the new life as Christians struggle through life's perilous path.

If any of these three ingredients are missing in the new life in Christ, the person will be overcome by the power of the bad. It will be almost impossible to resist for neither we nor this world are neutral, and the enemy seeks to destroy us.

## Calling for Commitment

*Christian perspective.* When Christians ask seekers to accept Christ, they are asking them to accept the gift of God who brings eternal life.

*Islamic perspective.* I have found that many Muslims misunderstand this part and think we are asking them to merely change religions and become a Christian, which is a negative concept. They may lose sight of who Christ is and view a call for commitment as simply changing religions. Muslims will think of the day of judgment and its consequences if they become Christians. Paradise is reserved for the true Muslims. Hell is for the *kafar* (unbelievers).

*Implications.* I believe it is helpful in the decision process to address the issue of judgment head on. In so doing we help the person keep focused on the real issues of life and who can give life. It is too easy to shift the focus on to the emotional issues of not changing religion for fear of the judgment of Allah.

*Alternative.* At this point, seekers can be asked if they want their inner good to be reborn. The key is what Jesus has done. Jesus allowed the power of evil to destroy Him completely through death and then overcame that power by coming to life again. Now He wants to give this new life to everyone who asks. John 1: 12, 13 states: "Yet to all who received him…he gave the right to become children of God" (NIV). The seeker needs to keep focused on the issue, not of changing religions, but rather of receiving life.

*Judgment Day.* When the judgment day comes, God will not look at the good deeds that we have done. Rather He will judge us as to whether we have new life and are alive to good inwardly. If the person is alive to good, then the person will go to heaven. If the person does not have this new life, it is too late to infuse life after death. Hell is the place for those who have not received life.

However, if the person has new life, then he or she will go to heaven. Heaven is not a reward for doing good works, but is reserved as a reward for those who are alive to good. In heaven, God promises to remove the bad in us and restore us to purity again as He originally created us. Though we do not know exactly what heaven will be like, we know that the bad in us will be removed and we will be fully what we were created to be.

## Conclusion

The Western world is changing greatly as the vast transmigration of peoples takes place in the twenty-first century. For the Christian, the task of communicating the gospel mostly with neighbors of similar background and belief system is quickly changing. The great challenge to the Western Church is to find ways to understand different belief systems, not just the religious beliefs but also the worldview behind those beliefs. As Christians go back to the Bible and prayerfully think through their presuppositions with new cultural eyes, they can find ways to share the wonderful message of Christ's salvation in a culturally relevant manner.

Christianity is about bringing new life, which people are unable to do for themselves. The purpose is to present this life clearly to all and call them into this new life in Jesus. Some will respond. Others will continue reflecting on the issue. When that happens, the Holy Spirit will work in the person's understanding. Some will not want this new life, for their life has been built around another set of standards. To accept Jesus and this new life would be too costly. For them we can pray that God will give them a vision of true life in Jesus.

My prayer for the Christian Church is taken from some paraphrased words of the Apostle Paul; Pray that whenever we open our mouths, words may be given us so that we will fearlessly make known the mystery of the gospel. Pray that we may declare it fearlessly, as we should (Eph. 6:19–20).

*Section 3*

# Models of Outreach
# to Muslims

# CHAPTER 7

# Organizational Models

## Hospitality Ministry

### Gerhard Wilch

### Introduction

Imagine yourself in another country where people speak a strange-sounding language and whose customs are quite different than yours. You have no family within thousands of miles. Now imagine you're going to school in that country and the date for a certain festival comes around. This is their biggest festival of the year for families to get together and the school is empty. You sit all alone in your dormitory room while all the other people have gone away to celebrate.

Now, of course this normally would not happen because usually the countries where North Americans travel practice hospitality and you would have been invited to a home. However, the unfortunate thing is that in North America, the majority of international students who come here—and there are perhaps hundreds of thousands of them—return to their countries after spending three to six years here without even once being invited to a Christian home or for that matter, any Canadian or Stateside home. The fact is that hospitality is not a big part of our culture. Perhaps it was at one time, but in our current culture, hospitality is not an important matter. But if you can put yourself in the kind of position imagined above, you can understand what it's like for people who come to our country and are never invited into a native home. They can only form their own opinions of our culture, based on ignorance.

Our ministry is actually named Philoxenia/Hospitality Ministry. However, I think hospitality is probably a big part of how most ministries work, so I do not claim to have any monopoly on the topic. Our ministry started in 1978 with Ernest Hahn who had been a

missionary in India for 25 years. He returned to Toronto and started
the work. I've been with him now for four years so I am still learning.

Our ministry takes a general approach. Our vision is to seek out,
not just Muslims, but also Chinese and Hindu and others. We work in
the areas of evangelism and discipleship. We also try to multiply
ministry by educating the church about this work. My work is primarily among the Iranian refugees, but I have contact with all kinds of
Muslims in the Muslim world.

We make contacts among our neighbors. God has blessed us with
a wonderful location. We have only a one-bedroom apartment, which
serves as my office, my ministry center, and also my home. However
we live in a building with 500 other families in the same building.
Within half a square mile, 30,000 people live and make their homes.
Authorities have identified 80-90 different people groups inside that
30,000-strong segment of population. It may be the most multicultural
and densely populated area in Canada. We're also near a subway
route, so our home is basically accessible to almost anybody living in
the Toronto area.

Many of our contacts are made simply by referrals because people
have known Ernest Hahn. They trust him because he has done such
outstanding work in building relationships and friendships. I've ben-
efited from inheriting that work. We literally meet hundreds of new
contacts every year just passing through our home. Some of them
stay in the area. Some of them move elsewhere. But along the way we
visit them, we care for them, we try to build some kind of friendship
and spiritual relationship too. We pray with them, and we invite
them to Bible studies if they are open to that. We have had in the last
couple of years, just over 100 students go through our Bible studies.
And new believers are counseled.

There is a weakness with our generalist approach. We cannot
really follow through with any one person. We're always trying to
find a church or some other source for follow-up. We like to pass
them on to someone else who can counsel them. We need to do this
because there are only two of us and we want to get the churches
involved. Perhaps one could say we are a kind of a conduit between
the Muslims and the Christian church. We do not do church planting
at this point because of our limited resources. We do, however, encourage the formation of ethnic fellowships.

We also disciple Christians. Right now we have a discipleship
course for a group of Christians from Ethiopia. The exciting thing
about these Christian Ethiopians is that most of their friends are
Muslims because they come from a people group in Canada and the

U. S. that is largely Muslim. They have more natural contact with Muslims than we have, so by discipling and training them we can multiply our ministry. Another way we multiply ministry is by reaching people who are coming to our shores temporarily. We disciple them, and they eventually go back to their own countries. If they come from unreached people groups, they will be the ones doing foreign mission work. They may be the future of foreign missions because these people already know the culture, the language, and the customs, and they even know the people there already. We have people in Iran and Pakistan who have done that already in the short time I've been with the ministry. We also hold awareness seminars for the church.

Last Thanksgiving we held three separate Thanksgiving dinners just to accommodate all our contacts. At the largest dinner, we had two turkeys and forty-three people in our small apartment. I still don't know how we fit them all in, but everybody seemed to be comfortable and shared a good time. We may need to work something else out for Christmas because we can't hold even one more person. God blessed us with people who were so eager to come and hear what Thanksgiving is all about. We share our message and it's almost like an informal worship time together as Iranians and Chinese and anyone else who wants to can come and celebrate Thanksgiving with us.

In this ministry, we need to address questions about what hospitality is from a biblical and cultural point of view. Hospitality is a very ancient tradition and most Muslims are strongly rooted in a culture of hospitality. This is a strong value for them, especially for those who come from a traditional culture. It's not just important because of tradition but it is also a way of building community. And how important hospitality is for building community, as well as strengthening our own ministries. We need also to look at some of the key customs of hospitality in the traditional cultures and see how we might adopt some of them. It is also helpful to look at some of the major barriers to hospitality. Why is it that in our own culture it is so difficult for Christians to practice hospitality? What are these barriers?

Another issue we might look into is how to develop a hospitality mentality among ourselves, among Christians, and among churches. The larger church community also needs to be hospitable. We need to see the kitchens, dining rooms, and living rooms of our homes as sanctuaries—places of refuge, warmth, and affirmation for the family, for fellow believers, and even for strangers.

The following is our model for hospitality ministry.

### Rationale and Biblical Foundations for a Hospitality Model of Ministry

The Biblical word for "hospitality" in the New Testament is *philoxenia,* which literally means "love or care for the stranger." God specifically instructed the Israelites entering the Promised Land regarding the strangers residing among them:

When a stranger sojourns with you in your land, you shall not do him wrong. The stranger who sojourns with you shall be to you as the native among you, and you shall love him as yourself; for you were strangers in the land of Egypt: I am the Lord your God (Leviticus 19:33, 34).

As Christians, redeemed by the blood of Christ and transferred into the kingdom of God, we are spiritually pilgrims and aliens in this world. Therefore we share a certain kinship and concern with those who are strangers in our land in a physical sense. Jesus reminds us that as we welcome strangers or those who cannot repay us for our kindness, we welcome and entertain Jesus himself (Matthew 25:31–40; Luke 14:12–14).

The motivation for Christian hospitality, however, is rooted even deeper, in the hospitality God has extended to us in Christ, who invites us—who once were his enemies—to the grand wedding feast with the saints. Among Christians, the celebration of the Lord's Supper is a foretaste of that feast. In fact, every meal shared with others (including strangers) in God's name is a reminder of the joy that awaits us. From God's gracious invitation and generous hospitality towards us, we draw our motivation for practicing the same towards the strangers among us.

The writer to the Hebrews was probably alluding to Abraham when he encouraged Christians with the following words: "Do not forget to entertain strangers, for by so doing some people have entertained angels without knowing it" (13:2). Abraham's reception of the three visitors under the great trees of Mamre is a good example of what hospitality is about.

Unfortunately, the practice of Biblical hospitality appears to be disappearing among Christians in the West, as the TV and computer occupy more leisure time and governments take over social responsibilities. Perhaps this is an important reason why the church has been quite ineffective in reaching Muslim immigrants in the West. While churches and missions prepare programs to reach out, the doors of Christian homes remain closed to them. And sadly, many who profess Christ later turn away disillusioned with the church and Christians. If we are to make any progress in reaching Muslims in North America, we need to relearn Biblical hospitality. One of the tasks of a *philoxenia* (hospitality) ministry is to instill a hospitality mentality among fellow Christians.

For a further study of the importance and practices of hospitality I would recommend Arley Loewen's article, "Refreshing the Stranger: Celebrating God's Hospitality" (1997).

### Description of Hospitality in Toronto

*Context.* Our ministry is located near the downtown core of Toronto, a major metropolitan city that receives at least 50 percent of Canada's immigrants and refugees, about 150,000 each year. Muslims make up a significant percentage of the refugees who arrive in Canada. Refugees usually are very receptive and welcome friendship with Canadians, although it may be more difficult for Canadians to identify with Muslim refugees.

Our "ministry center" in Toronto consists of a one-bedroom apartment, where we have managed to live and do significant cross-cultural ministry. The apartment is located in a housing complex where as many as 40,000 people, mostly immigrants and refugees, live within half a square mile. Although the center is not located in a predominantly Muslim neighborhood, it is not difficult to make contacts with Muslims. The center is also easily accessible by public transit, and so we frequently welcome guests who come from other parts of the city. Besides being a place to welcome newcomers and to fellowship with them, the center is also used for Bible studies, dinner parties, and social functions, as well as a small office and literature resource center. The central location of our center also facilitates visits with Muslims in the downtown area where refugees tend to settle at first, and for connecting with the government and legal services often required by refugees. We are currently seeking to move to a larger apartment to accommodate a growing house-fellowship (house church) and to provide space for the office and overnight guests and short-term missionaries.

The ministry center was located for many years in Mississauga, a suburban context. There the ministry dynamic was different: The house had a more relaxed and home atmosphere, with ample space in the garden for summer gatherings. However, it was less convenient for visitors to come. It also meant more travel time to meet appointments and often required picking up visitors. On the other hand, it provided more privacy and fewer opportunities for unexpected visitors to drop in. While availability is as an advantage, it is not absolutely necessary, nor always desirable.

*Purpose.* Philoxenia/Hospitality Ministry has always seen itself as a two-track ministry. One track involves direct contact with Muslims and refugees or immigrants. The other involves work with the church to encourage participation in ministry to Muslims. At this time our particular mandate is quite broad and virtually anything related to cross-cultural ministry is fair game. The reason for this was to allow me as a new missionary to gain exposure and to become familiar with a wide variety of ministry opportunities. The board of directors did not specify particular goals in terms of converts beyond a general involvement in some kind of cross-ministry with Muslims, Hindus, and other refugees, students, converts, etc. This lack of direct and specific guidance has been a source of frustration, and in the next year or so, we expect to formulate a more specific ministry direction with expectations more clearly defined.

*Ministry Structure and Support.* Ours is a very small ministry with only one paid missionary couple, a retired missionary couple, and a seven-member board of directors of pastors and laity from a number of local congregations. Guidance is provided through informal conversations with the retired missionary and occasional board meetings, to whom the staff missionary is accountable. The ministry had its beginnings in 1978 when Ernest Hahn returned to Canada from 25 years as a missionary to Muslims in India with the Lutheran Church-Missouri Synod. In 1987 the Ministry was incorporated and became a registered charitable organization. Currently it is a Listed Service Organization of Lutheran Church-Canada, which allows it access to congregations of that Synod who are its main supporters. About 4,000 copies of a four to six-page quarterly newsletter is sent out to supporters and congregations in Canada and the U.S., reporting on events and soliciting prayer support. A financial update is included from time to time. Start-up funds were received from Wheat-Ridge Foundation. We have not actively sought or received support from any other foundations. If we had more regularized formal programs to assist newcomers (e.g., a refugee reception center, host-family program, ESL classes, etc.) we would consider applying for support from foundations or government agencies.

Because of the small size of our ministry, staff members need to be well-trained and highly self-motivated. However, this type of ministry is not difficult to begin with someone who has had a few years of cross-cultural ministry experience and if started with the support of a church and some good oversight. As the ministry grows, it can develop its own board of directors, constitution, and charitable registration number.

*Expectations.* As mentioned above, our particular mandate is quite broad at the time and will need to be narrowed down in the near future. Basically, developing good relationships with Muslims so that meaningful faith-sharing can occur is a major object. The main ingredients that make this type of ministry work include a true concern for the well-being of the Muslims, coupled with a respect for them as fellow human beings, and a willingness to share one's life with them in a significant way. The context where we believe this happens most effectively is in the home, where the Christian life and faith is lived and modeled. The other aspects of a ministry of hospitality can take many forms and are probably best determined on an individual basis, considering the local needs, resources, skills, and opportunities.

*Outreach Activities*

1)   Contacts are made through referrals from other Christian ministries and other Muslims who introduce us to their own friends. A few result from outdoor evangelism, literature distribution, involvement in dialogues/debates, or door-to-door ministry. These latter means do not result in much fruit, but help to train us for sharing the Gospel and building a communal cause.

2)   Contacts are visited and invited to social functions (picnics, dinners) and suitable Christian content programs, such as a Christmas Eve service or an Easter pageant. Ideally, we would like to link up immigrant families with Canadian Christian "host families" who will keep in touch with them. We help with practical needs as far as we are able and offer to pray for their needs.

3)   The Gospel is shared in a sensitive way, including printed materials in the native languages. Those interested in further study are invited to a weekly ESL Bible study fellowship in our home (i.e., ministry center).

4)   New believers are followed up, discipled, and prepared for baptism. For this we have several small discipleship groups that usually include a new believer as well as a serious seeker together with a leader. Helping them find a suitable home church is also an important aspect at this stage.

5)   A monthly Christian leadership training course is provided for ethnic Christian leaders, including Muslim converts, who wish to serve in specific ethnic ministry or outreach to their community.

*Workers.* A ministry of hospitality can function with only a volunteer family who is willing to connect with newcomers and open their home to them. Paid staff can devote more of their time toward developing a more elaborate ministry involving volunteers. Volunteers currently assist with ESL Bible classes, Vacation Bible School and evangelistic outreach, meeting special needs of refugees, organizing social functions, or as host families. Training is usually quite informal for the friendship-type ministries, consisting mainly of "see and do."

For those seeking to understand the Islamic religion, on-the-spot individual instruction or group seminar instruction is conducted in conjunction with other missionaries to Muslims in Toronto. Training of missionaries always involves a good amount of practical hands-on experience. Some volunteers may join us as short-term contract workers, and receive a stipend. Seminary students who qualify for funding may also join our ministry for their practical ministry component. The current staff missionary is a seminary graduate and an ordained minister in Lutheran Church-Canada. This facilitates speaking engagements involving preaching in that denomination.

*Networking.* The small size of our ministry team dictates that we network with other similar ministries reaching Muslims in the area, involving about ten missionaries. The group is called Muslim Friendship Ministries, the ministry arm of Fellowship of Faith with Muslims, a long-established literature resource and prayer ministry for missions to the Muslim world. This group meets every other month to network in areas where we cannot conduct ministry by ourselves. Primarily we coordinate seminars on Islam and participate in large-scale outreaches, as for example, when a challenge to dialogue or debate arises. This group acts also as a clearinghouse for requests for publications or for sharing ideas and resources. Other ministries we network with from time to time include shelters for refugees, hospital and prison chaplaincies, and other community initiatives for newcomers.

*Final Comments.* Our very general approach to Muslim ministry makes it difficult to judge whether our particular ministry is being effective or not. We make numerous contacts and we encourage and facilitate the personal ministry of others with Muslims. At the moment we do not have a specific set of measurable goals, like that of establishing a church by such and such a date, etc. This can be a source of frustration. It is helpful, though, to reflect on the relationships that are being built, and to see how Muslims have come to know the Lord over time.

This type of ministry can work well in virtually any situation and could be duplicated in almost any area or by any congregation where

there is a core group of committed volunteers and prayerful supporters. It does not necessarily require a dynamic leader. Even a low-key
approach that is warm and sincere can win the Muslim heart. Patience and a long-term commitment to relationship-building is required, however, because the fruit often takes many years to develop.

## Major Issues

◆ Time is one of the biggest issues. If we are going to have time to
  entertain Muslims, we may have to cut out the soccer or basket-
  ball game or our favorite TV program. We might even have to
  cut back on some church activities and risk the reactions of
  fellow church members.
◆ Balance is also important—between instructing and modeling.
◆ Developing good relationships is crucial before meaningful faith-
  sharing can take place.

## Action Steps

◆ Model hospitality as well as encouraging it.
◆ A manual for a hospitality ministry to Muslims could be prepared to help others learn how to do this.
◆ Begin prayer and plans for a social function for your church that
  would especially attract immigrants.

# Refugees

### *Milton Clark*

To escape the horrors of nations in utter turmoil, thousands of
refugee families and individuals land at O'Hare Airport in Chicago.
Few know English. Some have less than 10 cents in their pockets. No
food. No jobs. No place to call home. The good news is, they do have
a few new friends: church members, volunteers, and World Relief
staff who greet them at the airport and devote months to guiding
them through the difficult, confusing process of making a new home
in a foreign land.

I work with World Relief in Chicago, and I will share a bit about
what World Relief does. We are a relief and development organization owned by the National Association of Evangelicals. Around the
world we are often involved in disaster response, but in the United
States we are involved in the special service of resettling refugees
(citizens of one country who flee across borders to seek safety in

another country). So we help those people who are fleeing their countries, often because of religious or political persecution.

The world contains more than 12 million refugees today, the Associated Press has reported from data furnished by the United Nations High Commission for Refugees. The UNHCR also reports about 1.2 million people presently seeking asylum in another country. More than 120,000 refugees in the past seven years have had some sort of contact with North American churches. Over the last 20 years World Relief has resettled more than 20,000 refugees from many different cultures, faith, and backgrounds.

One of the unique things about World Relief is that we work through the local church. So we offer the church an opportunity to touch people who are coming to this country for the very first time. People meet the refugees at the airport and welcome them into their homes. We are one of the largest resettlement agencies in Chicago, and we have about 27 offices across the country. Over the past 10 years or so, we have resettled more than 10,000 Bosnians in the Chicago area. That literally means that those 10,000 people have been touched and aided by Christian volunteers.

Many of those who come to America have been persecuted by so-called Christians in their country. But now they are able to receive the love of God through believers who meet them at the airport. It can be rather amazing to these refugees when suddenly they come into an airport, not knowing who is going to meet them, and suddenly they see a group of people standing there with the refugees' names on a sign saying, "Welcome to America." These volunteers come with flowers, maybe with gifts for the refugee children, expressing, "Come to my home, we want to welcome you to America." It makes a lasting impact in their lives.

This is a tremendous opportunity because most of the Bosnians coming to us are nominal Muslims. Their whole culture and faith has knitted them together in their home country, so they are not going to make a commitment to Christ overnight. We are talking about a long-term commitment and planting a lot of seeds for progressive growth. This can happen when you are part of the process of helping them get resettled. They live in your home for a while. You are reaching out to them in a very special way and you can become their friend for a lifetime. That gives you an open door.

Over the years we have seen a lot of interesting things happen. The first question is, where is the mosque? It is not that the mosque doesn't care—they are helping people too—but Christians can also help. Some of the families give a picnic for the refugees or a party of some sort so that everybody on the team can meet them. From 5 to 10 or 12 people may be on a team reaching out to a refugee family. And the refugees think, "Is this for me? I mean, why would you do this for me?" It has real impact on their lives.

Different people on the team are able to help in a variety of ways. One may help find a job. Others will help find housing. We train the volunteers, suggesting tasks to help the family so that these refugees will be able to adjust to this country. So a number of people are building relationships with them and performing special kinds of service to help their beginnings in America be free from a lot of hassles. This is one of the main things we do at World Relief.

Several volunteer opportunities are available through World Relief to impact the lives of refugees. The following is a short list that churches participate in:

1)   Church Sponsorship Teams. World Relief uses these teams to help newly arrived refugee families adjust to their new life in America for their first few months. Areas of involvement include helping with transportation to and from appointments, an orientation to the public transportation system, finding an apartment, finding employment, collecting needed housing items and/or financial resources. A significant part of this team includes a friendly and loving host family to temporarily house a new refugee family from three to seven days.

2)   "Good Neighbor Kits." Groups can provide kits of household items to refugee families. Refugees come with little more than the clothing on their backs. They are in need of such items as dishes, sheets, towels, and so forth, to start their new life in North America.

3)   Tutoring English. Refugee families are in need of learning English to survive and adjust to life in the States, make American friends, and find employment. Volunteers can tutor refugee families in their homes once a week for a couple of hours and help them learn the basics in English and American culture. World Relief provides an orientation/interview and one six-hour training session on a Saturday.

4)   Assist in Children's Program. Volunteers can help in an after-school program for approximately 30 refugee children (K-12) to facilitate their adjustment to America. The program encompasses children of all ethnicities and is designed to help them with homework and to build their English skills. Leaders help with one-on-one tutoring, small group instruction, and play activities during the week.

We have built some elements into our own organization, shaped around programs for the refugees, to be able to have a continued ministry. For instance, we have had to hire some of the Bosnians because of language and cultural differences. We needed some of them to help us with those factors, and that offered a challenge to us as Christians. Suddenly Muslims were on staff with Christians. But we didn't see that as a problem. We saw it as an opportunity. However, the pressure was on us to be who we said we were as Christians. That brings a tremendous amount of responsibility.

Even failure offers opportunity to exhibit Christian principles. We can offer forgiveness. We can repent when we are wrong. Those kinds of attitudes and behaviors have had a tremendous impact both on the Christians and on the Muslims who work with us. We are sensitive to them, but we still remain who we are. Sometimes we come together for worship and prayer, and oftentimes the Bosnians will attend the prayer sessions.

We have gone on World Relief retreats where some of them have come along. At times late into the night when we are rooming with them, they will have a lot of questions about Jesus. "Tell me about Jesus. Is he really the Son of God?" So we've been able to plant a lot of seeds in the hearts of these Bosnian families simply by having them on staff.

We have seen some of their other needs and have tried to be sensitive as an organization to meet those needs. We have started children's programs for their kids because they were concerned about gangs in the communities. We have offered space for activities and have been able to write grants and get money for those kinds of things.

Some of the older people who have come to our country are slow to learn the language and are not able to adjust well. They have had a tendency to become isolated. So we have created a place and atmosphere in our office that looks like a Bosnian living room where they can come in, sit down, have coffee, and just talk. We have discovered that, among other factors, this has improved the mental health of some of them. Also the interaction instills in some of them the desire to go to ESL classes so that they can learn English. There are many issues that need that kind of sensitivity.

Listed below are twenty comprehensive programs where we assist families whose lives have been shattered to become whole again.

### Children's Development
 ◆   "Mental Health" — counseling and therapy for traumatized and mentally ill refugee children
 ◆   "After School Program" — assistance and activities for refugee children adjusting to life and the "cultural shock" of urban America

◆   "Our Hearts" — culturally appropriate dance and fitness training

## Elderly Activities
◆   "Sijelo" — English language and citizenship instruction for elderly Bosnian refugees
◆   "Hand to Hand" — elderly refugees reaching out to assist newly arrived refugees with handmade goods

## Refugee Adjustment and Relief
◆   "Reception and Placement" — the initial housing placement, comprehensive orientation, and medical screening
◆   "Cultural Adjustment" — ongoing cultural orientation, counseling, problem solving, mediation, and translation services during the refugees' first twenty-four months in the USA
◆   "Family Resources" — introducing families to broader community resources including home ownership, college planning, and women's issues

## Jobs and Business Development
◆   "Employment Counseling" — basic job training/education on the U.S. job market, interview coaching, and resumé assistance
◆   "Job Development" — help employers find dedicated, skilled workers in the refugee community
◆   "Your Business Center" — helps the refugee start his/her own business through training, consulting, referrals, and resources with seventy-seven new start-ups in one year alone

## English Language Education
◆   "Pre-employment" — intensive English-language instruction to facilitate refugee employability
◆   "Immigrant Language Training" — honing immigrant English usage to enhance their functional skills
◆   "Lamplighter" — English tutoring, matching volunteers with newly arrived refugees
◆   "Special Needs English" — classes designed for students whose physical or mental abilities preclude intensive training

## Mental Health
◆   "Horizons Clinic" — individual and group psychotherapy/ counseling for refugees suffering post-traumatic stress disorder, depression, grief/loss, and other war effects

◆ "Activities and Resource Center" — psychosocial activities to promote healthy social interactions and prepare for the workplace

**Immigration and Citizenship Assistance**
◆ "Immigrant Services" — BIA-accredited legal aid on immigration-related issues; i.e., amnesty to work authorization, adjustment of status, family reunification, naturalization
◆ "Church to Community Services" — church based low-cost/high-quality immigrant legal services
◆ "Citizenship Education" — U.S. citizenship instruction to immigrants and refugees who wish to earn their citizenship

For many churches, refugee ministry is a new way of evangelism. But the immigrants are moving into our communities. They are coming. Here is a tremendous opportunity for North Americans to get to know the immigrant population and to be able to reach out to the Islamic community. Let us pray that Christians will respond all over our country.

## Major Issues

◆ The major influx of immigrants in the United States means that representatives from all the world religions will increasingly become a part of mainstream society. How will Christians deal with their attitudes toward these immigrants?
◆ Euro-American Christian Communities (EACC) are weak in faith and practice and often self-serving. The church is a sleeping giant in this matter. If local churches could be awakened to the need and opportunities, many exciting occasions for evangelism could occur.
◆ The area of missions is still being dealt with often as a matter of geographical borders rather than people groups, which hinders cultural, linguistic, and religious contextualization.

## Action Steps

◆ Imparting vision is crucial. Churches and groups can help inform educational leaders and professors, church leaders (both Euro-American and ethnic Christian communities), the laity (teens as well as adults), and business and professional people.
◆ Compiling a comprehensive list of resource material to aid in imparting vision and doing practical ministry is a need at present.
◆ Promoting training—who is my neighbor and how do I build bridges to my neighbor? World Relief provides training for their programs.

◆   Get your church involved in prayer and possibly later in refugee sponsorship. Contact World Relief for practical information on getting involved.

World Relief
Herb Snedden
655 Village Square Drive
Stone Mountain, GA 30083
Phone (404) 294-4352 X 252, E-mail Hsnedden@wr.org

◆   Remember, this is not a paternal situation. With adult refugees, the relationship must be conducted at a friendship level.

◆   Sponsorship may lead to friendship. Eventually it may come down to a one-on-one relationship connecting, assisting, mentoring.

◆   Sometimes focus groups can be developed out of these immigrant communities and formation of new communities helping each other can take place.

◆   Practice hospitality. The best kinds of ministry take place as these people are in our homes, and we are in their homes.

## Friendship Centers

### Samuel Naaman

**Introduction**

In urban settings today the spheres of influence are changing. Over four and one-half million Muslims call America their home. Their numbers are increasing by six percent every year (Alliance Video 1998). From its center of influence in the 10/40 window, Islam is aggressively targeting America as its mission field. The vision is to reach 75 million converts in the next 20 years. More than 500,000 American Hindus are also joining in this penetration of America. These immigrant groups are making inroads among our young people, captivating their minds and attracting them to their way of thinking. The President of the Christian and Missionary Alliance, Dr. Peter Nanselt, has said, "Our mission has a strategic plan to penetrate the 10/40 window. We're clearly serious about reaching this massive group of unreached people over there. But we are just as serious about reaching them around us."

I am from Pakistan and my dad is a Muslim convert. He accepted Christ in 1949. My younger brother was assassinated in Pakistan in 1990 by an underground Muslim movement. I think that factor played a major role in my staying in the Chicago area. First of all, there are plenty of ministry opportunities here for me, but secondly, it was not safe for me to go back home.

I studied for a master's degree in theology in Seoul, Korea, and earned a doctorate of missiology at Asbury Seminary in Wilmore, Kentucky. In the process of my studies, I met the Christian and Missionary Alliance (C&MA) people at Asbury. Since 1993, I have been affiliated with the C&MA. Basically, my wife and I are district missionaries, working among Hindus and Muslims. The C&MA helped fund our South Asian Friendship Center (SAFC) with other seed money coming from churches, individuals, and grants.

Chicagoland is an area where, at the time of this writing, we have more than 400,000 Hindus and Muslims. Our Center is located in the heart of the Indian marketplace. We are about one block from the closest mosque and two blocks from another mosque. This is a unique and strategic area with a large proportion of illegal immigrants, many blue-collar workers, and cab drivers with 18-hour days. Our landlord is a Muslim, but we have been very open with him about the nature of our Center.

The uniqueness of SAFC is that all of us are volunteers. None of us is paid by the Center. God has brought a wonderful interdenominational, biracial team together. That factor plays a strong part in our ministry. There are eight individuals on our team, some bi-vocational and others full-time missionaries. Three denominations support SAFC: the Assemblies of God, C&MA, and the Evangelical Free Church of America. This broad base of prayer, financial, and personnel support has made it possible for this Center to open.

Many of the Muslims and Hindus are shocked by our Center at first. They ask why in the world a bunch of Anglos would be involved. They could perhaps understand Pakistanis doing this, but why Americans? However, they are beginning to realize that we don't have a hidden agenda. We care for them; we love them. So we have opened up a Friendship Center. When they come, they have a safe haven. They can have a cup of tea and talk to someone. So sometimes they open up and really share their hearts with us. We do receive some subtle opposition with people being warned not to come.

We started an evening worship service a couple of years ago with an eastern, contextualized service in Hindi and Urdu. There are only about four Muslim background believers and three or four Hindu background believers.

## Aspects of Ministry

We have identified four areas in which we as a Friendship Center want to be involved.

*Bookstore.* The first aspect is the bookstore. There we offer books, literature, tapes, and videos in more than 15 languages of the South Asian community. These languages include Arabic, Bengali, Dari, English, Gujarati, Hindi, Persian, Punjabi, Tamil, and Urdu. Most of the literature comes from various multi-language media. With staff and various associates of SAFC making trips to India and Pakistan, we are able to purchase books, tracts, and new music releases on tape or CD from sources on the subcontinent and offer them at a reasonable rate. We get many walk-ins to make photocopies or use our fax service. See contact information under "Action Steps" at the end of this friendship center section.

*Practical Service.* Secondly, we have a service component. We want to be of practical service to the community, to legitimize the fact that we are here on a long-term basis, specifically to reach out to the needs of the immigrant and foreign communities. We do that by offering English as a Second Language (ESL) classes. They can be once a week for two hours or one and one-half hours twice a week. We have also offered business seminars, including small business taxation. We have held a seminar on immigration, and immigration consultation is available. We offer bone density scanning for women and have women police officers teaching on safety. Our women's ministry offers trips to points of interest in the Chicago area as well as day trips to various shopping malls.

*Outreach.* Our third facet is outreach. That permeates everything we do. This includes a passive evangelism where we are a presence in the lives of those who come and want to open up and share with us. But sometimes there is an aggressive angle as well, where we go out into the community.

We conduct a Kids Club to lay a foundation in the lives of kids. We are open about our programs being based on the Word of God. But this is a safe place and many parents will let them come. Some Christian children's videos such as "McGee and Me" teach biblical values common to Islam. Sometimes we have games and crafts. We have also read from *The Lion, the Witch and the Wardrobe* by C. S. Lewis (1950). And we are using some David C. Cook object lessons on the nature of God, focusing more on God and less specifically on Jesus. We sent a letter home with the children giving the title of each object lesson for the weeks to come.

One of our workers heads up a taxi-driver outreach, frequenting their hangouts and taking time to form relationships with them. One student trying to learn Urdu goes to the taxi hangouts and asks for help. We are looking for more opportunities to reach teenagers and women.

*Training*. Training is our fourth aspect. We train students from four Christian institutions that are involved here in the Chicago area. The Christian Colleges and Universities have service requirements for their students. Currently SAFC has 30-40 student volunteers, plus 20 volunteers from churches, who help in the various ministries. These students are trained and provided with contacts in the community. This hands-on approach is the best training for creating vision and compassion for Hindus and Muslims.

SAFC also services mission organizations that would like a place to train their candidates. In addition, students seeking internships to gain prefield training have come to SAFC. The varied knowledge and experience of the SAFC staff has a powerful influence on the students, in both formal and informal settings.

SAFC conducts seminars in local churches wanting to both understand their changing community and practically reach out to Hindus and Muslims. The Center also offers vision trips where groups come to the neighborhood and are introduced to the ministry, hear a testimony of a convert, visit a temple, eat in an ethnic restaurant, and are sent on a scavenger hunt to get them into the community and interacting with local people. This helps remove emotional barriers some may have about talking with people whose dress, language, and culture are radically different than theirs.

## The Need

One of our recent stories is of a person who came here from India with his family. When he arrived here he was given a cold shoulder by relatives and his community. He was very depressed and discouraged. Then he saw one of our advertisements for ESL. He came in the other day and said, "You know, the love and comfort that I received through this center, I have not even received from my relatives." He expressed his thanks for the Center's help and for the fact that we had cared for him unconditionally.

Many people within the South Asian immigrant community are extremely lonely. The sense of connection they had in their own country has been destroyed in our individualistic country—there's this whole idea of just making money and maintaining only surface friendships. Many of the women are lonely and are home alone much of the time, so there's a need for women to form relationships with them. There is a role to play as agents of reconciliation, helping to bring forgiveness between different ethnic groups, and convincing opportunities to display the unity we have in Christ. We have a tremendous role to play if we can find these people. We pray that God will bring us divine appointments with people who are at crisis points in their lives so that we can touch them for Jesus' sake.

However, we need to go out and make friends and form relationships. Then we can bring them back to the Center. We cannot just sit around and relax. "Now we have opened the Center and everything is fine." That will never work. Islam is aggressive, so we will need to be aggressive too. They will never just walk into our American churches. Why should they?

I ask my American friends, "How many times have you visited a mosque or a Hindu temple?"

Do we go? No.

Why? Because we don't feel a need to go. And neither do they.

The best place to meet needs is right in their marketplace. People sometimes ask me, "Where do you get the energy? Where do you get your passion for this work?" Whenever I'm depressed, my brother's face sometimes appears in my mind. The sacrificial life of my brother is always in my memory and that is probably my guiding force, along with the Holy Spirit.

### The Vision

"Little India," a commercial district located on the north side of Chicago, draws people of various ethnic backgrounds from Illinois, Indiana, Michigan, and Wisconsin. The initial desire was to open a Christian Center in this marketplace and make contact and establish friendships with them. The vision of South Asian Friendship Center and Bookstore is to maintain a positive and active Christian presence and to proclaim the uniqueness of Jesus Christ in Chicago's predominantly Hindu and Muslim marketplace on Devon Avenue.

By God's grace, the Center is not any one person's dream. The Lord started this ministry because of the concerned prayers of an Indian Christian Fellowship that goes back 15-18 years. In an all-night prayer session, they prayed for a friendship center in Chicago, and even claimed in prayer the property we now use. We started with five missionaries and now we have about 30-40 volunteers from Moody Bible Institute, Wheaton College, and Trinity Evangelical Divinity School. We also now have five converts. I am not a big "numbers" person, but certainly these statistics are encouraging and help satisfy some of the critics. We are so grateful to God for this beginning harvest.

This is the first center of its kind reaching South Asians in North America and this will not be the last. Our vision is that as we share this model, other cities will follow, modifying the plan as needed for their area. But programs are not possible if they are only plans. It is people who make the difference. God has honored us with a terrific team. They are second to none. And we are committed to the Chicago area. With vision, people, and commitment we believe such friendship centers can make a vital difference in immigrant communities.

**Major Issues**
- Much prayer and vision-raising must be done before opening a friendship center.
- Using a multi-agency and multi-church approach to friendship centers is a big advantage.
- With friendship centers, relationship-building is fundamental. Much time must be devoted to forming strong friendships.

**Action Steps**
- Carefully contextualize any worship services offered.
- Sometimes much forgiveness is needed between various ethnic groups. Take advantage of opportunities to act as agents of reconciliation.
- Ministry workers should be chosen who can display constantly a strong sense of Christian unity, humility, and incarnational ministry.
- If interested in more information on establishing a friendship center, contact:

> South Asian Friendship Center and Bookstore
> 6346 N. Talman Ave., Suite 101
> Chicago, IL  60659
> 773-764-6846 Bookstore
> 773-764-9945 Fax
> www. safcbookstore.com
> E-mail: safcptl@megsinet.com

# CHAPTER 8

# Models for Ethnic Ministries

## International Students
*David Philip*

### Introduction

In the mid-1970s, two Iranian Muslim sisters came to study at a university in Texas. Through the love and gentle witness of local Christians, both placed their trust in Jesus Christ as Lord and Savior. By their own admission, one of their greatest fears was that God would ask them to go back to their country, which in fact He did. They arrived back in 1978 to a country that hosted many missionaries. However, three months later when the revolution took place the expatriate missionaries and many of the minority Christians left the country. The sisters remained and for years ministered to the citizens of their country, many of whom were disillusioned with the Islam they saw practiced by their government. Finally, when their own lives were threatened, the sisters left but continue to have an effective witness to Persian-speaking people in the USA, Tajikistan, and elsewhere (Bringing Back 1995).

### The Potential

The story of the sisters illustrates the effectiveness of reaching Muslim international students studying in the USA. The exact number is not known but according to International Students, Inc., there are more than 600,000 international students in the USA. Of these, 44,000 are Indian and Pakistani, 30,000 are Arabs, Turks, and Jews, and 25,000 Malaysian and Indonesian (10/40 Window Reporter 1998). No figures are given for Iranians or African Muslim students.

Even if you assume that some students from these countries are from a Christian background, there are still probably at least 75,000, if not more, Muslim international students. These scholars are the future leaders of their countries in politics, education, business, and the military. They are also potential recruits and supporters for terrorist organizations. Eyad Ismoil, who was convicted in the World Trade Center bombing, entered the USA to attend Wichita State University. After three semesters he dropped out and joined a group of Islamic terrorists (Scott 2000).

Though they may not become Christians as students, if they have at least been touched by the kindness of Christians, they might some day be making decisions that contribute to the advancement of the kingdom of God. In my conversation with a Turkish pastor in 1997, he told me about a Turkish Christian leader in the mid-1990s who was seeking to rent an apartment flat for use as a church. After explaining his intentions to a potential landlord, the landlord responded that thirty years earlier he had been an international student in the USA. Every Wednesday the man had eaten lunch provided for international students at a local church. Despite his personal risk, the man rented the flat to the Turkish Christians to repay the kindness he had received so many years earlier.

My wife and I ministered almost 12 years in Turkey, Cyprus, and France. Most of the time was spent in Istanbul, Turkey, in campus ministry and church planting. I also served in an administrative capacity at our organization's headquarters for North Africa/Middle East ministries first from Limassol, Cyprus, and then Paris, France. Since 1992 we have been ministering to Muslim international students at a state university in the Midwest with a student body of 25,000 and another 25,000 in the surrounding communities. Of the more than 2,600 international students, there are probably around 350–400 Muslim students and another 200–250 of their dependents to whom we try to minister.

As we started our work on campus we realized some of the barriers we faced in Turkey did not exist or at least were not as formidable in the USA. For instance, I am no longer required to have a secular job to maintain residency. My hours are given to full-time ministry. The security issues have changed. I can freely say I am a campus minister without fear that authorities will ask me to leave. If someone is bothered by that fact, it still will not jeopardize my ability to stay in ministry on the campus.

Overseas, language was always an issue. We invested several years in learning Turkish. It is now an asset to be able to communicate in Turkish with the Turkish students, but since the majority of Muslims are graduate students proficient in English, I am able to communicate in English with Arabs, Iranians, Pakistanis, and others.

I had been able to stay in Turkey first as a university student and then as a businessman. My classmates and later colleagues were middle-class Turks. However, the university students we have contact with now are the elite of their country. In ten to fifteen years most of them will have substantial influence. Because of the friendships that have been started while students, I will be able to walk into their business or government office and be well received.

Still, ministering to Muslims in the USA has several disadvantages. We were warmly welcomed in Turkey. It was almost a status symbol to be introduced as someone's American friend, so we had no shortage of Muslim friends. They knew we were Christians but that was not threatening to them in a country of 65 million Muslims. However, it is different in the USA. I understand that Muslim students are warned before they come to the "Christian" USA that they will encounter people like us and they should be on guard to protect their own religion and culture.

So we do find a defense up already when we try to reach out to them—something we never encountered in a Muslim country. And Muslim students are certainly not as responsive to the Gospel as some other international student groups, such as the Chinese. One could choose to spend one's time with the most responsive groups and not share the Gospel with Muslims.

However, I have chosen to restrict my efforts to Muslims. This could have potential negative consequences if they feel targeted. So that is why I conduct Muslim ministry in the context of general international student ministry. I am part of a team of three workers from different parachurch organizations and one church staff person that gives leadership to a general international student ministry. My Muslim friends are usually comfortable attending events because it is international rather than Muslim specific.

Although they are potentially the future leaders of their countries, the majority of international students do not return to their country. In my conversation with a former State Department employee in 1995, I was told that U.S. State Department statistics show that 67 percent of foreign students will stay in the USA after their education. Our hope and prayer is that of those who are Christians whom God is calling back, more than 33 percent will obey God and return, as did the Iranian sisters.

## The Ministry

Our ministry activities fall into three categories: felt needs, events, and direct ministry.

### Felt Needs

A dividing wall is automatically up with many of the Muslim students. They are guarded when we initially approach them. I have found, however, that the wall comes down as we come alongside and help meet their felt needs. They have many needs when they first arrive, often in August before the fall semester starts.

We have made a friend for life if we can help them settle in, acquaint them with the university and town, familiarize them with the transportation system, take them shopping, and so on. Sooner or later they figure everything out, often through the help of students from their own country. But if they initially bond only to those from their own country, it will just make it more difficult to penetrate their new world in the weeks following.

Longer-term, they experience loneliness, so we have different social activities to help meet this need. Often they have come from large families and miss interaction with children. We have volunteered for a host family program established by our university. We request and have been assigned Muslim students who have become a part of our family's activities for a semester.

Also the spouses of these students often have a problem with English. The husbands have excellent language ability as graduate students, but they are away from home for long periods of time each day. This means the wives are often isolated or restricted to contact only with women from their countries who speak the same language. Our church has a well-established multi-level English program for these women, and my wife teaches there. The teachers are all Christians who volunteer their time so the only cost is for textbooks and a modest fee for childcare. These teachers engage in activities with their students outside of class, which often leads to opportunities to share Christ. They also plan social events that the husbands attend and this enables us to meet them also.

Medical emergencies have occurred where we have been asked for advice and assistance. This can be a frightening and costly time for the students and their families. I have also become aware that Muslim students sometimes get into trouble with the local or campus police. That defensive wall I have referred to comes down quickly when they have been arrested for some deed (they may or may not be convinced it was wrong), and I am the first one to come to their assistance. We have helped in incidents involving domestic abuse, shoplifting, sexual assault, burglary, public intoxication, traffic violations, divorce/child custody, and others since 1993.

The first time I just happened to be in the right place at the right time to be in a position to help. But now I make it a daily practice to read the "On the Record" and "Police Blotter" sections of the local and campus newspapers to see if any Muslim students are in trouble. If so, I contact them and offer to help. Sometimes I will be able to clarify the law to them, explain their options, or help them contact a lawyer. Other times there isn't much I can do other than lend a sympathetic ear, visit them in jail, or attend a court hearing. But that is especially appreciated if they have been abandoned by the Muslim community because of their offense. I have had some of my best spiritual conversations when a Muslim student has been at a time of crisis.

The "On the Record" newspaper section also announces births at the local hospital. Our three children were all born overseas so we know what it is like when there is no family present to celebrate that joyous event. When a Muslim couple has a baby, I try to send them our congratulations and a prayer that their child grows up to obey God and bring joy to the parents. Romans 12:15 says to "rejoice with those who rejoice" as well as to "weep with those who weep."

Recently I worked with the Turkish Student Association to collect donations for earthquake victims. It was a good thing to be able to work with the Turkish students collecting donations from Christian students given to the Red Cross.

### Events

When working with American students we like to sponsor events where we can gather crowds, present the Gospel, and then follow up with students who express interest in learning more. I thought a long time about what kind of event we could sponsor as Christians that would draw large numbers of Muslim students. Then I realized that we did not need to sponsor events. Rather, we could attend theirs.

The Muslim Student Association sponsors one or two lectures each year when they bring in a speaker to talk about some aspect of Islam and/or disparage Christianity. These lectures are well attended by the Muslim students. I go to see how many students I can meet. Then later when I see them on campus I can in a natural way begin speaking with them again. Every year an Islamic Awareness Week is held on campus. I go to their book tables and displays to meet and talk with those attending.

Since the international student population is so large at our university, students from the various countries have formed associations. We have Bangladesh, Indonesian, Malaysian, Pakistan, Sudanese, Turkish, and Arab student associations. The university allots these associations money each year so they can sponsor a cultural event with dinner, folklore, music, dancing, etc., for the university community to know more about that country. At Turkish night, every Turk within a 25-mile radius will be there, so I attend in order to meet as many of them as I possibly can.

Another event sponsored each week on campus draws several hundred Muslim students. This Friday Prayer is held around noon in the largest room in the Student Union. Some of my colleagues make it a practice to go to the prayers on campus or at the mosque to observe and then engage the students in dialogue afterwards.

These students also have respect for and curiosity about our church services. I have on occasion invited Muslims to Sunday morning, Christmas Eve, and Easter services. Not only do they hear the Word of God, but they also have the chance to sense the presence of the Spirit of God and observe the community of believers. This is an area where we need to be even more active, since they are generally willing to come at least once.

### Direct Ministry

How can we intentionally give Muslim students the opportunity to receive a Bible and Jesus video in their own language, the chance to study the Bible, and meet with a Spirit-filled Christian? The Muslim Student Association is bringing in high-powered Muslim evangelists and paying these speakers from university student fees. We thought, "Well, why should we just stand around, trying to minister to one at a time when that's definitely not what they are doing?"

So we tried a lecture on campus, "Christianity and Islam: Two Paths to the Same God?" The Muslim students came because they were curious as to what I was going to say. They brought copies of rebuttals to pass out—even before I actually spoke.

I talked about Islam, I talked about Christianity, and the similarities and differences. My conclusion was that in fact, there are two paths to two different Gods. But since they are both monotheistic religions, one has to be right and the other wrong, or else they are both wrong. But the two cannot be right at the same time.

I invited them to bring their Qur'ans and other literature to pass out to students while we made Bibles and Jesus videos available, so each person could decide for himself.

They objected to me presenting Islam. They wanted a Muslim to present Islam, so we agreed to hold two debates six months later at two of the state universities. After much negotiation and preparation, we held the events. They were well attended (300 both nights), and probably two-to-one Muslim to Christian. The Gospel was clearly presented and some literature was taken, but the Muslims did not fill out comment cards (possibly out of fear of the disapproval of the Muslim community) so there was basically no follow up. But we have used both lecture and dialogue.

I have found an individual approach is probably more effective. The greatest tool to use in identifying Muslim students is the student telephone directory. It is quite easy to go through the directory and pick out the students with names like Ali, Hasan, Khadijah, Mohammad, and the like. I have developed a short telephone survey ending with the question, "Would you like to meet together to discuss Christianity and your religion?"

Through that process, I have found some good contacts. Even if they were hesitant to meet, I offered to lend them the Jesus video or send them a piece of literature with my business card, inviting them to contact me if they ever wanted to discuss religion further. It didn't take long to have made at least one contact with every Muslim at our university...and gain a reputation as an evangelist. Yet, as I was involved in meeting felt needs, many of them began to look at me as a friend.

After helping one student from Bangladesh, who had been arrested for public intoxication, a week later I got a call from a guy with that same accent and with the same problem asking for advice. He did not identify himself but later I found out it was another student from Bangladesh. The first student had told him I was the person to talk to about this problem.

It was satisfying to know that every Muslim student at our university had at least one chance to hear the Gospel, but I began thinking about the thousands on campuses all across the USA who would spend 2–6 years here and never once be presented with the claims of Christ. I realized we have the Christian workers already on these campuses, but they did not have the time to be involved in all these activities to reach out to the Muslim students.

Short-term missions is a hot issue in the mission world today. In our organization we have sent as many as 100 full-time staff and students a year, for the last 15 years, on short-term summer missions projects to predominantly Muslim countries: Albania, Egypt, Jordan, Kazakhstan, Kirghizstan, Morocco, Turkey, and Uzbekistan. Part of my work is to communicate to them that they can continue to be involved in Muslim outreach on the campuses right where they are after they have returned from their short-term trip. We provide them with a number of ideas.

I ask them, "If I can identify open Muslim contacts at your university, would you be willing to follow them up?" Many say yes. They then send me their student telephone directory. I identify the Muslim names and contact them by mail offering a free Bible correspondence course, a Bible, and a Jesus video.

When they respond, I send the Bible and the course directly to the Muslim student. But the video I send to the staff member at that campus who sent me the directory. The Jesus videos are then delivered by Christians at that campus so they can meet the Muslim student and follow up as appropriate. Through this direct mail strategy, in the last seven years we have been able to make contact with nearly 18,500 Muslim students at 75 universities and have had almost 360 responses. You may think, "Well, that's not a whole lot." But it's about two percent. And what we do not know is how many times that videocassette is watched when it goes into the Muslim community. In how many countries might it end up being watched?

Nor are we able to document how many search out the answering-Islam.org website, which is mentioned in each letter. We have received enough response to know that some are at least looking at the website regardless of whether they ask for the materials. We feel the Lord is telling us to sow the Word of God as broadly as possible and wait for Him to bring forth fruit in his timing.

Our goal is to see that every Muslim student in the United States is prayed for by name and then has the opportunity to receive a Bible, Jesus video, a chance to study the Bible, and a chance to interact with the body of Christ and see Christians in action. For those who respond, we want to see them discipled, trained, and then put in contact with Christians in their home country. That is what we are always working toward.

We also conduct some training programs during the summer. We have done six-week training programs at Ohio State, Penn State, University of Maryland, and in the Seattle area. In addition we have a 24-hour conference that we conduct for Campus Crusade staff in Muslim ministry.

Our ministry is definitely relational. We are trying to meet felt needs, we show an interest in their events, and we try to assist them when they are in trouble. At the same time we want to systematically expose every Muslim student in the United States to the Gospel at least once. And we want to see each one of them prayed for by name.

The Lord has impressed on us the truth of Ephesians 6:12 (NIV), "For our struggle is not against flesh and blood [we are not battling with the Muslim students], but against the rulers, against the authorities, against the powers of this dark world and against the spiritual forces of evil in the heavenly realms." And II Corinthians 4:3, 4 (NIV) says, "And even if our gospel is veiled, it is veiled to those who are perishing. The god of this age has blinded the minds of unbelievers, so that they cannot see the light of the gospel of the glory of Christ, who is the image of God."

Muslims come to Christ when the Spirit of God uses the Word of God to convict them of sin and reveal the Savior to them. This often happens in response to prayer on their behalf by believers. That is why three of us have gathered most Fridays during the school year for the last seven years to pray for the Muslims in our community while they are reciting their prayers. And each letter sent out in the direct mail strategy represents a person who is prayed for by name. We are powerless to convince them apart from the Spirit of God. We love them, we sow the Word of God among them, and we pray that God will work in his time to establish his church among those who have come to Christ from an Islamic background.

**Major Issues**

&#9670;   The conservative leadership of the mosque, the small, tight Muslim communities, and possible vulnerability of newly-arrived Muslim students all mean that the Islamic community is warned against Christians.

&#9670;   Christian students rarely demonstrate long-term interest in Muslim students. But students who go on summer missions to Muslim countries can be mobilized to come back and reach out to Muslims on their campuses.

&#9670;   The importance of deep, caring, long-term relationships is seldom displayed by North Americans. American families can share holidays, such as Christmas and Easter, and/or special family events, such as birthdays and picnics, with international students.

&#9670;   Cultural sensitivity to Muslims will help gain openness to the Gospel.

♦   Student ministries need to cooperate to maximize their effec-
tiveness, build vision, and be a model. Ministries such as InterVarsity
Christian Fellowship, Navigators, Campus Crusade, Baptist Student
Union, Chi Alpha, etc., need to partner closely together to reach
Muslim students effectively.

## Action Steps

♦   Get a campus directory from a campus in your area and send
to David Philip, P. O. Box 1392, Ames, IA 50014. He will select the
Muslim names and send a mailing to those persons, offering a correspondence course and free Jesus video. For those who respond, he
will mail the correspondence course material and a Bible, but he
sends the videos to local contacts and asks that they take the Jesus
video directly to the student and begin to form friendships.

♦   Inform David Philip about other Bible correspondence courses
that might be effective. It would be good to find one, not only with
solid content, but also with contemporary graphics that looks as good
as the materials Muslims are accustomed to receiving at the university.

♦   Compile a master list of surnames of Muslim peoples for
those who are wanting to engage in a mailing ministry or who are
looking for Muslim contacts in their local area. This could be done for
other groups such as Pakistanis.

♦   Create internships in ministry, ESL, cross-cultural studies,
etc., recruiting students to be involved with Muslim ministries.

♦   Encourage Christian students to live in buildings, dorms,
and apartment buildings where the Muslim students live.

♦   Train other international Christians from countries with large
Muslim populations to reach out to the Muslim students (assuming
you can overcome their prejudices against Muslims in their own
nations). Korean students might also be a helpful group since they
are motivated toward missions.

♦   Use the Urbana mission conference as an opportunity to
motivate, envision, and train American students to reach out to Muslims on their campuses.

♦   Recruit and train host families who are sensitive to Muslim
students.

♦   Come up with ideas for moving from training (academic) to
modeling (experiential) in mobilizing Christian students to reach out
to the Muslims.

♦   Write articles on Muslim student ministry for parachurch
magazines, especially those oriented toward students.

♦   Get students who are ministering to Muslim scholars to share their ministry testimonies with other Christians. Students often can motivate other students to reach out to Muslims.

♦   Develop Muslim specialists among international student ministry (ISM) workers, but these specialists should usually work as part of a larger ISM team.

## The Keys to the Iranian Heart

### Ashton T. Stewart, Jr.

"Yet I will restore the fortunes of Elam in days to come, declares the Lord" (Jeremiah 49:39, NIV).

When the history of Iran in the twentieth century is written, the year 1979 will be seen as a defining watershed. The events that unfolded that year have forever changed the lives of the Iranian people. That year the Shah of Iran, Reza Pahlavi, was forced to abdicate his long reign in Iran and flee into uncertain exile. It was also the year that Ayatollah Ruhollah Khomeini flew into Iran on his chartered Air France jumbo jet and established the Islamic Republic of Iran. These events shocked the Iranian people as has no other event in modern times.

Just as an earthquake sends out shock waves, the events of 1979 sent out its own series of tremors. The people of Iran at best could have been called nominal Muslims, but now the full weight of Islamic law and practice was placed on them. Women were forced once again to cover themselves with the "chador," a veil that covers women from head to toe. All alcoholic beverages were destroyed, movie theaters were closed, and Western music was eliminated from the radio and T. V. programming. A countrywide reform was begun to bring every area of personal and public life into compliance with Islamic law. It is far beyond the scope of this brief article to try to give a full description of the revolutionary changes that hit Iran. Suffice it to say, the Islamic Revolution turned life upside down all over the country.

The results were catastrophic. Iranian society began to erupt. Thousands of educated Iranians and those with ties to the previous regime began to flee the country. It was difficult to book a seat on a flight out of Iran. The great Iranian Diaspora was on. It is interesting to note in Jeremiah 49:34–39 that God will bring his judgment against the Elamites (one of the ancient names for the Iranians) and He will humiliate their king and scatter them to the ends of the earth. In the

17 years since the Islamic Revolution, Iranian people have literally been scattered to every continent. A 1993 study done by Iranian Christian Internationals, Inc. (ICI) shows significant numbers of Iranians in 33 different countries and on every continent. The total number of Iranians scattered worldwide was cited then as more than three million. Today that number has climbed to four million. It is estimated that two million of these displaced Iranians live in North America.

The next shock wave was the surge of Iranians who began to turn to Christ as a result of the Revolution. Of course, this was not evident to all at first as many Christians fled Iran along with others. My wife and I had the privilege to be in Iran that first year of the Revolution, and we were firsthand witnesses to the devastation that the exodus of Iranian Christians had on the churches. However, at the same time we saw the heightened interest in the Christian faith as churches began to fill up with seekers.

Iranian Christians International reported the number of Iranian believers in 1979 at less than 3,000. Today, 17 years later, estimates range from 25,000 to 40,000. It is very difficult to get statistics that can be verified but the point is clear: there has been a dramatic growth of Christianity among Iranian Muslims. In 1969 Dr. William M. Miller wrote his landmark book entitled, *Ten Muslims Meet Christ,* and it was heralded as a breakthrough. Today if Dr. Miller were to write a book he would have to call it the rise of the Muslim Background Believer church; for since the Islamic Revolution more than a hundred Iranian fellowships have arisen outside Iran.

This fact prompted Greg Livingstone, the founder of Frontiers, to comment that the Iranian Church is the most mature Muslim Background Believer church in the world. Iranians are coming to Christ in unprecedented numbers with more of them turning to Christ in the last 17 years than in the previous 1,000 years. The Iranian harvest field is white but awaiting workers. Today there is only one Christian worker for every one million Iranians.

There was one more shock wave yet to consider in understanding the Iranian context. That was the persecution of the church in Iran. The Christians in Iran fled from the grip of the Islamic Revolution because they intuitively knew Islam's stance on Christianity. They knew firsthand that Islam would make every effort to stamp it out. Again, it is beyond the scope of this article to go into depth describing the persecutions that the Iranian church has undergone; suffice it to say that five pastors have been martyred since the beginning of the Revolution and countless others have been persecuted and martyred.

Today Iranian believers are routinely persecuted for their faith. The blood of the martyrs has indeed become the seeds of revival. Pastor Mehdi Dibaj, one of those martyred for Christ, often said, "The Church in Iran is like a rose petal; the more you press it the sweeter the perfume."

In summary, the Islamic Revolution has changed the contour of the Iranian mind and heart. Iranians have been driven from their homeland by forces beyond their power to control or even to understand. They have been ripped from the close and intimate relationships of family, causing devastating emotional consequences. They have suffered the ravages of war and possibly have had members of their family executed by the Islamic courts. They have witnessed the unmasking of Islam and may now hate all religion and religious leaders.

Iranians may mistrust other Iranians and want to lose themselves in their new country of residence. They are strangers living in a new culture. If they do not know the language, they must work for other Iranians and be at their mercy for survival. Many Iranians living in the West are well educated but have had to settle for very menial occupations. Still others have become successful in a great variety of careers and make great contributions to society as productive citizens. However, the events of the Islamic Revolution still affect them deeply and stir up a host of basic questions about the God of history and the purpose of life. Within the Iranian community there is a full range of conclusions about life, but also there are some of the most open and searching souls on earth. God has prepared them for such an hour and He is calling us in the Western church to respond.

You will not regret the time you give to your Iranian friends for they will teach you much more about friendship than you will be able to teach them. You will find them more interested in spiritual matters than your Western neighbors probably are, and you will find that God may well touch your life afresh as you observe God at work in them.

## The Key of God's Love

By now it should not come as a surprise that your Iranian friends need love. They have been greatly hurt. They have lost so much—their homeland and perhaps their fortunes. By the time they get to the West they may well have been abused by smugglers who promised them easy access to the West, and they have experienced harassment by Western government officials. They need friends who can love them with the unconditional love of Christ. They need someone who can help them find their way in their new country.

As I listen to the countless testimonies of Iranian Christians, one of the keys God has used in their lives is the unconditional love of Christians. Iranians are social people and do not thrive alone. They would rather be with a group of people. So when they come to the West they are amazed at how separatist we are. They may find us to be friendly on the surface but are surprised at how poor we are at friendships.

When they come to our churches we smile and greet them but we seldom invite them to our homes or open our lives to them. This would not be the case if we were in their home country; we would very quickly be invited to their homes. When we understand this about their culture it becomes a key bridge into the Iranian heart. Become a friend. Open your life to them. Learn about their culture and enjoy their foods.

One aspect of Iranian culture that you must quickly master if you are going to have successful interaction is what Iranians call "tarof." The best way I can explain "tarof" is to say that it is a formal politeness that may disguise the true feelings of the person. For example, if you ask Iranian friends if they would like something to eat, they will probably say no. However, what you should do is bring them something to eat anyway. They are not likely to share with you their real wants. If you go to their homes, it is customary to take flowers or a small gift. The best thing to do is to ask your Iranian friends to tell you about how "tarof" works. For a fuller description of the Iranian culture and holidays, l would recommend *Sharing the Gospel with Iranians* by Don M. McCurry (1982).

### The Key of God's Truth

The events of the Islamic Revolution have caused a great many Iranians to be disillusioned with religion. They have seen the hypocrisy of their religious leaders. They know the powerlessness of Islam to change the human heart. As I have listened to dozens of testimonies I hear this theme over and over again. Their disillusionment is with the "Mullahs" who rule Iran with merciless adherence to the Qur'an. Many of them have a story to tell you about their discovery of the emptiness of Islam. They might tell you about their experiences of searching for the truth and how they brought their questions to the Mullah, who told them to believe blindly.

One of my good friends who taught the Qur'an for many years, and who today is a follower of Jesus Christ, shared with me how he had been taught. He was told that if he would repeat a certain verse from the Qur'an a thousand times, God would give him anything he desired. He prayed and fasted for three days and repeated the verse thousands of times.

He told God there was only one thing that he desired and that was for God to change his character. He had a terrible temper. Once he had finished his spiritual exercise he had great hope that God would answer and make a new man out of him. When he emerged from his room he saw one of his children doing something annoying and he exploded with anger. Within moments he was in great despair because, not only had he gotten angry, but he had discovered his faith was powerless to change him. So great was his despair that he plotted to take his life. Instead he was led to the cross of Christ and to the One who makes all things new. Iranians are experiencing a great paradigm shift in their souls. They are going through a time of great questioning and the key to witnessing to them is to present the truth in love.

It is extremely important to note at this point that all our confessions of the truth must be accompanied by a life that demonstrates it. Iranians have been so disillusioned by religion and religious leaders that they will not easily be convinced by insincere Christianity. It is the reality of Christ that they are seeking, not a formal nominal Christianity. This must put us on the alert to be the fragrance of Christ.

We can begin to demonstrate Christ's reality in our lives by praying with Iranian friends. I usually say, "I like to pray with my friends. Would it be all right if we close our time together with prayer?" Never once has an Iranian objected. When I pray I always make it a very personal and intimate communication with God because they generally do not know God that way. I also always include specific requests for my friend. God is so faithful and almost always answers those prayers. Our prayer times serve as a spiritual lab session in which they see how much I depend on God, and they see God at work. It does not surprise me when a Muslim friend calls back to tell me God answered my prayers, and would I now be willing to pray for another matter? Now I have an open door to begin to share with him how he can know God as I do. As you can see, I have not argued my friend toward faith in Christ but have led him to taste and see that the Lord is good.

As we pursue this matter of truth the good news is that in general, Iranians still believe in absolute truth and revelation. (The exception here is if the Iranians have completed their formal education in the West; then they may well have become a Western relativist.) They have been taught that the "Injil" (The Gospels) is a holy book and that they should read it. They may have been told that it has been tampered with, but my experience shows that they are anxious to read it. I find that Iranians gladly accept a gift of the New Testament. Sometimes I will say, "Now that you are living in our country you probably would like to know what Christians really believe." Then I present them with a New Testament.

I am always careful to caution them about thinking that all Westerners are Christians. I go on to tell them that as they read they should underline the sections that are hard for them to understand. I assure them that it is all right to make marks in the Bible since it is a guidebook to God and his peace. This may come as a surprise for them since they revere the Qur'an but seldom read it, let alone dare write in it. The first verse I like to read to an Iranian seeker is Matthew 11:28–30. The Lord's invitation to give rest to those who are weary and burdened always seems to cut into their hearts.

Two cautions are in order here. One, you must be forewarned that the Iranian mind is very much a literal mind. By that I mean they will take the Bible very literally and you will have to help them understand it. Be patient as they ask you questions you may never have heard before.

An example might be: "You say Jesus is God but here he is praying to God. Now if he is God who is he praying to?" Iranian seekers also will need help with many terms that are very familiar to us. They will not know what a Pharisee is or what the Jewish feasts are all about. As you encourage your Iranian friends to read and ask questions, be patient and explain everything. Do not assume they are getting the message on the first reading. It is better that you discuss these things with them alone. Never ask them questions about their faith in front of other Iranians but set times to be alone. It is also better that they initiate these times. Iranians are very polite and may agree to meet with you just to please you. So tell your Iranian friends that you are at their service any time they want to discuss their Bible reading. As this point the best thing you can be doing is to be praying for them.

The second caution is that the Iranian tends to see truth not so much as objective truth but embodied in a position or person. For example a young Christian might give a seeker a totally correct answer from the Scriptures, but the seeker will not accept it as truth because it did not come from the mouth of a pastor. This means that you may need to find a way to link the Iranian seeker with a person whom he or she accepts as authoritative in the matter. Take them to your pastor or an older leader in the fellowship and let them get answers there. This is especially important if the Iranian you are dealing with is an older man.

Now we are ready to get down to some specific discussions with our Iranian seeker. At this point I cannot over-emphasize how important it is not to debate the weaknesses of Islam. It is far more productive to use the New Testament and simply discuss who Christ is and what He offers the sinner. It is also advisable to present Christ as Savior of sinners and leave the question of his divinity for later.

The first problem you may run into is that in the mind of your Iranian friend (I will use a man as an example), the terms you are using mean different things. You may not pick this up at first but it is a major hurdle that must be overcome. For example, if you suggest that your friend is a sinner he may well become insulted. The reason for the indignation is that in his mind sins are horrible crimes against God like murder, adultery, and stealing. He will be insulted if you suggest that he is such a person. You will need gently to go to Genesis and show him the story of the Fall and explain that he may well be a good person in comparison to other human beings but in God's sight all have sinned, and he has inherited his sin from Adam and Eve. You will need to show him that all human beings are sinners not because they sin; rather they sin because they are sinners. I have often spent an entire evening laying a sure foundation for the sinfulness of man.

As you continue your discussions with your Iranian friend you will want to begin to define for him, from the Scriptures, many key terms. Jesus' true identity will quickly become a focal point. Your friend will likely say that he believes in Jesus. But before you celebrate his conversion, you need to know what it is that he believes about Jesus. Generally Muslims believe Jesus was a great prophet, that He was born of a virgin, that He lived a sinless life, and that Jesus Himself did not die on a cross; rather it was someone who looked like him. Jesus ascended into heaven before the so-called crucifixion. Now you will begin to realize you are up against a system of thought that has carefully eclipsed Jesus's divinity and atonement. All your arguments will not reveal the truth of Christ to your Muslim friends; it will take the revealing work of the Holy Spirit.

A day will come when your Iranian friend will want to have a serious discussion with you about the divinity of Christ. He may now find himself drawn to Christ but the Trinity may be his stumbling block. Here are the steps I have used that God has blessed many times.

1. "Do you agree that God is Almighty and can do anything He wills?"
2. "Do you agree that God is a Spirit and can take any shape he wills?"
3. "Do you agree that God is infinite and beyond human comprehension except as He chose to reveal Himself to us?"

I have yet to meet an Iranian who disagreed with these statements. After laying the foundation I share this illustration. I ask my friend to compare the vastness of the ocean with that of God. We can not possibly explore the entire ocean. But then I ask, "What if I took a glass and filled it with water from the ocean and brought it to you? Now you can taste it, touch it, and smell it. You could put it under a microscope and you would see that in essence it is the same as the ocean. It is separate from the ocean but it is in essence the same as the ocean."

Then I read John 1:1, 14 and Colossians 1:15. I show how God emptied Himself and became a human being so that we could taste and see who He is. This illustration has been the key for many Iranians to begin to understand the divine nature of Christ. Throughout the discussion you will want to underscore the Christian belief in one God by reading 1 Corinthians 8:6.

You will need to carefully help your Iranian friends see what the Scriptures teach about the character of God, the nature of heaven, salvation, grace, and faith, You can safely assume that they have non-biblical concepts for most of these precious truths.

When you talk about prayer, your friends' experience with it is probably that they recite memorized prayers in Arabic that they really doesn't understand and that while they are praying their minds are wandering. When you begin to pray with them they might even repeat what you are saying because they have never really talked to God. This is to illustrate how important it is to get the Iranian seekers into the Word. Be sure to provide them with good solid evangelical literature in Persian. One very good resource is Dr. William Miller's book, *The Beliefs and Practices of Christians* (1975), in Persian.

### The Key of God's Touch

In the storeroom of tools we have with which to share Christ with Iranians, we still need to remember the greatest one. The greatest truth is that God has chosen to touch the Iranian people at this point in history. Jesus told Peter that it was not flesh or blood that had revealed to him that Jesus was the Christ; rather it was the Spirit of God. Today the Spirit of God is touching Iranians around the world. That means that God has already gone before you in witnessing to the Iranians in your location.

As you grow close to Iranians you will hear more and more stories about the dreams they may be having. You may find these stories hard to grasp, but I have found that almost every Muslim convert I know has had some type of dream that he understood to be a revelation of Christ. These dreams seem to awaken a hunger for Christ. I have come to see them as God's calling his own out of the world because we, his church, have failed to go to the Muslim world as commanded. Still today only two percent of the Western mission force is serving among Muslims, who make up twenty percent of the world's population. The approach I take with dreams is to celebrate them and then invite the seeker to get to know Jesus through reading the New Testament.

Over the years I have catalogued the types of dreams Iranians are having about the Lord. Most of them have a rescue motif. For instance, the person may be drowning when a hand comes down into the water and saves him. Or a person is ill and a being in radiant white robes enters his room and tells him he will be healed, and he is. Not only do they have dreams; they also may have a vision while awake. The point is that God is calling these dear people, and we need to be sensitive to the work of the Holy Spirit and be ready to follow up with good biblical discipleship.

The other evidence of the touch of God is the stories of the transformation of those who have been saved. Iranian Christians have miraculous testimonies. I never get tired of hearing them. Their testimonies are full of stories of how God intervened in their lives. One Iranian man told me that while he was visiting Los Angeles, he was walking the streets to pass the time of day when a painter on a ladder said "hello" to him. That began a two-hour conversation that led the Iranian to trust Christ. He confessed, "God sought me out."

I strongly encourage you to get to know the Iranian Christians in your area and get them to tell you about how they came to faith in Jesus. It will thrill you. The next important step is to introduce your Iranian Christian friends to your seeker friends. There is no power like the testimony of one Iranian believer telling his or her story to another Iranian. Another important insight is that if you feel you have led an Iranian to Christ and he refuses to meet with other Iranians, it may well be a sign that he has not really come to faith. A good acid test of true faith is when new believers are willing to confess Christ before their own peers.

Another powerful testimony to the touch of God in the Iranian community is the Iranian Church. When true Iranian believers gather for worship and fellowship, this is another tool you want to use in reaching other Iranians. The Muslim who attends a worship service in Persian usually makes comments like, "I have never experienced such peace!"

In our Persian language fellowship we have many Muslims who come to church just to feel the peace of the presence of God. But there is yet another unseen difference that you and I as Westerners will probably miss. That is the different social flavor a gathering of Iranian believers has in comparison with a secular gathering of Iranians. I have heard numerous times from Iranians, as they tell me their testimonies, that it was the transformed relationships in the Iranian Body of Christ that convinced them Christ was real.

There is no doubt about it; Iranians have been uniquely prepared for the Gospel. God has brought them to our shores and He is calling us to be available to minister to them. In many of our larger cities there is probably a small fellowship of Muslim Background Iranian Christians already worshipping and fellowshipping. If we are open to God's Spirit we can be God's link between the unbelieving Iranian and the Iranian Church. It might surprise you that an unbelieving Iranian would rather have you as his friend in contrast to one of his own unknown countrymen. But this happens. We need to use the favored position that we as Westerners hold, and use it for the advancement of our Lord's Kingdom.

## Major Issues

◆   Many Iranians have suffered deep loss. They are looking for friends who will love them with unconditional love.

◆   Many Iranians have become disillusioned by religion and religious leaders. Faith-sharing with Iranians must be accompanied by a life that demonstrates the truth.

◆   Rather than debating the issues of Islam, it is far more effective to discuss who Christ is and what He has to offer as Savior of sinners.

## Action Steps

◆   Get to know Iranian Christians in your area and encourage them to tell you about how they came to faith in Jesus.

◆    In general, Iranians still believe in absolute truth and revelation and will accept a copy of the New Testament.

◆    Introduce your Iranian Christian friends to your seeker friends. There is no power like the testimony of one Iranian believer telling his or her story to another Iranian.

◆    Put your Iranian friends in touch with an Iranian church if there is one in your area. Attending services in their own Persian language will be deeply moving for them. Also in worship, many Iranians respond to music and drama.

◆    If you need help in locating Iranian Christians in your city get in contact with ICI at (719) 596-0010 and they will assist you.

◆    If you would like more information on how to minister to Iranians you may contact: Rev. Ashton "Tat" Stewart, Jr., Talim Ministries, Inc., P. O. Box 471736, Aurora, CO 80047-1736, (303) 873-6611, tatstewart@compuserve.com

## Kurds

### Robert Blincoe

Greetings to all the people who have given their hearts and lives to the Kurds and endured suffering for that. They are my heroes. Now let's look at some models for ministry in the United States among the Kurds.

Imagine this. You pour hours into helping a Muslim Kurdish fellow find a job. You talk to the boss of a company to give the new guy a chance. You offer your phone number, asking the boss to call you if he ever has problems with this new employee. Three weeks later the phone rings. It's the company boss. Your Kurdish friend hasn't been to work for two days. You subsequently discover that he quit work without notice because his newer friends advised him about how to get on welfare. Now, he's too ashamed to see you anymore. And you are humiliated before the boss of the company. Is this a model for ministry?

Another example. You hear about a convert in another town. You call him up and send him some literature. He says, "You're great." He seems happy. The next call you get is from a lawyer in that town asking if you know that this friend is in jail. Is this a model for ministry?

Or maybe a picnic seems like a good idea. You reserve a picnic table in the park, you send out letters in the mail. Lots of Kurds and Americans come, and a good time is had by all. Then a stranger walks toward the group. He's wearing a suit. A few Kurdish men go over to meet him, and they whisper back and forth. He is from a political party. The Kurdish picnic breaks into two parts, those for and those against the politics of the stranger. You decide that to show the offended Kurds this was not your idea, you must leave your own picnic. Is this a model for ministry?

Perhaps you have a Kurdish friend, and you and she talk for hours over tea. You cook together, laugh together, travel, and then one morning your friend takes a deep breath and says, "I don't have any person in the world I can trust." You fall silent. Your heart beats rapidly and your forehead is moist. You reply, "What about your husband, of course?" She replies, "I said, I have no one in the world that I can trust except for you." A veil has been lifted for a moment and she speaks unveiled. Then the curtain falls again. But your relationship is forever clearer, dearer, and nearer. Is this a model for ministry?

A repeated experience for many who love the Kurdish is that they have borne Christ's words and his wounds. We are in prayer that Kurds too might bear his words, works, and wounds more and more. Perhaps we can take on Samuel Zwemer's life verse: "Lord, though we have fished all night and caught nothing, yet at your command we will launch out once more into the deep." So we resist despair for "we have this ministry as a mercy from God, so that we do not lose heart" (II Cor. 4:1).

I have learned a few things along the way. The first is that over in Kurdistan, most foreigners developed a patron/client relationship with Kurds. We walked around as gigantic North Americans with passports and finances in our pockets. Our relationship was based on our patronage and their purchased loyalty. But as they come to America, our ability to continue that dissolves. Here, our purpose is to get them to stand on their own. But they have lost the hierarchy of who they are, in relationship to us and to everyone else. So in this new country they tend to fall back to the hierarchy they knew among Islamic people. I am not so sure that we have done right to give them no structure of relationship except equality.

I would like to recommend a structure with which they are already familiar called the *tarika*—the Arabic word for "the way." *Tarika* is a highly structured model for ministry centering around a spiritual leader who gathers others around him for the purpose of spiritually examining one another and providing accountability. But the structure of *tarika* is well known. We have 350 Kurds in my city, two of whom are believers. As I have approached them, they are both interested in joining a *tarika* where two or three would gather in His name and be in spiritual relationship, accountability, and testing one another—examining themselves to see that they are in the faith in terms of the structural context with which they are already familiar.

We also haven't done enough with the shame/honor worldview. Kurds have a proverb, "No man admits his yogurt is sour." That is, no one takes on shame. We may need to approach them (as outlined in an earlier chapter) with Christ's victory not only over death, devil, and sin, but over shame as well. Christ is the one who bore our shame. There's no shortcut to spending all afternoon with Muslims telling them about our God. Friends of the Kurds ministry is a ministry to encourage American Christians to get involved with Muslim friends who've come among us—those strangers about whom Christ said, "In ministry to these, you have done it as unto me."

Some Americans can more suitably reach the first generation immigrants, others the second and successive generations. Xenophobic types should avoid working with first generation immigrants. Young people are sometimes better at working with second and third generations.

I give a fuller explanation about the *tarika* and my own ideas about missiology in a book I've written, *Ethnic Realities and the Church: Lessons from Kurdistan* (Blincoe 1998).

One exciting development in Kurdish ministry is an internship program here in the United States where Kurds live and where we are now sending American Christians who want to minister long-term with Muslims in the future in their homelands. But as interns they can spend time meeting Muslims and living in Muslim communities. This is our first internship of that kind.

The internship program has several distinctives. 1) Participants receive hands-on opportunity for service among Muslims. 2) They get mentored experience (usually from nine to twelve months). 3) This is a team-based ministry with extensive field experience to draw on from agency staff. 4) The internship experience takes a holistic approach emphasizing personal communion with Christ, character building, community formation (peace-making and team building), competence in ministry, and evangelism content.

Ministry workers to Kurds must never lose heart. Christ's sufferings will spill over into our lives (Col. 1:24). Prayer is vital for peace in Kurdistan so that the work can go on there. Pray also for Bible translation, radio broadcasts, Jesus film distribution, Christian ESL teachers in the USA and Canada, more volunteers doing friendship evangelism, and for the very few scattered Kurdish believers to become strong spiritual leaders. North America is the field for ministry to Kurds at this time and the American church needs to be awakened to this idea.

A video, "In Harm's Way," produced by Friends of the Kurds is now available for use in recruiting helpers from local churches.

## Major Issues

◆ Many more workers are needed.

◆ It is difficult for Kurdish believers to cooperate together. Their loyalties tend to be tribal. Kurds need to find peace not only with God but also between themselves.

◆ Kurdish ministry is difficult and takes time to bear fruit so recruit workers who do not discourage easily.

## Action Points

◆ Befriend the Kurds.

◆ Translate the Bible into Kurdish.

◆ Emphasize developing relationship-building programs when working with Kurds.

◆ Exposure generates motivation. Most American churches do not realize that the mission field has come to them. Gather materials such as books and the video mentioned above and expose the local church to the great need for work among Kurds.

◆ Work toward mobilizing youth as well as adults. Young people seem to be responsive to opportunities to get to know Muslims.

◆ Stress willingness to learn about and adapt to Muslim culture. Very few Anglos ever attempt to learn any Kurdish, not even a few words.

◆ Books about Islam are being placed in libraries by Muslim educational trusts. Gather resource materials and place books about Christianity and the Muslim context in college and university libraries.

◆ For more information, write to: Friends of the Kurds, Box 58319, Seattle, WA 98138-1319. E-mail: friends_of_kurds@home.com

# CHAPTER 9

# Interfaith Dialogue Models

## Muslim-Christian Dialogue

### Jeff Morton

I live in Orange County, California. According to the latest statistics in the *Los Angeles Times,* Orange County has about 97 percent occupancy in all residential areas. Basically there is no more room. Don't plan to move there! However, Muslims continue to come, and they arrive in large numbers. We just had a refugee family staying with us for the last month. We did finally locate a place for them to live, fortunately inexpensive, although it took us a month to find it. But in many ways this is tremendous news. Muslims are arriving at Orange County in large numbers.

I work with the SIM mission agency and we have a small division called Ethnic Focus Ministry. Even though we are the only "SIM-ers" in Orange County, we work together with a number of other folks and agencies in a group called Church without Walls. This is not a building program. We call ourselves a bridge team. Bridge teams are groups of Christians willing to go to mosques to have "Meetings for Better Understanding" between Muslims and Christians. I remember the first time I introduced myself as part of a bridge team, some others thought, "Well, where's your deck of cards?" Seriously. Especially the Muslims. They wanted to play cards. But we don't use the term "Church Without Walls" as much as simply saying we are a "bridge team." When we meet with a mosque, which I will explain later in this chapter, we call it a Meeting for Better Understanding (MBU).

A really memorable experience for me was during the time just before we left Guinea at the end of our third term as missionaries. We had moved up to northern Guinea, very close to Mali. For our earlier ministry (because frankly my language skills were poor), we had lived in Liberia, where I could use English and Mandingo. But then we moved to Guinea because of the war and I had to use Maninka and French. What a struggle I had! I would sit at a book table where Muslims would pass by. Some of them would sit down and between English, French, and Maninka—and my Maninka was horrible—we would discuss the issues in these little pamphlets. That was my first introduction to the Church Without Walls. It was a good time of sitting down one-on-one with a Muslim, not just to share Christ, but to learn how to be a friend and form a relationship with this person.

We were living in a town called Siguiri, a gold mining capital of Guinea. Siguiri was a wild and wooly town—where people might kill others just to get their gold—something like the Wild West in the United States. You could go out to the gold mines and lose your life. You could also lose a fortune. Fortunes were made and lost like that. And that is where I cut my teeth, so to speak, on dialogue and intense discussion with Muslims. But not based on differences, just based on the fact that I knew this person, he knew me, we had a relationship, and we could debate intensely and still be friends.

What we are doing in Orange County is similar, but it didn't originate with us. It started with a fellow named Anees Zaka. The idea is to introduce Christians to Muslims. If there are any two groups that are going to be totally separate by will, it will be Christians and Muslims. I don't think I know any Christians (except maybe for a few interested for some special reason) who go out of their way to meet Muslims. I don't know any Christian in my church who goes 100 yards down the street to one of the Middle Eastern grocery stores for any reason. Orange County has Muslim dentists, Muslim doctors, and Muslim lawyers, but Christians do not go there. We just do not do things with Muslims.

So Church Without Walls, and the bridge teams, is an attempt to span the gap—to bridge the chasm that exists between Muslims and Christians with dialogue and discussion. But of course, that is not the end in itself. This is a church planting ministry and we are encouraged by some of the other bridge teams that are working throughout the United States.

In Orange County, we are one of four bridge teams. We all do things a bit differently. But here are a few guidelines. Identify a mosque that might be willing to have MBUs and develop a good relationship. Plan out a specific format for MBU meetings, agreed to ahead of time by both Christians and Muslims. After choosing a meeting time and place, then publicize the meeting ahead of time at churches and mosques. One Muslim speaker and one Christian speaker should be chosen (important that it be only one each). The speaker must be a man, and should be an older, more mature man. A soft and gentle demeanor (not combative) is an asset. Fridays and/or Sundays seem like good times usually. Average attendance might be around 50 Muslims and 30 Christians.

When approaching Muslims about having MBUs, say, "We know we don't understand you very well, and you probably don't understand us very well, so could we have meetings for better understandings?" Agree upon the amount of time for each speaker (usually 30-45 minutes).

At the meeting, the two speakers speak, with the Muslim going first. Then a moderator leads in a question-and-answer time, which sometimes has lasted as long as two hours. The Q&A time should be confined to matters of understanding and clarity, not polemics or additional debate. Sometimes it may be better to have the questions submitted in a written form, to avoid too much "heat" or getting too far off on tangents.

If the meeting takes place at a Christian church, a meal or at least refreshments makes a better social/relational setting, so that it seems more than just a debate.

Attitudes are extremely important, going into the meeting. This is not for just anybody; only more mature Christians who are definitely interested in ministry to Muslims. The Muslims may give an invitation to convert to Islam. A skillful Muslim speaker can easily convince a weak, unprepared, or untested Christian. Prayer is important beforehand, and an attitude of prayer should be maintained throughout the meeting. Another important attitude is simply, "I'm here to learn," and "I'm here to meet at least one Muslim friend with whom I am willing to spend time." Never respond in the same spirit with which they attack. "Relate, don't debate" is a good principle for these meetings.

You could possibly do this in a Hindu temple as well. We generally have a debriefing time the following week among members of the bridge team to see what we have learned, to pray for results, and encourage the forming of relationships.

These meetings will likely run their course in due time and will need to end. We have been conducting them for three to four years with no plans for closure yet. However, everyone on the bridge team now has enough Muslim friends that they can continue to relate, even when the bridge group shuts down. A lot of friendship evangelism is going on. Don't be in a hurry to end the meetings, because they are extremely valuable for getting Christians involved in the lives of Muslims.

Typical topics covered in such meetings are:

| | |
|---|---|
| Who is God? | Forgiveness |
| Who is Jesus? | Homosexuality |
| Inspiration of the *Bible* | Social Issues |
| Inspiration of the Qur'an | Cultural Issues |
| Problems Raising Kids in America | Values (not just theologies) |

A key issue is to stick closely to the Bible. Which version of the Bible should be used? It perhaps does not matter much. Using the New American Standard Version could possibly be a problem because it has the word "America" in it. Also, some Bibles with highlights or certain commentary notes could be a problem.

We have found it a good idea to identify ourselves as "Bible-believing Christians" but not from any specific denomination or group. It needs to be made clear that the speaker is presenting the biblical view. This may be contrary to what Muslims have heard about the Christian view. So you will need to continue saying, "This is what the Bible teaches."

It would be well worth your time if you are interested in this type of ministry to get a copy of the book, *Muslims and Christians at the Table,* by Bruce McDowell (1999).

The first part of the book is on the vision for reaching Muslims in the United States and some of the background about movements of Muslims here and the growth of Islam.

The second part discusses the importance of understanding— understanding the Muslim background and gaining a cultural and historical understanding of Islam. There's also a theological background concerning major doctrines in Islam and Christianity and how they compare.

The next major part of the book is about reaching Muslims. Sections are devoted to such topics as the theological basis for evangelism, how to reach Muslims, guidelines for friendship evangelism, meetings for better understanding, and studying the Bible with Muslims. The chapter on meeting for better understanding talks about a number of topics that can be discussed at these meetings. Muslims and Christians meet at a mosque or a church, and they alternate places. They perhaps meet on a monthly basis and may do this over a period of years. The Christians develop relationships and make presentations of the Gospel on whatever topic they have chosen to discuss. A Muslim will speak on the same topic as the Christian speaker and then afterwards they may have some question/answer time.

This book can be a help as we address the major issue in our society of coming to grips with the immigrants in our communities and achieving better understanding of their cultures, backgrounds, and worldviews. If we are not willing to expend time and conscious effort at this, we will find it difficult to impact their lives for Christ.

## Major Issues

◆   Relate; don't debate. Meetings should be used intentionally to develop ongoing relationships with Muslims.

◆   Always stick closely to the Bible. Keep coming back to it, stressing, "This is what the Bible teaches." This is important because what the Bible teaches is not necessarily what Muslims think Christians believe.

◆   It is important to have a support group of mature Christians who are strongly concerned about ministry to Muslims.

## Action Steps

◆   Contact Dr. Anees Zaka to speak to your Bridge Team, or have him conduct a seminar: Dr. Anees Zaka, Church Without Walls, P.O. Box 27276, Philadelphia, PA  19118.

◆   Identify those in your church (or a group of churches) who are interested in Muslims. Begin meeting for prayer and vision, sharing together for weeks and even months before launching such an effort.

◆   Identify a mosque in your area that would be willing to have an MBU. To make contact with mosques, some members of your group might be willing to take Arabic courses there, or go to Friday prayers, or to an Islamic Awareness session (which they often conduct on Fridays or Sundays).

## The Internet

### Jochen Katz

There are many reasons why it is difficult for Muslims to attend Christian events. But Islam is a mission-minded religion and they have their own outreach events. Why not attend? While a student, together with a couple of other Christians, I went to a number of "Introduction to Islam" classes offered by the Muslim Student Association. We observed that while we were there, the numbers of Muslim students were higher than usual. Often there were Muslims who came because they knew we were coming. We used the "Question and Answer" time after the talk to ask some critical questions and sometimes we heard some of them murmur, "Good question, good question." They came because we were asking questions they did not

dare to ask, but they had those questions on their minds. This experience is not specifically about the Internet, but using their mission
events to make contacts with Muslims is worth considering, and this
story introduces one of the reasons for using the Internet.

I have been asked to give a small overview of the most important
features of the website that I maintain, www.answering-islam.org,
and then introduce a few projects suggesting other possibilities for
outreach. Perhaps there will be some who would like to join in and
help transform these opportunities into reality.

## Motivation

Where do people increasingly go for information these days?
They go to Internet search engines. They type in the words they want
to know about and then see what comes up. Where will Muslims who
have questions go? Asking critical questions is not very welcome
within the Muslim community. But Muslims do have questions. Where
can they go and securely ask those questions? The Internet is one way
they can research issues that they are not supposed to read about.

## Overview

We have two locations, one in the U.S. and one in the UK (mirror
sites), and we have offers for maybe having a mirror in Australia
soon. This setup has various advantages. First, speed. If you are
closer to the site, you get the content faster. But also, security. If you
have the site in several locations, then the motivation of trying to
attack one site to bring it down is not so great because the information
is still there somewhere else. Currently we have about 7,500 pages,
and new content is constantly added. We have about 50,000 visitors a
month requesting some 200,000 pages total. Most visitors read about
3, 4, or 5 pages. Of  those, about half, we estimate, are Muslims,
because the site is advertised mainly in the Muslim newsgroups and
chatrooms. On Yahoo! the site is listed in the Islam section, not the
Christianity section. Also from the feedback we get, a little more than
half is from Muslims who ask further questions, or who vent their
anger about the site, or give some other kind of response.

We have begun adding material in different languages. Answering Islam currently has a Turkish sub-site, an Indonesian and Malay
sub-site, and a French sub-site. We would love to add more if people
who speak different languages will provide material for Muslims in
these languages, be it evangelistic or apologetic materials. We hap-
pily host these sub-sites for free. We just need people to create the

materials and give them to us. Urdu would be one language very high up on our wish list.

Regarding content, the site has several areas. The apologetics part is the largest currently because the website grew out of my observing Muslim attacks on Christianity in newsgroups. I felt compelled to respond to these attacks and misunderstandings. That is how I got into the dialog on the Internet. Therefore the apologetics section is the largest. We also have quite a bit of non-confrontational evangelistic material; partly on the Answering Islam site, and partly on the website www.injil.org which also belongs to us. The latter is still small, but it tries to be non-confrontational, more contextualized, presenting the gospel only without getting into arguments.

The Answering Islam site is giving answers to the various questions asked by Muslims or maybe questions not yet asked. But the site does not do only "answering." Muslims make many claims—not only about what is wrong with Christianity, but also why everyone should believe in Islam. We take a good look at those claims and critique them, show where they are flawed in their logic, false even in the "facts" supplied, or whatever other reasons there might be why we cannot accept their claims.

For example: Why should Muslims consider reading the Bible? For most Muslims this is an irrelevant issue because they are so convinced that the Qur'an is the word of God and that the Bible is corrupted or of less value. Why should they even bother?

In the process of the discussion we ask in return, "Ok, why do you believe the Qur'an is the word of God?" Next we let them present their claims. Then we request, "Ok, what is the evidence for that?" So in a kind, friendly, but questioning and critiquing way, we try to elicit responses as to why they believe what they believe. And we pray that many will realize that, actually, they don't really know why they believe what they believe.

The questioning part is important because when they come to realize that they do not really have so many good reasons for their faith, then the Bible becomes more of an option. Then we invite, "Well, let's investigate both books and see what the support is for these books." The critical investigation of the Qur'an is done on every level where there are claims from Muslims; i.e. textual purity (variant manuscripts), miraculous eloquence, scientific miracles, numerical miracles, no contradictions, and so forth. All these discussions can be found under the section "Qur'an" on the website.

The third area, in addition to the answering of Muslim questions and the questioning of Muslim claims, is presenting training materials for Christians. Six years ago I started the site mainly in order to communicate with Muslims and to reach them. But the longer I maintain it, the more responses I get from Christians in Malaysia, Pakistan, Egypt, and so on, who say, "This is exactly what I need. We don't have this here. Thank you very much." For many Christians in these countries, it becomes a resource where they can now get answers and then give them to their Muslim friends. Often they are under attack and don't have answers because this kind of literature is not allowed in their country. In these cases, the site became a resource for these groups of people as well.

The most effective part of Answering Islam contains the testimonies of Muslims who have become Christians. Because a testimony comes from the heart, it is about life and it touches lives. It is personal instead of only argumentative. We have had a number of Muslims become Christians through these testimonies. Not only the text of the testimony is important, but the opportunity to correspond with these converts via e-mail. This happens under pseudonyms. Even in the "free West" security is still an issue, as we all know. But the Internet is now making it possible for them to witness to Muslims, when they could not have done this in their community. Going under a different name they can tell their story, correspond with the seekers who want to ask further questions, and can lead them step-by-step.

A few of the testimonies on the site are even by people who have come to Christ basically through correspondence with other converts who give their testimony there. Several more have not yet written their testimonies. This is not only an opportunity for Muslims to hear the gospel, but it is leading to growth for the converts themselves. Often, in real life, they don't know where to start. It's dangerous. It's difficult. But in a safe environment, they can tell their story and then be challenged to deeper thinking by the Muslims who ask further questions. They can find answers and give reasons for their hope and for what has changed them. So the involvement in witnessing helps the converts to grow themselves. They may also develop a deeper prayer life as they pray for those with whom they are corresponding.

For those of you who minister among Muslims, you probably have contacts with converts. This could be an effective growth opportunity for them. Ask them whether they would consider sharing what they have found in Christ. It is a shock for many Muslims to find that converts exist. Most of them say, "I have never met a Muslim who became a Christian." It is a shock for them and for some, a wholesome shock.

I would like to have at least 10 testimonies from every country with a substantial Muslim population—some men and some women.

Then when people come to the site, their reaction may be: "Oh, here is my country, my language…let me see." At this point, the testimonies are organized in countries, but maybe as the numbers grow, we can also organize them into ethnic units. If you have contact with Muslim background believers who would like to share their testimony in this way, we have a guide that will help them in the process of writing. Please let them contact me at the e-mail address given below.

We have rebuttals to the material of the main Muslim writers or speakers (Ahmed Deedat, Jamal Badawi, Shabir Ally, etc.). We are extending this section to as many of the popular Muslim writers as possible. We try to show where their arguments are wrong, first to the Muslims who build their faith on those books or videos, but also to let Christians see, "O.K., here are solid answers we can give in response to their attacks."

Muslims are constantly going around challenging Christians to debates. Often, the Christians are overrun because they don't know how to respond. In this rebuttal section they can find the arguments that a certain speaker uses over and over again. And they see that these are possible answers. It can also have another effect. There are debates that Muslims love to bring up where the Muslim speaker has won. But we can later look at the debate, analyze it, and make our own rebuttal. Maybe in the actual debate, the Christian speaker failed to answer, but that doesn't mean that Christians don't have any answer. We may be able to neutralize some of the most harmful debates.

## One Possible Project

I would love to develop a Muslim Study Bible. America has wonderful study Bibles. But they are written for the "white middle class American" who already has a Christian background. Muslims ask very different questions than Christians do when they read the Bible. Folks in Muslim ministry have probably done some one-on-one or small group Bible study with Muslims or converts from Muslim background. They may have used several texts many times and know what kinds of questions are asked and what needs to be explained.

We invite you to send study notes that you may already have made for yourself, or to condense your experience with biblical texts into study notes that can then help Muslims around the world read the Bible with understanding. If we could develop this on the Internet we would not have to wait for publication until an entire biblical book is complete. Even one text would already be useful and help many around the world.

Another great plus for the Internet is that those short study notes can then contain links to more in-depth articles in the Bible commentary or in the apologetics section. Those who want to can dig deeper when certain terms or ideas appear in the text, which the notes themselves cannot supply. The notes themselves should be explanatory, not "debate material." The notes should just be help in reading and understanding the text. No reference to Islam is necessary. But with certain terms and concepts where Muslims always come with protest, we can supply the necessary discussion easily with a link, something not possible in a printed book. If anyone finds this vision fascinating to create such a Study Bible for people from Muslim backgrounds and would like to contribute in some way, please contact me.

In general, this site can offer you an extension of your ministry with little extra effort. If you have developed things that work well in your smaller group, and if you will make it available on the Internet, these tracts or articles may help Christian workers all around the world—not just here, but particularly in countries where they desperately look for good ways of approaching their Muslim friends and neighbors.

Bringing your materials to the Internet can also help you improve them; just add an e-mail address and you have the chance to get feedback from Christians and Muslims—what questions they raise and how you could refine your arguments.

Why should you consider joining Answering Islam instead of opening your own website? Answering Islam is already well known among both Muslims and Christians. If you place your materials here, they will be found and read—not lost in an ocean of websites.

## Major Issues

◆ Putting Muslim ministry materials on the Internet multiplies your audience and greatly increases the chances of feedback.
◆ The Internet offers many opportunities for cooperation between Muslim ministry workers and organizations.

## Action Steps

◆ If you want to be involved in ministry to Muslims via the Internet (contributing study notes, recommending good materials, etc.), contact Jochen Katz at jokatz@gmx.de and let him know your ideas or questions.
◆ If you have any ideas for a Muslim Study Bible, let Jochen Katz know.

*Section 4*

# *North American Road to Relevancy*

# CHAPTER 10

# Muslim Ministry Workers in North America

*Richard M. Bailey*

## Introduction

The information in this database describes workers doing Muslim ministry in North America. The data has been collected mainly by contacting workers and asking them about their ministries.[1] At present approximately 35,000 different bits of information are stored. These bits of data range from address to language proficiency to ministry focus information.

This database is designed to be a tool for research and networking of ministries and workers in North America. It can be especially useful for collecting and analyzing information around questions about ethnic ministry (i.e., Persian work), types of ministry (i.e., campus work), and regional characteristics of ministry (i.e., work in Dallas).

The biggest limitation at this point is 'soft' data. For many workers complete information is not available. The existing data is based only on a self-analysis of one's ministry (or secondhand descriptions about workers who could not be contacted directly). Some people may not have described what they are doing accurately. The data also was not collected with potential data entry problems in mind. Because of this a worker's description may have been misunderstood and entered incorrectly. Considering these factors, some of the data is less meaningful than one would ideally hope for. But in spite of its present shortcomings, the database does reveal valuable information for knowing where energies need to be focused.

### Number of Workers

The database presently has 643 names listed in it. About half of these people (324) directly contacted us either by e-mail, letter, or phone about their ministries. The other half (319) of the records contain secondhand information.

About one-third of the names listed in the database (208) are believed to be presently inactive in any type of Muslim ministry in North America. Some of these people formerly were active in North American Muslim ministry, but are no longer so. Others possibly never were active, but were incorrectly described as active by other North American workers. Yet others plan to become active in North American ministry in the future but are presently held back by other responsibilities. Retirees who ministered in the Muslim world, but are known presently to be inactive in Muslim ministry in North America, are also included in this category. They are viewed as potential part-time workers.

The remaining two-thirds of the names in the database (435) are believed to be active at some level in ministry to Muslims in North America. It is important to realize that these workers are not all professional full-time workers focused only on North America. In fact less than 20% of all active North American Muslim ministry workers (72) fit this profile.[2] Beyond those listed in the database, it is clear from known information that other workers (at least 100) are active in North America who are still not documented. Existing information strongly suggests that almost all of these undocumented workers are casual, part-time laypeople with no ministry outside of North America.

How high is the Christian worker-to-Muslim ratio for North America? Most sources assume a North American Muslim population of about five million. Because most Christian workers reaching Muslims in North America are not full-time professionals, it does not seem appropriate just to use the total number of workers active at any level as the basis for determining the amount of effort being spent to reach Muslims here.

In order to compensate for this problem, the number of full-time workers working only in North America has been doubled. This represents an approximate estimate of the total energies that are being spent to reach Muslims in North America by all Christian workers (78 [72 full-time professionals + 3 full-time laypeople + 3 full-time retired professionals] + 78 [for all the efforts of part-time workers] = 156). This yields a ratio of North American workers to Muslims (about one worker for 32,000 Muslims) that is considerably better (nearly five times better) than the seven-to-one-million ratio found in the Middle East, according to *Operation World*.[3] Whether it is appropriate for North America Muslims to receive this level of attention relative to the Muslim world as a whole is a question in need of further reflection.[4]

However, there is another perspective to the question of whether workers are giving appropriate attention to the Muslims of North America. Since North America has one of the highest concentrations of Evangelical Christians in the world, and Christians here do not need to go anywhere to reach Muslims, does the number of active workers suggest a lack of vision, understanding, and concern for North American Muslims by the church? That the number of laypersons involved in ministry to Muslims in North America (including the 100 presently undocumented lay workers) is only about two-thirds the number of paid professional workers (about 200 lay to 288 professional workers) suggests that something is wrong.

Thousands of laypeople across the country have taken Muslim awareness seminars and formal classes on how to witness to Muslims. Many thousands more interact with Muslims on a daily basis at their jobs. Why are so few of them actively reaching out to their Muslim neighbors? If we look at the ratio of lay workers who appear to be reaching out to Muslims to the number of Evangelical Christians (*Operation World* estimates 50 million Evangelical Christians in America[5]), the rate of lay involvement is shockingly low (one worker from every quarter-million Evangelical Christians).[6] Is the problem with the North American church, our training programs, a mixture of both, or something else all together?

## Worker Profile

*Age.* No direct question about the age of workers was asked. But about two-thirds of all workers provided some information from which their minimum age could be guessed (i.e., they recently graduated from college or have been active with Iranians for 20 years). The results of entering minimum possible ages suggested that the age distribution of workers is not heavily weighted toward retirees or the very young. The age bracket where most workers end up is the 40-50 age bracket (about 20% of all workers) with significant numbers in all other age brackets. Since newer workers tend to be more difficult to spot (they have no history to report), the remaining one-third of workers whose age cannot be guessed are more likely to be young workers than old. In short, the evidence, while tentative, gives good reason to believe that the age distribution of workers is well distributed among all age brackets. This suggests that ministry to Muslims in North American is neither a dying ministry (which would be the case if most workers were 65+) nor an immature ministry (which might be the case if most workers were in the 20-30 age group).

*Education.* Those who minister to Muslims in North America are well educated. While no specific information on education was asked, workers often volunteered such information or provided other information that strongly suggested their education level. (We can assume, for example, that most pastors with certain denominations have a masters degree.) Based on information provided, either exact information or a reasonable guess about an individual worker's education level was possible for two out of three respondents. Virtually every worker who could reasonably be analyzed had at least a B.A. (42%). Eleven percent indicated that they have a masters degree and 14% clearly have a doctorate (often determined by their name being preceded by the title Dr.). In summary, there is good reason to believe that at least two-thirds of all workers to Muslims in North America have at least a B.A., with some 25% of all workers holding higher degrees. The data, at this point, is inadequate to answer the question of how relevant their formal education is for ministry to Muslims in North America.

*Ethnic Identity.* About two-thirds of all workers (67%) appear to be Caucasian Americans. The remaining one-third, either by name or other information provided, are clearly not Caucasian Americans. This group appears to be divided between about 25 different ethnic groups (30 if we sub-divide Arabs into different groups such as Egyptian or Iraqi), the vast majority of which are ethnic groups from the Islamic parts of the world. Ten percent of all active workers in North America (45) were born Muslim. This 10% comes from 18 different ethnic groups (23 if Arabs are sub-divided).

*Marital and Gender Status.* One-third of all workers gave no indication about their marital status. Fifty-six percent are clearly married (usually determined by the mention of a spouse). Thirteen percent appear to be single. While several workers volunteered information about divorce or remarriage, no meaningful information on these questions was collected.

Most workers are doing ministry as couples (46%). Their information suggests that both are doing ministry together, but it is not clear who is doing exactly what. The next largest group (40%) is men who appear to be doing ministry on their own. If they are married (most of them are), this usually means that their spouse does not appear to be active in ministry to North American Muslims. In a few cases the spouse is active in ministry to Muslims in North America, but she is doing such different things from what he is doing that they have been entered into the database separately.

The last group are women doing ministry on their own (14%). Most of these are single. The few who are married usually do not have spouses active in Muslim ministry in North America. If their husbands are active, their ministries are so different from each other that they have been entered into the database separately.

Data on the workers' marital standing suggests a stable group of workers. The information about whether they work as couples or individuals suggests that a significant percent of females who are married to male workers are not active in ministry to Muslims. The female dimensions of ministry to Muslims also have an overall under-representation as compared to males.

### Distribution of Workers

The distribution of active workers between the United States and Canada is 87% and 13%. This would appear to be a reasonably good distribution of workers between the two countries, though exact numbers on the Muslim populations of either country are not available.

Within Canada, the distribution appears to be reasonable, based upon where the Muslim populations are most likely to be concentrated.[7] Ontario, which contains the city with the largest Muslim population in Canada (Toronto), has the largest number of workers (24). The western Canadian provinces of Alberta and British Columbia, where the second largest concentrations of Canadian Muslims are likely to be found, have the second largest concentration of workers (12 and 11 respectively).

The distribution of workers in the United States, on the other hand, shows some problems. Among the three regions in the country where the largest concentrations of Muslims are found—these being, in order of importance, the greater New York area, California, and Illinois—the concentration of workers is completely reversed. Illinois appears to have the most workers (48), California a close second (43), and the greater New York area, which would include New Jersey and Connecticut, a distant third (NY=15, NJ=13, CT=1, Total=29).[8] Why are there so few workers in the New York area? The most likely reason is that the New York area has fewer Protestants, containing more Jewish people, Catholics, and non-Christian immigrants. This means that the pool of potential volunteer workers is considerably smaller than what would be found in Los Angeles or Chicago.[9]

Another state that seems to have too few workers is Texas. Houston, with one of the top ten concentrations of Muslims in North America, has only one known active worker.[10] Texas as a whole has only a little over 2% of the total ministry work force (10 workers). We also know of no workers in 16 states and 3 provinces. Most of these are unlikely to have considerable Muslim populations (i.e., North Dakota, Alaska, Wyoming). But a few of these states potentially could have sizable Muslim populations (i.e., New Mexico, Nevada, Delaware).

The severity of the distribution problem of workers among Muslims in the United States can be seen by comparing the ratio of workers to Muslims in Arizona and the greater New York Area. If we estimate 20,000 Muslims for Arizona (with 22 workers) and 500,000 for the greater New York Area (with 29 workers), the effect is a concentration of workers in Arizona that is 15 times greater per 1000 Muslims than in New York.[11]

What is the underlying cause of this inequity in worker distribution? While it may be partly due to ignorance of where Muslims are concentrated, the best answer seems to be that workers are deciding to do ministry to Muslims after they have decided to live someplace for other reasons. They may want to live near family or do not like big cities. While there is nothing wrong with giving other issues consideration, the big picture suggests that Muslim ministry in North America may be suffering from such choices. More emphasis needs to be placed on workers choosing to do their ministry where the Muslims are living.[12]

### Types of Ministry

Each worker's ministry has been categorized according to 26 possible types of ministry.[13] The types that most workers are involved in are listed below.

| | |
|---|---|
| Friendship Evangelism | 39% |
| Teaching and Training of Workers and Churches | 35% |
| Administration | 23% |
| Campus Ministry | 20% |
| Resource Development and Distribution | 17% |
| Writing and Translation Work | 15% |
| Church Planting | 13% |
| Social Work | 13% |
| Convert Work | 11% |

This information suggests that most ministries to Muslims in North America are focused on the preliminary stages of contacting people and starting friendships rather than the more developed stages of church planting and discipleship of converts. The reasons for this are open to discussion.

*How many of the 27 possible ministry types are most workers involved in?* The database shows that 25% of all active workers (107) appear to be involved in only one type of ministry. Another 25% (114) appear to be involved in two types of ministry, and 19% (81) are involved in three. The remaining 30% of the workers are involved in anywhere from 4–11 different types of ministry (4=13%, 5=8%, 6=5%, 7-11=3%). The data suggests that most workers are not making the mistake of trying to do too many different types of ministry at once.

*How much of each worker's ministry time is going toward direct and indirect ministries?*[14] The data suggests that about 50% of all workers are totally or mostly focused on direct ministries to Muslims. Another 25% of all workers give about 50% of their time to direct ministry and 50% to indirect ministry. The remaining 25% of workers are focused mostly or totally on indirect ministry. Almost all the indirect ministry in North America is being done by professional and retired professional workers. Because of this, professional worker time is only slightly more focused toward direct ministry than indirect. Lay workers, on the other hand, are focused heavily in the direction of direct ministry. Overall, this data suggests that North American ministry to Muslims has a healthy mix of direct and indirect work.

*Are some types of ministries not receiving enough attention?* Many opinions exist on this topic. But if we ask where Islam is most likely to be vulnerable and where Islam is most likely to have success against the Church, two types of ministry loom large. In the western context, Islam's role for women would seem to open up special doors of opportunity. Yet ministry to women is receiving little attention (7%). On the other hand, the type of work that Muslims are presently using most effectively to penetrate nominal Christians is prison ministry.[15] Yet at present this ministry is receiving virtually no attention by those interested in reaching Muslims (under 2%). In both the areas of prison and women's ministry there are some problems of accurately measuring what is actually occurring. But there is no doubt that neither is presently a priority among workers to Muslims in North America.

*Are some types of ministries that are receiving adequate attention not effective?* The effectiveness of friendship evangelism (39% of workers involved) and teaching and training of workers and churches (35% of workers involved) should be questioned. How many Muslims have been brought to Christ through friendship evangelism? Are there some ways *not* to do friendship evangelism? Are our teaching and training programs for workers and churches producing better professional and lay workers? Does the apparent lack of lay workers suggest that there are wrong ways to teach and train workers and churches?

**Ethnic Ministry**

The way workers described their contact with Muslims varied widely. Twenty percent (90), who are all involved in indirect ministry, do only 'non-ethnic based ministries'.[16] About 20% more described their contact without any mention of the ethnic identity of the Muslims they are reaching. These workers would say they are reaching out to "Muslims." Approximately 40% more mentioned that they are reaching out to one or more specific ethnic groups. These workers would say they are reaching Arabs or Turks or both. The last 20% mentioned that they are reaching out to both a specific ethnic group and also doing some general outreach towards "Muslims." Some of this last 20% will be more focused on the ethnic group, others more focused on the general non-ethnic type of outreach.

Muslims in North America can be divided between five different ethnic groups, each making up very roughly one-fifth of the Muslim pie. These categories are Arabs, Persians, South Asians, African Americans, and others.[17] The percentage of the total Muslim ministry work force focused on each of these ethnic groups is as follows:

| | |
|---|---|
| Arabs | 21% |
| Persians | 8% |
| South Asians[18] | 8% |
| Afro-Americans[19] | 2% |

In the "other" group, the percent of the total Muslim ministry work force focused on each ethnic group is:

| | |
|---|---|
| Kurds | 8% |
| Turks | 3% |
| Somalis | 2% |
| Bosnians | 1% |
| Sub-Saharan Africans | 1% |
| Indonesians | 1% |
| Malays[20] | 1% |

The above information shows no clear relationship between the number of Muslims in North America from a specific ethnic group and the number of workers trying to reach them. The ethnic group with the most serious lack of attention by ministry workers is African Americans. South Asians are also receiving less than half of the attention they deserve. If all the presently active workers who know a South Asian language or have past experience in South Asia were to focus on South Asians now, the percent of total workers active with South Asians would double (from 8% to 16%). In other words, many workers do not seem to be prioritizing their past ethnic experience in deciding what type of Muslim ministry they are doing in North America.

While there can be many legitimate reasons for doing this, most workers are probably not aware of how valuable their linguistic and ethnic experience may be in the North American environment. Some ethnic groups have virtually no workers active among them in North America, even though some workers presently doing other types of Muslim ministry in North America know how to work with those ethnic groups.

The ratio of White to non-White workers in each of these ethnic ministries is different. Among Arabs the distribution is 40% white, 60% other.[21] Among Persians it is 50% White, 50% other. Among South Asians the rate is 60% White, 40% other. Among Afro-Americans the percentage is 12% White, 88% other.[22] Among Kurds it is 94% white, 6% other.

Differences also exist between the ethnic ministries in what types of ministry they emphasize. The most significant difference lies in what percentage of ethnic workers are involved comparatively in church planting and in convert work. Among ethnic workers to Arabs the numbers are 11% and 10% respectively. Among Persians the rates are 52% and 60% respectively. Among South Asians the percentages are 25% and 6% respectively—and among Kurds 18% and 6% respectively.[23]

The best explanation for why Persian ministry is so heavily focused on church planting and convert work compared to the other ethnic ministries is that the Persian people are more responsive to the gospel than other ethnic groups in North America. This raises the question of whether a person's religious or ethnic and cultural identities are more determinative of whether they will consider the gospel. This data would suggest that ethnic identity outweighs religion. If this should be correct, workers in most situations should be discouraged from reaching "Muslims" and instead be encouraged to reach "Arab Muslims" or "Kurdish Muslims."[24]

Finally, the data shows that among those who are working with specific ethnic groups, at least 50% are either foreign fluent or native speakers of the language which that ethnic group speaks. This suggests that many workers with specific ethnic groups come to their ministry either having been born in that culture or having had extensive experience overseas in their homelands.

The one exception to ethnic ministries that are linguistically and culturally prepared are workers among Kurds. Here two-thirds of all workers appear to speak only English. Only a handful speak Kurdish fluently. This problem may largely be due to: 1) the inability of most Kurdish workers to stay in Kurdish-speaking parts of the world for extended periods of time, and 2) the relative newness of most Kurdish work. In the long term this problem, if not addressed, will probably reduce the potential effectiveness of Kurdish work in North America.

### Organizations

The database was originally designed around individual worker information. Later it became clear that workers were providing enough information about the organizations they were associated with that an organizational dimension was added to the program. This information has been grouped according to 14 different types of organizations. The most important of these are Ministry Organizations (146), Churches (81), Mission Societies (46), Secular Schools (31), and Christian Schools (25).[25]

The worker need not be a formal member of an organization to be listed with it. Many, for example, do campus work on secular campuses. These workers are listed under the name of the campus where they minister. It is important to realize that most workers are associated with more than one organization. A campus worker, for example, will be listed under the campus he is working on and the ministry organization he is ministering through.

Our information on organizations is not as complete as what we have with workers.[26] But the information is extensive enough to give a general profile of the way workers are tied to organizations. Of those workers known to be associated with "ministry organizations," 58% appear, in terms of their North American Muslim ministry, to be one-person operations (84). Only 10% (14) of the organizations appear to have more than 3 North American workers. The largest ministry organization listed presently has only 14 active workers in North America.

The picture this information suggests is one of excessive organizational division. While most would agree that division of resources in North America among many organizations is wise,[27] excessive division can produce undesirable results. These would include unnecessary duplication resulting in poor utilization of limited resources, and loss of effective networking. There do not appear to be any strong Evangelical organizations primarily focused on North American Muslim ministry. Without such organizations, our prospects of successfully addressing the larger issues that Islam is attempting to introduce into the North America environment will be greatly diminished.[28]

## Conclusion

The data supported many of the areas addressed during the consultation. Improved networking, more attention to ministry to women and Afro-Americans, and concern for the apparent ineffectiveness of training programs to produce more lay workers are all issues that the data suggests are important for workers doing ministry in North America.[29]

The data also clarifies some questions that workers to Muslims in North America need to be asking.

- Am I living in a good place in North America to do my kind of Muslim ministry?
- Do I have ministry gifts for an under-reached ethnic group that I am not using?
- Am I involved in the types of ministries that are most likely to stop Islam's advance and exploit its weaknesses in North America?
- Have I made appropriate efforts to involve my spouse in Muslim ministry?
- Am I wasting limited resources by not cooperating more with others?

# Table 1
## Number of Workers by Work Status—Location—Ministry Level

NOTES: The database contains 435 workers active in North American ministry to Muslims. This report lists these workers based upon: 1) whether they are lay workers, professional, or retired, 2) the percentage of their ministry that is in North America, and 3) whether they are full or part-time in Muslim ministry. This report shows that those active in North American ministry are as follows.

1) Overwhelmingly professional workers (66%) rather than lay (23%) or retired (7%).

2) Focused totally in North America (69%) instead of mostly in North America (9%), half in North America and half overseas (14%), or mostly overseas (8%).

3) One-to-one ratio between full-time workers (35%), serious part-time workers (33%), and casual part-time (13%) or unknown workers (10%).

The true number of casual part-time lay workers active in North America is known to be at least 100 greater than what is presently documented (13%). This report also shows that virtually all full-time workers are professional (though many professionals are also part-time workers), almost all laypeople are part-time workers, and almost all of those who have some active ministry overseas are professionals.

### LAYMAN

**1) Completely in N. America**

| | | |
|---|---|---|
| A) Full-time | 3 | 0.69% |
| B) Half-time | 2 | 0.46% |
| C) Part-time (significant) | 52 | 11.95% |
| D) Part-time (occasional) | 14 | 3.22% |
| E) Part-time (hrs unknown) | 2 | 0.46% |
| F) Active (hrs unknown) | 6 | 1.38% |
| **Total:** | **79** | **18.16%** |

**2) Primarily in N. America**

| | | |
|---|---|---|
| A) Full Time | 3 | 0.69% |
| B) Half-time | 4 | 0.92% |
| C) Part-time (significant) | 7 | 1.61% |
| D) Part-time (occasional) | 1 | 0.23% |
| Total: | 15 | 3.45% |

**3) Mixed N. America/Overseas**

| | | |
|---|---|---|
| A) Full Time | 2 | 0.46% |
| C) Part-time (significant) | 3 | 0.69% |
| **Total:** | **5** | **1.15%** |

**Worker Status Total:** 99  22.76%

### PROFESSIONAL

**1) Completely in N. America**

| | | |
|---|---|---|
| A) Full-time | 71 | 16.32% |
| B) Half-time | 13 | 2.99% |
| C) Part-time (significant) | 55 | 12.64% |
| D) Part-time (occasional) | 26 | 5.98% |
| E) Part-time (hrs unknown) | 2 | 0.46% |
| F) Active (hrs unknown) | 20 | 4.60% |
| **Total:** | **187** | **42.99%** |

**2) Primarily in N. America**

| | | |
|---|---|---|
| A) Full Time | 13 | 2.99% |
| B) Half-time | 3 | 0.69% |
| C) Part-time (significant) | 2 | 0.46% |
| Total: | 18 | 4.14% |

**3) Mixed N. America/Overseas**

| | | |
|---|---|---|
| A) Full Time | 36 | 8.28% |
| B) Half-time | 4 | 0.92% |
| C) Part-time (significant) | 7 | 1.61% |
| D) Part-time (occasional) | 3 | 0.69% |
| F) Active (hrs unknown) | 1 | 0.23% |
| **Total:** | **51** | **11.73%** |

**(continued)**

**4) Primarily Overseas**

| | | |
|---|---|---|
| A) Full Time | 21 | 4.83% |
| B) Half-time | 3 | 0.69% |
| C) Part-time (significant) | 2 | 0.46% |
| D) Part-time (occasional) | 5 | 1.15% |
| F) Active (hrs unknown) | 1 | 0.23% |
| **Total:** | **32** | **7.36%** |

| | | |
|---|---|---|
| **Worker Status Total:** | **288** | **66.22%** |

## RETIRED LAYMAN

**1) Completely in N. America**

| | | |
|---|---|---|
| D) Part-time (occasional) | 2 | 0.46% |
| **Total:** | **2** | **0.46%** |

**1) Mixed N. America/Overseas**

| | | |
|---|---|---|
| C) Part-time (significant) | 1 | 0.23% |
| **Total:** | **1** | **0.23%** |
| **Worker Status Total:** | **3** | **0.69%** |

## UNKNOWN

**1) Completely in N. America**

| | | |
|---|---|---|
| C) Part-time (significant) | 1 | 0.23% |
| F) Active (hrs unknown) | 7 | 1.61% |
| **Total:** | **8** | **1.84%** |

**Unknown**

| | | |
|---|---|---|
| F) Active (hrs unknown) | 5 | 1.15% |
| **Total:** | **5** | **1.15%** |
| **Worker Status Total:** | **13** | **2.99%** |

## RETIRED PROFESSIONAL

**1) Completely in N. America**

| | | |
|---|---|---|
| A) Full Time | 3 | 0.69% |
| B) Half-time | 2 | 0.46% |
| C) Part-time (significant) | 11 | 2.53% |
| D) Part-time (occasional) | 6 | 1.38% |
| E) Part Time (hrs unknown) | 1 | 0.23% |
| **Total:** | **23** | **5.29%** |

**2) Primarily in N. America**

| | | |
|---|---|---|
| A) Full Time | 1 | 0.23% |
| B) Half-time | 2 | 0.46% |
| C) Part-time (significant) | 2 | 0.46% |
| **Total:** | **5** | **1.15%** |

**3) Mixed N. America/Overseas**

| | | |
|---|---|---|
| C) Part-time (significant) | 1 | 0.23% |
| F) Active (hrs unknown) | 1 | 0.23% |
| **Total:** | **2** | **0.46%** |

**4) Primarily Overseas**

| | | |
|---|---|---|
| A) Full Time | 1 | 0.23% |
| C) Part-time (significant) | 1 | 0.23% |
| **Total:** | **2** | **0.46%** |

| | | |
|---|---|---|
| **Worker Status Total:** | **32** | **7.36%** |

# Table 2

## Distribution of Workers by State and Province

NOTES: This report shows how many active workers in North America live in each state or Canadian province. They are listed from the states with the largest worker populations to those with the least. Since we do not have state addresses for 14 workers presently believed to be active in North America, the totals do not equal 435 or 100%. It is important to notice that a worker's location is not necessarily where his/her ministry occurs, though this is usually the case. A good example of this is to be found from those listed with overseas addresses. They are active in North America on a part-time basis. Due to extremely good data collection from Illinois, their worker count is probably more complete than most other states listed. States with no known Muslim ministry workers are Alaska, Arkansas, Delaware, Idaho, Kentucky, Montana, Nevada, New Hampshire, New Mexico, North Dakota, Rhode Island, South Dakota, Utah, Vermont, Washington D.C., and Wyoming. Provinces with no known workers are New Brunswick, Newfoundland, and Nova Scotia.

| State | (#) | (%) | State | (#) | (%) |
|---|---|---|---|---|---|
| Illinois | 48 | 11.03% | Iowa | 5 | 1.15% |
| California | 43 | 9.89% | Missouri | 5 | 1.15% |
| Virginia | 24 | 5.52% | North Carolina | 4 | 0.92% |
| Ontario, CAN | 24 | 5.52% | Wisconsin | 4 | 0.92% |
| Arizona | 22 | 5.06% | Maryland | 3 | 0.69% |
| Colorado | 20 | 4.60% | UNITED KINGDOM | 3 | 0.69% |
| Michigan | 18 | 4.14% | West Virginia | 3 | 0.69% |
| Pennsylvania | 17 | 3.91% | CANADA | 3 | 0.69% |
| New York | 15 | 3.45% | Mississippi | 3 | 0.69% |
| Georgia | 13 | 2.99% | Oregon | 2 | 0.46% |
| Minnesota | 13 | 2.99% | Manitoba, CAN | 2 | 0.46% |
| New Jersey | 13 | 2.99% | Alabama | 2 | 0.46% |
| Alberta. CAN | 12 | 2.76% | Quebec, CAN | 2 | 0.46% |
| Indiana | 12 | 2.76% | Oklahoma | 2 | 0.46% |
| Florida | 12 | 2.76% | Massachusetts | 2 | 0.46% |
| South Carolina | 11 | 2.53% | Connecticut | 1 | 0.23% |
| British Columbia, CAN | 11 | 2.53% | CYPRUS, Republic of | 1 | 0.23% |
| Ohio | 10 | 2.30% | Maine | 1 | 0.23% |
| Texas | 10 | 2.30% | Nebraska | 1 | 0.23% |
| Kansas | 8 | 1.84% | Saskatchewan, CAN | 1 | 0.23% |
| Washington | 7 | 1.61% | PHILIPPINES | 1 | 0.23% |
| Tennessee | 6 | 1.38% | Louisiana | 1 | 0.23% |

# Table 3
## Types of Ministry

NOTES: This report shows all of the types of ministries in which those who are working with Muslims in North America are active. It is listed in descending order, from those ministries they are most active in to those they are least active in. This report does *not* tell whether they are full or part-time in these ministries, or whether they are active in these ministries totally here in North America, or also active overseas. Most workers are active in more than one type of ministry, so the total number of workers cannot be determined by adding the numbers up for each type of ministry. The last 6 types of ministry listed (except for "Prison Ministry" and "Unknown") were added later in the data entry process or were not developed adequately to be meaningful at this time.

| Type of Ministry | # Workers | % |
|---|---|---|
| Friendship Evangelism/Home Hospitality/Enquirer Mtgs | 168 | 38.62% |
| Teach/Train Workers/Churches (Seminars—Workshops—Trips) | 154 | 35.40% |
| Administration/Advisor/Networking of Workers | 98 | 22.53% |
| Campus/Foreign Student Ministry | 85 | 19.54% |
| Resource Development/Distribution (Print, Audio, Video) | 76 | 17.47% |
| Writing/Translation Work | 64 | 14.71% |
| Church Planting/Home Bible Study/Fellowship Groups | 56 | 12.87% |
| Social Work/Development (Medical-Mercy-Refugee-Sports) | 55 | 12.64% |
| Convert Work (Discipleship-Training-Assistance) | 50 | 11.49% |
| Speaker/Motivator in Churches/Schools/Small Groups | 39 | 8.97% |
| Pastor/Missions Pastor/Missions Elder | 38 | 8.74% |
| Evangelism/Witnessing/Outreach/Evangelist | 36 | 8.28% |
| Radio/TV Ministry | 35 | 8.05% |
| Muslim/Christian Meetings (Debate-Dialogue-Discussion) | 34 | 7.82% |
| Prayer Ministry | 34 | 7.82% |
| Women/Children/Marriage | 32 | 7.36% |
| Language Study Programs (TESL-TEFL) | 31 | 7.13% |
| Mailing Ministry (Personal or Mass Mail—Ads—Mail Courses) | 31 | 7.13% |
| Research/Scholar | 30 | 6.90% |
| E-mail/Website/Newspaper Editorial Ministry and Witness | 25 | 5.75% |
| Volunteer Recruitment/Co-ordination | 19 | 4.37% |
| General Missionary (Ministry Undefined) | 17 | 3.91% |
| Prison Ministry | 8 | 1.84% |
| Unknown | 6 | 1.38% |
| Minister to Workers/Fellowship/Encouragement | 3 | 0.69% |
| Human/Religious Rights/Asylum Assistance | 2 | 0.46% |
| Home Maker/Assist Husband's Ministry | 1 | 0.23% |

## Endnotes

[1] The method has been to start out with e-mail contact when possible. If this is not possible letters have been sent via the post office. Phone calling has not been used due to the cost involved. Each potential worker has been contacted three times. If no response was received after three contacts, no further efforts have been made at directly contacting them. However, all secondhand information provided by others has been kept. This data has been processed into the database along with information received directly.

[2] See "Table 1: Number of Workers By Work Status—Location—Ministry Level."

[3] It should be noted that *Operation World* does not seem to distinguish between full and part-time workers as we have here. But, while many workers in the Middle East may be 'tentmakers' whose formal ministry may not be full-time, all workers in the Middle East should be viewed as seriously involved in ministry. In North America, since local church members can easily be involved at a casual level, it seems more appropriate to use some qualifier that Patrick Johnstone does not. If someone does not agree with this qualifier, the ratio of workers in North America to Muslims including the 100 or so that are not presently documented, would be about one worker for every 9,000 Muslims, or about 107 workers for every million Muslims. This would be about 15 times greater than the worker-to-Muslim ratio in the Middle East.

[4] This question has been addressed in a paper entitled "Some Reflections on the Evangelization of Muslims in North America."

[5] This is the number of Evangelical church members in 1993. Attendees were estimated at 70 million.

[6] Let us assume that we have missed most of the laypeople and that there are actually 800 lay workers (instead of the present estimate of 200) who are actually reaching out to Muslims in North America. This would still leave a worker-to-Evangelical Christian ratio of 1-to-62,500. If the average Evangelical church has 100 attendees, this would mean that only one layperson for every 60 Evangelical churches is actively trying to reach Muslims in North America.

[7] See "Table 2: Distribution of Workers By State and Province" for complete information on the distribution of active Muslim ministry workers in North America.

[8] Since our database probably has better data for Illinois than for

California, Illinois may, in reality, be slightly behind California in number of active workers. Depending upon how many more Muslims there are in California than Illinois, the distribution problem may still exist.

[9] The New York area also has few Bible colleges or seminaries from which to recruit workers as compared to Los Angeles or Chicago.

[10] Because complete information from the Southern Baptists has not yet been obtained, it is possible that they are doing some Muslim work in Houston.

[11] While many of the workers in Arizona are active in indirect ministries that are not geographically sensitive (i.e., office workers), it is also clear that many of those doing ministry there are focused on direct ministries, trying to reach the local Muslim population.

[12] We are referring to professional workers here, not lay. Of course lay workers cannot be expected to do ministry anywhere except where they are living. Since three-fourths of those listed in the database as active workers are either professional (66%) or retired professional (7%) workers, the overall distribution picture that the database presents primarily reflects what professionals are choosing to do. While some professional workers cannot choose where they do their ministry either (i.e., pastors), a large percentage of professional workers do choose where they live to do Muslim ministry.

[13] See "Table 3: Types of Ministry."

[14] *Direct* ministry would include anything that is for Muslims or convert discipleship. Examples would include such things as witnessing, friendship evangelism, literature or radio ministry designed for Muslims, and social programs such as TESL that are directed toward Muslims. *Indirect* ministries, on the other hand, are directed toward the worker or Christian community. Examples of indirect ministry would include such things as administration or training of Christian workers, speaking in churches about ministry needs, literature or radio ministry intended for Christians or workers, and research, such as is found in this database.

[15] Muslims also have a lot of attention focused on campuses. A significant percent of this (perhaps most of it) seems to be directed toward keeping Muslim students Muslim rather than trying to convert non-Muslims.

[16] Some examples would include someone who teaches general classes on Islam at a Christian college or someone who publishes literature designed to mobilize churches to reach out to their Muslim neighbors.

[17] The numbers given for each of these groups will vary widely. Some, for example, will argue that the Black Americans make up 40% of the Muslims of North America. Others, however, view this group as a phantom Islamic group because of the high dropout rate from those who convert to Islam while in jail. Whatever one's view on this, most will agree that the four ethnic groups identified above are the largest in North America.

[18] South Asians here are understood to include Afghans, Pakistanis, Indians, and Bengalis.

[19] The numbers are probably less complete for Persians and Afro-Americans than for the other two groups. It would not be surprising to discover that the total number of workers among Persians might be around 15%. There is great uncertainty about how to categorize Afro-American ministry. At this point we may not properly understand how ministry is being done in the African American Christian community toward Islam. Nevertheless, there can be little doubt that this is a seriously neglected ministry.

[20] We know of many more lay volunteers for Kurdish work than are presently documented, so this percentage, in reality, is probably closer to 15-20% of the total Muslim ministry work force. We may not have complete information on some of the refugee groups such as Bosnians and Somalis. The guess is that we do not yet have a full picture on what is going on with refugee types of ministries.

[21] The "other" category in the cases listed here are 80% or more from the ethnic group under consideration. The one exception to this is with Kurds, where the identity of one non-white worker is Arab and the other is unknown. It is very possible that no ethnic Kurds are involved in Kurdish ministry in North America—though there are at least two that are active among Persians.

[22] The percentages presented on Afro-American workers are based on only 8 workers. This is too low a number to be able to view the percentages as statistically meaningful..

[23] There were too few Afro-American workers to generate any kind of meaningful reports on this question.

[24] Some possible exceptions would be general campus ministry and some ministries to second- and third-generation immigrants.

[25] The other categories are: Publisher/Distributor, Radio/TV Ministry, Training Program, Community Center, Denomination, E-mail Network/Website, Secular Institution, Islamic Organization, and Magazine.

[26] A network in one major city, for example, presently only has a couple of names listed. It is known, however, that the true number of workers in this area who are associated with the network is far larger—perhaps 40 or more. But since most workers did not mention in their personal ministry summaries that they attend these meetings they are presently not listed as being associated with it.

[27] Some reasons would include: 1) We don't want to give Islam an obvious target to aim at. 2) If problems develop in one organization, it will not do damage to the whole of ministry in North America.

[28] As Muslims, for example, attempt to change the "Judeo-Christian Tradition" to the "Judeo-Christian-Islamic Tradition" in textbooks, what small organization would have the resources to successfully counter this? A successful strategy to counter this would require significant resources that can be focused over a long period of time in very carefully chosen directions. The consequences of the general public accepting such a change of view would be profound.

[29] Earlier less refined data was supplied to the steering committee as they considered what to focus on at the consultation.

# CHAPTER 11

# The Call to the Church in North America

*Richard P. Bailey*

## Introduction

The vital question of how to mobilize the church for mission has no easy answers. Many workers ministering among Muslims have invested a large amount of time and effort trying in various ways to motivate God's people here in North America to get involved in sharing Christ with the six million Muslims God is bringing into our midst. One can envision the massive effect that an army of some 50 million born-again believers could have if they were mobilized. Such potential! Yet we often feel frustrated by the lack of any substantial involvement. Is there some key to this situation that we have not found? Maybe our efforts are ineffective because they are based on certain wrong assumptions. Do we have blind spots in our thinking? Or is the laity of North America so far beyond revival that there is no hope?

We will take a look at a survey I conducted among Muslim ministry workers in North America but first, by way of analysis, a classification of both workers and types of Muslims.

## Classification of Workers

Workers could have been classified in various ways, likely with subgroups. But for simplicity, I have used four classifications:

1) Euro-American Lay Workers
2) African American Lay Workers

3) Foreign Born Workers
4) North American Born Cross-Cultural Workers

Euro-American Lay Workers are usually called Anglo-Americans. But we are addressing not only Anglo (British) but other Europeans as well—Germans, Italians, etc., so I prefer the term Euro-American.

Foreign Born Workers (whether lay or professional) are those who have grown up in a Muslim society and understand the language and culture of the Muslim people in their part of the world. Some are professional Christian workers and others are lay workers.

North American Born Cross-cultural Workers are missionaries who have learned the language and culture of a particular Muslim group. Either they went overseas and worked in a Muslim society for a time but now are working in North America—or they went overseas to learn the language and culture of a people group specifically in order to work with them here.

A few workers may not quite fit into one particular classification, or may belong in more than one. Nevertheless, these four major groups should serve our purposes here.

## Categories of Muslims

The Muslim Groups can be divided into four major categories:

1) African American converts to Islam (2.1 million - 35%) - Rapid growth; future growth will depend on trends in the black community.
   a. *First generation converts from professing Christian background*
   b. *Second generation Muslims raised in Muslim homes*
2) Euro-American converts to Islam (180,000 - 3%) - will continue to grow to perhaps 300,000
   a. *Women married to Muslim men* - convert for sake of marriage
   b. *Men converts* - "revolving door" - many leave after a while
3) First generation immigrants from Muslim cultures (2.25 million - 37.5%) - largest group
   a. *Core culture group* (1.75 million - 29.2%) - mix only as much as necessary with North Americans; will continue to grow to a critical mass of 3 million
   b. *Fringe group* (500,000 - 8.3%) - doctors, businessmen, diplomats, and 250,000 foreign students)

4) <u>Children of first generation immigrants</u> (1.5 million - 24.5%)
   a. *1° generation* (450,000 - 7.5%) - will increase to 700,000
   b. *Second and third generation descendants of immigrants* (1 million - 17%) - unlimited potential for growth; will double each 30 years to become the largest group; will have the greatest, most  permanent impact on N.A. culture and government; "The invisible Muslims"

1) First are the African American converts to Islam. Carl Ellis has given us a figure of about 2.6 million in this group. I am estimating about 2.1 million. Numbers for these categories are not exact. African American converts, therefore, probably account for somewhere between 35–45 percent of all North American Muslims.

The potential for continued rapid growth in this group will depend on trends in the Black community in the future. I have divided this group into first generation Muslims (most of whom were professing Christians before converting to Islam) and then their children, who are growing up in Muslim homes. This group of children will continue to multiply as the first generation group grows unless the trend toward conversion to Islam slows down. The question before us concerning this group is: who is best able to reach the first generation African American converts to Islam, and who is best able to reach succeeding generations?

It should be stated here that any worker in any one of the four worker groups who is really concerned and determined will be able to reach a Muslim in any of the Muslim groups. I am not saying that there are only certain groups who can reach specific other groups. But I am saying we need to determine which type of worker would be *best* able to reach each of these groups of Muslims. More specifically, the purpose of this paper is to help us realize which Muslim groups lay Christians are best able to reach, so we can encourage them to develop strategies targeting those specific Muslims.

2) Euro-American converts to Islam may number about 180,000 (three percent of the North American Muslim community). I am estimating that this group will grow to approximately 300,000. Most of these converts are women married to Muslim men. In most cases they convert to Islam for the sake of their marriages. From figures I've seen, these women may account for around two percent of the total number of Muslims in North America. Many of the men converts are becoming Muslims on university campuses. This is largely a revolving door, since many of them later leave Islam. Again, I am asking the question, "What kind of worker is best able to reach these Muslims?"

3) The third group consists of first generation immigrant Muslims. They come from many different Muslim nations around the world. They may number about 2.25 million and account for 37.5 percent of all North American Muslims, the largest group of the four. As long as the immigration policies of the United States and Canada continue as they are, this group will grow until it reaches a critical mass somewhere around three or four million. At that point new immigrants will simply replace the earlier ones who are dying of old age. This very real cross-cultural foreign mission field will continue to need workers able to reach them effectively for Christ in their own languages and cultures.

I have divided first generation immigrant Muslims into two groups—a core culture group and a fringe group. The core group contains those who are not educated here and usually have limited English. They are from a foreign culture, married usually to a spouse of the same culture, and have few social relationships with North Americans. These people are something like, say, a piece of Pakistan in New York city living their whole lives within the Pakistani community—both in New York and Pakistan.

Others are farther out on the fringes. They have more relationships with the Canadians or Americans around them. Most of these Muslims are doctors, businessmen, technicians, diplomats, or foreign students who come with advanced degrees, or to get advanced degrees. Others are married to North Americans. Many of the Muslim background believers who have come to Christ here are in this group and have been attracted to Jesus through contact with North American Christians.

4) In the fourth category fall the children of immigrants who either have come here as small children, or were born here. This group, now about 25 percent of all North American Muslims, will continue to grow larger with each generation.

These children of immigrants are also divided into two groups: the "one-and-a-half" generation and then the second and third generations. The "one-and-a-half" generation young people came here with their parents between the ages of 10 and 15. They obtain only part of their education in North America. They are "half-culture kids" who usually speak English with an accent, and often desire but fail to achieve deep social relationships with North Americans. Christians who befriend these young people, embracing their differentness, will find them more responsive than most Muslims.

The most important group is the second and third generation immigrants. This group already accounts for probably about one million, and the potential for growth is endless. If Muslim families continue to have at least three or four children, this group will double every thirty years. Looking into the future, this is the group with which we need to be most concerned. They receive their education in North America. They speak English without an accent. They are culturally North American while still being accepted in their parents' culture. Except for the women who wear the Muslim *hijab* (head covering), these Muslims are what we sometimes call "invisible" Muslims because they speak, dress, and act just like we do. They may be working in the same office with born-again Christians who have no idea they are Muslims. This important group is the future of Islam in the U.S. and Canada, and they are already busy preparing very effective videos and web sites presenting a contextualized Islam according to our North American cultural understanding.

My opinion is that this group of immigrant descendants is where most North American lay workers should expend the majority of their efforts. Others should focus on North American converts to Islam. First generation immigrants are more difficult for the laity to reach because of language and cultural barriers. Yes, there are some lay workers providing a valuable ministry among first generation immigrants in such programs as ESL and hospitality, etc., but the fruit of such effort can only be "picked" by those who can communicate the gospel clearly in the language and culture of those Muslims. I believe lay workers will generally do best among those who speak English fluently.

Now with this background, let's look at the survey and its results.

## Workers' Statistics

These statistics are from a data base of workers among Muslims in North America as of August 20, 1999.

Out of the 273 units who are involved in ministry:

- 50 are lay people (35 North American lay workers and 15 foreign born lay workers),
- 223 are "professional" workers. Of these 223:
    - 15 focus mainly (90% of their time) on seminars and speaking in churches.
    - 69 spend about 40% of their time speaking in churches and conducting seminars.
    - The other 173 spend about 10% of their time speaking in churches.

This means that as a group of workers (not counting the lay workers) we are spending about 25 percent of our effort speaking to lay people in seminars and churches about Islam and reaching Muslims. Are the results commensurate with such an investment of time and effort?

## Survey Results

Out of the above group of 223, I contacted 92 people who have some involvement with lay people in their ministry among Muslims here in North America, sending them a questionnaire about mobilization of the laity. Twenty-four of them responded. Although this was an unscientific and incomplete survey, nevertheless it has yielded some interesting insights. Much of this chapter comes from those responses.

### Methods of Approach Being Used by Laypeople to Reach Muslims

Out of the 24 respondents, the following number were successful in involving lay workers in ministry among Muslims using the following methods of approach:

Direct:
12 (50%)  developing friendships through various means of contact
12 (50%)  helping immigrants to learn English through ESL and private tutoring. If some kind of one-on-one structure was incorporated, friendships often developed.
9 (38%)  helping to meet other felt needs, such as painting walls, teaching driving, cooking classes, job placement, simple kindnesses, etc. Many times these efforts led to developing friendships.
3 (12%)  teaching one-on-one Bible study
2 (8%)  joining a group doing dialog with Muslims
2 (8%)  showing the "Jesus" video
2 (8%)  involvement in girls' or women's clubs
1 (4%)  socials/picnics
1 (4%)  surveys house to house
1 (4%)  Internet outreach
1 (4%)  learning a language from Muslims

Indirect:
3 (12%)  involvement in prayer groups
5 (20%)  helping with mailing programs, data entry, etc.

## Types of Programs involving Laypeople

The types of programs mentioned by the same 24 respondents which have involved lay workers include the following:

ESL   - with lay tutors assigned to homes to teach individuals
        - with lay people assigned to be conversation partners of individuals

Dialogues in mosques and/or churches

Classes for immigrant parents on topics such as, "loving your teenagers into becoming beautiful people"

A "cooking exchange" for Muslim and Christian women

A girls' club, or after-school tutorial class

Host families for international students and foreign diplomats

Christian students befriending Muslim students

Refugee ministry

Ministry center with various felt needs approaches

Door-to-door survey of ethnic and country background

Short terms abroad followed by local involvement

Socials and picnics

Internet outreach

Prayer meetings with MBBs involved

Direct mailings

## Desired Lay Involvement

The respondents felt that the greatest needs for lay involvement are in the following areas:

1. Greatest need - informed, strategic prayer for Muslims
2. Second greatest need - love for other races and cultures, including Muslims
3. Third greatest need - genuine, enduring friendship with individual Muslims
4. Involvement in programs reaching Muslims, especially those in English
5. Financial support of full time cross-cultural and national workers here in North America
6. Encouragement of workers and potential workers involved here
7. Providing facilities for ministry to Muslims
8. Obtaining training and mentoring (for those already involved)

## Strategic Questions

In most cases the laymen mentioned above are Euro-Americans and the target groups are mostly first generation immigrants plus some international students. Will the same kind of programs mentioned above be effective when used by lay workers to reach second and third generation immigrants and North American converts to Islam? Or are different approaches and programs needed? What kind of training is needed for the laity to carry out such programs?

The following fourteen questions arising out of the survey responses were dealt with in later discussion sessions at a Muslim ministry conference. Each question is followed by some of my own thoughts and then by selected comments from the discussion groups:

*Question 1. Although we are spending one quarter (25%) of our time speaking in churches and conducting seminars for lay people, most of us are mobilizing very few lay workers to help us reach Muslims. Could it be that most of us are more focused on support raising and recruiting for overseas than on mobilizing lay people to reach Muslims here in North America? Should we be more focused on motivating and training lay workers to reach Muslims here? If so, how? One person candidly wrote, "I am not convinced that we Christian workers are serious about mobilization of the laity. What we want is money to do our own thing, or money to do something overseas, or a job of speaking to Christians about the evils of Islam..."*

It is popular today in our churches to be well informed on all subjects. It seems that information is the answer to everything. My own experience with church seminars, however, has led me to believe that in most cases the more information we give the laity about Islam, the more fearful and withdrawn they become from Muslims. Some of us first began realizing this in the 80s after a number of "awareness" type seminars, so we began holding "outreach" seminars where we included in the program visits in the homes of Muslims. This made a profound difference in the attitude of those lay people toward Muslims. They realized Muslims in most cases are warm, friendly people.

We were disappointed, however, because our efforts still did not result in any long-term outreach. We surmised that a longer period of exposure to ordinary Muslims was needed, in which they could develop genuine, personal friendships with individual Muslims. Our conclusions were based on the successful Summer Training and Outreach Program (STOP), which Christar (formerly International Missions, Inc.) designed to train full-time workers. This program has proven repeatedly since 1980 that it is possible to enable trainees to gain a lifelong love for Muslims. STOP includes a minimum of 15 hours per week of required, supervised visits in the homes of Muslims for four weeks, with extra emphasis placed on return visits to the same Muslim homes.

Of course a month-long program is not feasible for lay people, so we began trying seminars of six consecutive Saturdays, full weekends (Friday evening through Sunday evening except for Sunday morning church time), or six days in a week of vacation. I must confess that in spite of rave reviews by participants, I am still disappointed in the lack of long-term lay involvement in ministry among Muslims.

Now I am beginning to wonder if the problem may be that we have been exposing trainees to first generation immigrants rather than their children or American converts to Islam. Can we instead develop training programs which will introduce lay Christians to second and third generation American Muslims in high schools, colleges, and in skilled job situations? Or in light of the many conflicts between first generation immigrants and their children growing up here in a very different culture, would seminars and discussions on topics such as family conflicts or the foundations of North American culture be an effective way for lay Christians to reach the second generation?

*Comments from session participants:*

"Indications were that the World Perspectives course has been effective in many places in helping mobilize lay workers (www.uscwm.org)."

"Much laity help is in the area of TESL, but in some areas more volunteers seem to come from the college student population than from local churches. Using one-on-one volunteers as conversational partners seems quite successful. Churches should encourage hospitality and TESL ministry locally with internationals to create more awareness and recruit more volunteers."

*Question 2. Is most of the effort we are making to mobilize the laity instructional rather than modeling? In other words, do we tell them from the pulpit and in our seminars how to reach Muslims but fail to take them with us and show them how to reach Muslims? Does this in turn cause lay Christians to approach Muslims in the same "telling-but-not-listening" impersonal way? If so, how can we correct this?*

Instructional methods include Muslim awareness seminars or talks by missionaries on furlough from Muslim countries. Modeling consists of more action-oriented events such as visits to Muslim homes, field trips to mosques or Muslim areas of a city, picnics, hosting Muslims, etc. These activities help the laity learn to talk with and really get to know actual Muslims.

*Comments from session participants:*

The general agreement seemed to be that more instructional methods are presently used, rather than modeling. Some participants felt that more attention needs to be paid to Muslim ministry from the pulpits of North America, though this would be largely instructional. Also, much of the mobilization effort is instructional because it is conducted by itinerating missionaries who are raising support and are not around long enough to engage in modeling activities.

"Jesus used both instructional and modeling techniques, so a balance between the two is needed. But modeling seems especially pertinent in Muslim ministry because so few North Americans know how to relate to Muslims. Also the modeling activities are, for the most part, more enjoyable than the instructional seminars."

"Relational skills with Muslims should receive attention before giving detailed theological explanations of what Muslims believe. Frequent evaluation of modeling activities is essential to see what is really effective, and good follow-up is required to keep volunteers on track."

*Question 3. Do we have our eyes open for lay people who could have a ministry among Muslims locally? If we don't take the initiative to speak to such people about the opportunities God has given, how many lay workers will come forward on their own initiative?*

*Comments from session participants:*

"It may be too much of an assumption to think that lay people will naturally have a heart for other people groups. Once some of the congregation's world interests have been discovered, it can then be pointed out how many people from those countries live in the area."

"Natural interest groups should be used where possible. Professionals can perhaps reach Muslim professionals. Auto workers or taxi drivers may enjoy getting to know each other."

Other important factors repeatedly mentioned included 1) securing the backing of the pastoral staff; 2) each experienced person intentionally taking a volunteer along for training when conducting Muslim ministry; 3) developing an apprenticeship program; and 4) utilizing available training materials (written and/or taped) that will be helpful to volunteers without scaring them off—such as the Thirty Day Muslim Prayer Guide (www.ywam.org/prayer/

30daysmuslim.html), Praying through the Window (Johnson, 1996; www.ywam.org), or Global Prayer Digest (www.uscwm.org),

*Question 4. Muslim international students are quickly absorbed into Muslim Student Association (MSA) groups and local mosques soon after arrival on campus. Most student ministries are failing to reach them because other more open, non-Muslim students are holding their attention. How can we target this need? Is there an effective way of focusing Christian students' interest and efforts to reach Muslim fellow students?*

*Comments from session participants:*

"Some people may need to focus specifically on Muslim students and let other groups minister to more responsive students such as the Chinese. It helps to remember that most Muslims truly want American friends, and Christian students should be proactive at forming one-on-one relationships with Muslim scholars. Since a friendship takes time to form, it will help to meet Muslim students as near the beginning of their program as possible."

"Often, taking Christian students for a visit to a mosque will help develop sensitivity in the students as to how Muslim scholars feel coming to the West. Host-family activities are crucial for campus ministries. Local churches can encourage their families to join such a program. Meeting Muslim students at the airport can be an important ministry. Americans usually bond with the people they pick up at the airport. We may need to train laity to recognize the 'invisible' generations of Muslims."

*Question 5. Are we in most cases trying to mobilize the laity to do something for which they are poorly equipped? That is, are we encouraging them primarily to win the more visible first generation immigrant Muslims, whose dress, accent, and food cause them to stand out? Should we be focusing lay workers' attention on this group when they are without either a fluency in the Muslims' language or an understanding of their culture? Instead, should not we be pointing them primarily to the less recognizable, more westernized second and third generation descendants of Muslim immigrants as well as to American converts to Islam, whom they can reach in English with American culture? If so, how can we best train them to recognize these "invisible" Muslims living among us?*

One suggestion is to distribute and discuss the increasingly frequent newspaper articles about North Americans converting to Islam. These are people lay Christians can reach, and reading their "testimonies" will increase understanding as to the needs and motives behind such conversions. Knowing that a high percentage of these converts to Islam do not "stick" should encourage us to search them out and share true Christianity with them.

One survey respondent points out the "lack of ability or willingness of laity and congregations to adequately mentor and befriend converts so they integrate into a Christian family (church)." I believe in the cases where these are first generation immigrants it is more a lack of ability. In the church in New Jersey where I am a member we have four Muslim converts, two of whom are American born. The third has been here 25 years and is married to an American. These three were led to Christ primarily through the efforts of American lay Christians. They are well integrated and accepted into the church because they are culturally Americans. The fourth came to America as a college student, was helped in his journey to Christ largely through a cross-cultural worker (myself), and struggles more than the others to integrate into the fellowship. It is obvious that lay people in our church will have great difficulty attracting and integrating an immigrant who has even less education and has come here later in life.

*Comments from session participants:*

"We can't impose the E-3 evangelism model [different culture and language] upon the whole church."

"In some areas, the laity can give valuable help in reaching the first generation. For instance, newcomers will learn English better with lay workers who do not know their language. However internationals will share more deeply with the workers who can speak their 'heart' language."

"Some cultural help and supervision needs to be offered for the lay workers. For instance, "pork police" may need to supervise potlucks and picnics."

"Some of the first generation withdraw into cultural ghettos, but their children quickly adapt to a Western lifestyle. This creates big gaps."

*Question 6. North American Christians are constantly confronted with needs, and each one claims to be greater than the others. In our efforts to mobilize lay people to reach Muslims in North America shouldn't we be stressing "opportunity' rather than "need"? Spirit filled believers are looking for the most strategic opportunities because they know they can never meet all the great needs. Are we convinced that reaching Muslims in North America is a strategic opportunity given to us by God at this time? If we are apologetic about working here instead of overseas where the need is greater, will we be able to motivate lay people to join us?*

We may think that stressing the great needs of Muslims "over there" or "worldwide" will somehow cause lay Christians to reach out to the local Muslims around them, but mostly we will only reinforce the well understood need for either going overseas or praying and sending money to support those who go overseas. Of course the need is greater over there, but reaching the Muslims God is bringing here may be a greater strategic opportunity. Are we ourselves convinced or are we backpeddling with a soft-sell approach?

*Comments from session participants:*

Conference attendees felt that because we can reach groups here in North America that cannot be reached overseas, we should never be apologetic about recruiting workers for North America. Several important points need to be stressed. 1) Specific prayer should be planned for the laity to be mobilized; 2) Don't restrict lay people too much. Be willing for Muslims to be exposed to various Christians with vital witness and testimony;   3) Remember that enthusiasm strongly communicates when recruiting lay volunteers. Success stories will be greatly encouraging for the laity.

*Question 7. In our seminars are we unknowingly insulating lay workers from Muslims by giving them all the arguments to use, and warning them to always go as a team to protect themselves? In training lay workers, shouldn't we put most of our emphasis on developing genuine friendships with Muslims as real people? In other words, shouldn't we be enabling families to reach families and individuals to reach individuals of the same sex on a one-on-one basis, while relating to a support group of lay Christians who pray for and encourage each other?*

*Comments from session participants:*

Muslim ministry workers suggest developing lay training seminars with balance. Cover topics such as prayer, relationship building, discipleship training, finding opportunities to be exposed to and relate with Muslims, offering help with personal spiritual issues, providing information on Islam, methods of ministry, and modeling. Be sure there is a balance between information imparted and practical training. After a minimum of training, get folks involved. Involvement helps breed commitment.

"Training the laity through learned arguments may be too cognitive. More research needs to be done about why Muslims convert, and why they stay in or leave the Christian church. What can be done to help the laity gain and utilize such information?"

"One church has four consecutive sessions in Sunday school. The first session includes, 'Guess Who's Coming to America?' The second

Sunday treats immigration policies and anecdotes about how people can help each other. The third session addresses the biblical view of hospitality and how to treat strangers. On the fourth Sunday, the teaching is devoted to learning how to demonstrate love to Muslims."

"Create relational experiences—make opportunities for lay people to relate with Muslims, but give them some awareness and training ahead of time. Putting Christians and Muslims together so they can interact takes away some of the fear from both groups."

"Create houses or centers where resettled refugees can drop in. Also have laity volunteers to the center to cook, fix a fence, or paint a room. As refugees move in and out, the groups can interact."

"Start support groups for those married to Muslims or for relatives of Muslims, etc." [Note: there is an e-mail forum for Christian women married to Muslims called "Lam" (Love a Muslim).]

*Question 8. One respondent stressed that lay outreach to Muslims especially should be "relational oriented" rather than "proclamation focused." If that is true, then how can we structure our programs (ESL, special events, dialogs, etc.) in such a way as to promote the development of personal friendships with Muslims, instead of just dropping gospel bombs on them?*

Another worker responded, "We have formed the classes around the philosophy that the key to language learning is relationship and real conversational experience. Therefore we attempt to place each student or two with a tutor...this puts our real American in a position to fall in love with the students. This works wonderfully!"

*Comments from session participants:*

"Personal relationships can be developed in dialogue meetings, possibly followed up that same evening with small group discussions and one-on-one conversations afterward. It is also important to have social times outside such group meetings. We must invite them to our homes and learn to serve halal food."

"We can train workers to talk with Muslims before handing out tracts or other literature. Three questions could be: 1) What country are your parents from? 2) How old were you when they came here? 3) A needs based question—this is strategic because we can then pray for them regarding that need. An example might be: 'Is it difficult to raise children here in the West?'

"Attending local Muslim parties and other events can be a means to a relationship. However, the worker should be intentional about proclamation wherever possible, so the friendship is not merely social. Workers should mention upfront that they are Christians and take appropriate opportunities to bring up spiritual issues."

*Question 9. The vast majority of lay people involved in reaching Muslims in North America are doing so as individuals, some with and some without their church's encouragement. There are teams of lay workers from several different churches working together in a number of metropolitan areas. How realistic is it to pursue the idealistic dream of mobilizing entire churches for outreach among Muslims?*

One worker reported, "The thirteen members of our group attend six different churches and come from five different ethnic backgrounds."

*Comments from session participants:*

"Lower expectations on how many will be involved in Muslim ministry. Concentrate efforts on those who show an interest, and then form a core group. Expose as many as possible to Muslim awareness, but look for one or two who can be followed up for deeper Muslim ministry. Be realistic. Ministry to Muslims is not God's call to everyone. Qualities needed include a heart full of compassion for minorities, a maturing Christian walk, a strong interest in other cultures, and a willingness to accept and love other people."

"Mobilizing the entire church may be unrealistic. Cooperation between volunteers from several denominations and churches in reaching out to Muslims should be emphasized. Muslim ministry is difficult and working together with other churches will be encouraging."

"Young people are key, so target and train them. Generation Xers are very family-oriented, but also very involved in many things, and it may be a challenge to get them involved. If the pastor is hands-on and passionate about missions, he can be a key for Muslim evangelism. Among the youth, emphasize looking for purpose plus taking risks for God that really matter."

"It is important to have small groups in churches that can receive new converts appropriately."

*Question 10. In our mobilization of the laity, shouldn't a major emphasis be put on the need for us to expect and desire to adjust to Muslims (entering their cultural world) in order to win them, rather than waiting for Muslims to come to our church programs and adjust to our Christian culture? How can we best teach lay people to love Muslims and enjoy their culture?*

As I have studied this subject, I have found our own North American (European) culture to be one of the great barriers. Repeatedly we see that it is not so difficult to find volunteers to help with structured, impersonal, office type programs where there is no direct contact with Muslims. It is a bit more difficult to find people willing to face a group of Muslims in a setting such as a mosque or classroom. Even fewer are prepared to face individual Muslims in a structured, pre-arranged, one-on-one Bible study or similar program,

The most difficult of all is the most needed. North Americans find it almost impossible to spontaneously initiate a friendship with a Muslim, to accept an invitation to go alone into a Muslim home, or to invite a Muslim into their own home. It is what Robert McIntyre calls "actually sharing your home and table for a period of time." Since our culture tells us that it is "improper" to speak of "personal" matters like religion in public, most North American lay Christians never share the gospel with anyone—let alone someone from another religious culture. Yet a few people really are finding creative ways to involve lay workers in authentic friendships with Muslims for Christ.

We all like to feel like we are accomplishing something. It is natural, therefore, for lay workers to prefer helping with a mailing or media program that can report hundreds of letters or broadcasts, rather than spending time with individual Muslims repeatedly perhaps for several years before a decision is made for Christ. As a result we spend lots of money and time on such programs and continue to have "no time" to do the follow-up with individuals that could result in their coming to Christ. The majority of the soldiers of any army has to be in the trenches ready to occupy the ground "softened up" through air and artillery bombardment. It is imperative that we find ways to help lay people get into the trenches by developing personal relationships with individual Muslims.

In addition, we need to confront some other difficult cultural issues with clear teaching:

- strong North American cultural biases against Muslims
- racism which we somehow cannot recognize in ourselves
- an ingrained tradition that says North America is not the "real" mission field
- misinterpretation of biblical teaching that Muslims are under God's curse (because He has promised to bless Israel, because "they have already rejected Christ," or because "they are descendants of Ham").

*Comments from session participants:*
"There must be incarnational identification (Phil.2:5–11), so lay volunteers need to be taught about Muslim culture. However, they also need to maintain their own distinctiveness. They don't have to become Muslims to win Muslims."

"Network with ethnic churches to learn from them."

"Make visits to Muslim mosques, shops, and homes. Let Christians get to know 'flesh and blood' Muslims, and learn to love them. Then they will grow to love their culture. Mono-cultural people often need to take 'baby' steps; going with a Muslim ministry worker to have a meal with a Muslim, or visiting a ministry center that conducts outreach to Muslims."

"In Muslim cultures, the greater honor is in being the host; laity must be willing to go into their homes and honor them by receiving their hospitality."

"When sponsoring dinners, consider asking Muslims to help with the food, bringing dishes popular in their homelands."

*Question 11. What kind of effort are we making to mobilize lay people for serious prayer for North American Muslims? How can we best do that? Will praying through the 10–40 window or the 30 days of Ramadan automatically focus their prayers on North American Muslims? Is it wrong to have a special prayer effort just for Muslims in North America? Will personal friendships with Muslims or the sharing of testimonies by MBBs help?*
One respondent wrote, "If you want people to pray, just start praying. You'll get more people to pray with you by praying, than you will by preaching on it."

*Comments from session participants:*
"Utilize other internationals in prayer efforts."

"Pass the vision on by sharing a convert who came to Christ here. Have them share their testimonies. This will often promote more prayer. Adopt a convert or Muslim international student and entertain them in homes to stir up prayer interest."

"Adapt available prayer materials to teach prayer for Muslims in the U.S. and Canada: Prayer for the Persecuted Church Sunday (www.idop.org), Ramadan Prayer Guide (http://ramadan. everypeople.net), 30 Days of Prayer (www.ywam.org/ prayer30daysmuslim.html) Mission America Lighthouse Movement (www.lighthousemovement.com) or Global Prayer Digest (www.uscwm.org)."

"Have a prayer walk in local Muslim areas."

"Pray specifically for Muslims in local communities and neighborhoods after doing research into their different ethnic backgrounds and origins."

"Get maps of cities with Muslim communities marked. Use the map for your area to get lay people interested. Pray with them for the communities on the map."

"Some system of small 'pray for Muslims' groups can lead to more intentional prayer."

"Join a prayer support group for prison ministry. Watch for local news reports of Muslims in prisons and pray for them specifically."

*Question 12. Among the greatest needs for lay involvement in prison ministry are people to do one-on-one Bible study with inmates and to visit the families of inmates. According to one chaplain I spoke to, a few lay workers are willing to do the first, but none are willing to do the second. What can be done to mobilize the laity for these vital ministries?*

It is now common knowledge that the two arenas where Islam is gaining the most converts are the prisons and the university campuses. While there are many (but not enough) good evangelistic programs in both settings, almost none of them target Muslims and Islamic influence specifically. Little is being done to prepare lay workers to effectively serve the Lord in these arenas. It is time to focus our attention on these strategic venues by finding ways to effectively involve laity in the lives of those Muslims.

*Comments from session participants:*

"It is important to not reinvent the wheel. Prison Fellowship and many others already offer lay training, Bible studies, contacts, etc., and volunteers can link up with them. Laity can join the Angel Tree Project through Prison Fellowship (703-478-0100, www.angeltree.org) —providing Christmas gifts, camping trips, etc., to the families of prisoners. But laity are probably twice apprehensive—once about prisons in general, and secondly, about Muslims in particular."

"Another avenue of service would be to offer training to Christian prisoners so they can witness to Muslim prisoners. In addition, existing general prison ministries in churches can be taught how to minister specifically to Muslim prisoners. Ministry groups need to produce these."

"How about adopting the Muslim prisoners in a local prison or several local families who have a Muslim family member in prison? Pray for them and visit them like our own family."

*Question 13. Can we motivate lay workers by sending them overseas on short-term mission trips to some part of the Muslim world? Perhaps a local form of this is an organized tour of mosques and ethnic businesses. A deliberate effort must be made, however, to relate the short-term or local tour experience to local outreach afterwards.*

The comments of three respondents show the benefits of such programs for lay people: 1) "Some of the first steps are getting lay people over to Central Asia to do short-term work in the areas of their professional expertise. Those that go are touched positively and are more likely to help with the work locally to Muslims." 2) "I have led short-term mission trips with Muslim converts from Iran...These trips have resulted in the growth of the (local Iranian) church and several who went on these trips are now in full-time ministry." 3) "Ethnic tours (of mosques, etc.) are the biggest attraction. Many Americans within the church are really interested in knowing other cultural people, but they are afraid to explore and do not know how to do it."

*Comments from session participants:*

Nearly all conference attendees voted "yes" to the strong possibility of motivating lay workers by sending them overseas on short-term mission projects, or even to visit local mosques.

"Short-term mission trips need to be linked to local ministry because they often do stimulate mission awareness locally."

*Question 14. Would it be good to put together some of the best material being used in seminars so all of our presentations would improve and be of more benefit to the laity? Would we be willing to make such material available for others to use? Could such material be made available only for reference, but not for duplication?*

We all agree that cooperation in this area would be good, but most of us like to present things our own way, so this may not happen easily. A course similar to the Perspectives Course but specific to reaching local Muslims could become a powerful tool.

*Comments from session participants:*

"The alarming number of churches that have now become mosques could be presented to stir motivation. Perhaps some ministry group could produce a 'high-octane' video of pictures of such facilities with commentary to stimulate the audience with the reality of what is happening in this regard."

"To stir interest, use videos and testimonies of those who have gone short-term. More good training material is needed for lay workers. Perhaps some ministry organization will feel led to compile a list of materials for Muslim awareness and training."

# CHAPTER 12

# Ministry to Muslims in the Third Millennium

*Roy Oknesvad and Dotsey Welliver*

## Introduction

"There is no question that we are all crying out for help. When I was starting my ministry, at first I did not know anyone else [conducting Muslim ministry]. And churches often look at people like me, and don't understand." This statement by a Muslim ministry worker reveals clearly the felt need most workers have for encouragement, additional help, and guidance as they follow God's call to love and minister to their Muslim friends and neighbors.

One of the things commonly mentioned among these ministry workers in North America is that they often feel as though they are alone. There seems to be a strong consensus among them to have some kind of an ongoing network that would involve a steering committee, consultations at various points, circulating information about resources, and a database that could be accessed by members for information they need to network with other people or pass along information.

Conference evaluations, surveys, and other collected information reveal the following priorities.

## Database

It seems crucial to have knowledge available—who is reaching whom, the expertise each worker has, and where they are located. A structure needs to be in place where any ministry worker could call and get information.

The database presented earlier in this volume (see Chapter 10) could be developed to collect and assemble more material and make it available as appropriate. Uncertainty still exists, for instance, about the number of organizations that work among Muslims in North America. Network members need to continue saying, "Hey, what about this ministry that I heard of?" Collecting and disseminating more information seems to be a strong priority.

The present database functions well around three topics—geographical regions, types of ministry (women's or campus ministry), and ethnic ministry. Reports can be generated around those three aspects. For instance, if a worker is looking for all the people who are working with Muslim women in North America, she could go through the database, do a data search, and come out with names and addresses to contact. A person could check under the language resources they need, check the sources available in that language, and would not need to thumb through an entire catalog.

Some information is available about people involved in Christian/Muslim meetings—dialogue, debate, and/or discussion. A list of people who are willing to debate once or twice a year are listed in the database so a campus group can find out who is available. For people interested in organizing a debate, the database could help connect them with speakers within a certain area or nationwide, and could show the ones that have the most experience or who are more debate-oriented.

The database is obviously in development and help is welcomed in collecting more information. As structured now it applies mostly to North America. There are also excellent resources in South Africa and Africa itself, India, Pakistan, and England but limited time and resources have not allowed for those to be included in the present database.

**Literature and Other Resources**

A magazine called "Learn and Share" is an occasional publication of SIM's Life Challenge Africa (Box 50770, Nairobi, KENYA). This magazine is good to share with younger people or younger families in churches who are just beginning to learn how to reach out to Muslims. Geared to help African Christians have an effective ministry to Muslims, it is equally good for a wider readership.

One key distributor would be the South Asian Friendship Center and Bookstore (Phone 773/764-6846, SAFCPTL@megsinet.com). They handle as many as 200 titles designed for Muslims and Hindus.

Another organization to highlight would be the South Asian Ministry (253/756-7310, maxted.mgl.sam@juno.com) with materials designed mainly for workers among South Asians. Their catalogue lists more than 2000 titles and includes not only books but calendars, tracts, posters, tapes, videos, commentaries, dictionaries, and grammars.

Two top places to check for scriptures are Multi Language Media (717/738-0582, mlminfo@multilanguage.com) and Gospel Recordings (213/250-0207, Minfo@gospelrecordings.com).

When looking for tracts, two good places to start would be American Scripture Gift Mission (asgm@flash.net) and the Fellowship of Faith for Muslims in Canada (416/778-6702, ffm. toronto@sympatico.ca).

The Center for Ministry to Muslims (417/866-3313, 76243.2762@compuserve.com) produces effective booklets geared for the American church audience and also sensitive tracts for Muslims. Iranian Christians International (719/596-0010, 74521.230 @compuserve.com) is an outstanding resource for materials in Farsi and Dari for Iranians and Afghanis.

Another good source to know about is Ahl-I-Kitab in England (P.O. Box 16, Manchester, UK M35 9QL). This store has a wide variety of materials relating to Islam. Their tri-annual two-page newsletter is valuable as a review of books published in Europe that frequently go unknown to the North American reader.

An e-mail network is operating but a future possibility would be to streamline the e-mail by interest group, so that only those things significant to a particular interest would be received.

One question has been how workers can get more specific focused lists—for example, information only about prayer for Muslims or a very specific discussion on "What can we do on the Internet?" A mailing list that is not North America-focused but more on general ministry to Muslims with a certain focus on the Internet is called LTM—Love the Muslims. They can give prayer requests, what Muslims are doing in various areas, projects, and sometimes theological discussions. LTM is open to input and to creating more mailing lists. They are willing to combine lists or split them for more focus. E-mail (http://answering-islam.org/Christians/) for a descriptive list of what they offer.

As Christians share with other ethnic groups, they are finding that much of the resource material is written about what the ethnic groups are like back in their homelands. However, as ministry people work with ethnics, they are increasingly finding that they need to know more about how the USA or Canadian culture has affected the group. More literature is needed to address the westernization aspect of the immigrant population. There are several helpful books now coming out such as *The Changing Face of Islam in America* (Poston 2000) and a volume entitled *Good News for Muslims* (Haines 1998).

## Consultations

Many Muslim ministry workers are seeing the need for consultations. Some would like to see more regional sessions. They find that meeting other people working in their own region is most helpful. Also recommended are interest group meetings, such as groups working with women or international students or refugees.

Need has also been expressed for conferences for Muslim Background Believers. Sessions held in the New York area proved to be a rich blessing. But more regional ones may be needed, or even a national conference for believers with a Muslim background from all different ethnic groups. Others could be held for one particular ethnic group. A need is also felt to hold a conference to get pastors together and talk about Muslims in North America. Such meetings could present them with information now available and encourage them to do more Muslim ministry with their congregations.

When women talk about women's issues in Muslim ministry, a surge of excitement takes place addressing very practical issues and relationships. A conference could be designed to address such issues but with men included, because many of them have people coming to them with questions. Women have some answers for Muslim ministry but because of the dichotomy of Muslim work in terms of the separation of women and men, sometimes that information is not moving back and forth between men and women in the Christian community.

## Issues

Muslim ministry workers see a certain amount of overlap in ministries and some areas that are not being addressed at all. As organizations strategize about the future of their ministries and the direction they need, it becomes crucial to avoid reinventing the wheel. Ministry workers would like to see strong accountability in this area because of the amount of work to be done and the scarcity of workers and other resources. Networking becomes a large issue in terms of preventing duplication of ministries and increasing overall effectiveness.

Data so far points up several issues of increasing importance to Muslim ministry in North America. In addition to improving networking, two other areas frequently mentioned are paying more attention to ministry to women and African Americans, and concern about the apparent ineffectiveness of training programs to produce more lay workers.

Data also clarifies some questions that workers to Muslims in North America need to ask.

◆ Am I living in a good place in North America to do my kind of Muslim ministry? The New York area seems to be strongly lacking in workers and that is where the biggest single concentration of Muslims live. Statistics thus far present an uneven picture concerning how many workers serve in each region.

◆ Do I have ministry gifts for an under-reached ethnic group that I am not using?

◆ Am I involved in the types of ministries that are most likely to stop Islam's advance and exploit its weaknesses in North America? (This one applies particularly to women's ministry and jail ministry.)

◆ Have I made appropriate efforts to involve my spouse in Muslim ministry?

◆ Am I wasting limited resources by not cooperating with others?

Another strategic issue concerns returning missionaries and other cross-cultural workers and the almost overwhelming need for Muslim ministry workers in the U.S. Several hundred returning workers from Muslim worlds, for one reason or another, return to North America and cannot find a place of ministry. Missiologists believe that nearly every missionary takes about two years to adjust to coming back to North America. To not be able to find anyone who can talk the same language, think the same, or have the same heartbeat and vision for the Muslims is heartbreaking.

Resources should be marshaled both to help them and to offer them places to serve. If a missionary from a certain agency comes back from working with South Asians overseas and that organization doesn't have any work with South Asians in North America, they could possibly connect the missionary with others who do. Perhaps also human resources departments connected with mission agencies could look at the returnees and connect them with further opportunities to serve in areas of their cross-cultural expertise.

Another group to watch might be retirees who have finished one career, but all their lives really wanted to work with Muslims, and now don't know where to go to find out about this. Maybe their churches or some agency could send them for a vision trip to some area where a working team could adopt them and offer places to serve.

Opportunities develop rapidly. So many ethnic groups exist in the United States today, with many other religious traditions represented. Missiologists generally believe this is the work of God's Spirit. For instance, a Tibetan people's resource network is now beginning to have a section focusing on Tibetan people in the United States. A couple of projects are trying to develop a similar kind of networking for people working among Hindus in the United States. Some are also looking at Canada.

A coalition of ministries and denominations called the Ethnic America Network has the goal of praying for, caring for, and sharing Christ with every person in ethnically-diverse America. An ethnic workers' summit was held in the Los Angeles area in April, 2001. People working among Tibetans and Hindus are facing some of the same things that Muslim ministry workers share and grieve about. A strategic matter would involve keeping alert to what workers have been developing and finding workable among Muslims and then sharing the results with those in other fields of ministry as well.

## Future Opportunities

Below is just a partial list of the many dreams and desires mentioned by Muslim Ministry workers.

♦ The development of a CD to carry around with a computer. The CD would contain a handout section where tracts and pieces of literature could be printed one by one. If a worker shared with someone and had an opportunity to go into the CD, there he or she could find hundreds of tracts catalogued according to subject matter and be able to print them as needed.

♦ The development of certain specialized groups, such as writers and authors, who could write to specific topics which could be put on a CD and made available.

♦ The development of a list of professionals who would be willing to help—perhaps some with a digital data background who do web page design. If available people with certain kinds of expertise could be targeted, then ministry workers with specific projects could contact people who are willing to help.

♦ The development of a phone center where volunteers could call folks in Muslim ministry periodically and pray with them on the telephone. Perhaps they could call the pastors also and encourage pastors to pray with and pay special attention to their Muslim ministry workers. In this often discouraging ministry, they need to know they are not alone. They need to know that they belong somewhere, and that their work is valued, even in long periods with no results.

◆ Someone is needed to take responsibility to keep a list of training programs for Muslim ministry in North America updated with current dates and particulars.

◆ A volunteer is needed to take responsibility for a bibliography that has been started with books about Islam in North America or ministry among Muslims in North America.

◆ A definite need is felt for a literature group. Workers sometimes feel a desperate need for literature written for Muslims in North America. Most of the literature is published overseas, which is good there, but doesn't quite meet the need of North American Muslims, specifically African American Islam. Or, for example, in work among Pakistanis, literature is needed that uses both English and Urdu in the same book.

◆ Possibilities should be explored for a translation service and a publishing house. Groups of believers are interested in doing the writing. And an abundance of books written about Islam need to be translated into Arabic or from Arabic to English.

◆ People are needed who would be willing to help with the responsibility for an ethnic network. There should be a key person for every ethnic group. Then if someone wanted to know how to get in touch with others who are ministering among Turks, they could contact that person.

◆ Muslim workers need a prayer network—someone who would take on the responsibility of gathering information on prayer needs and communicating those needs to people who want to pray specifically for Muslim ministry.

◆ Needs have been expressed for an underground railway, halfway houses, and other safety places—a net for Muslim converts who are in trouble and need a place to go.

◆ Much more work needs to be done and help made available concerning reconciliation and the matter of racism.

◆ Some workers dream of counseling and discipleship services for Muslim converts themselves. This would provide more fellowship for them as they go through their various difficulties.

◆ A strategic need is to develop a Bible commentary that would be most useful for and directed toward Muslims. One idea is for someone to start building a database, with others e-mailing comments on particular verses to that person. For example, for someone writing on Deuteronomy, they could use a standard abbreviation such as DT, then chapter and verse, and add their Muslim-specific comments. Over a period of years perhaps someone could take this and shape it into a useful form. This would help capture and incorporate workable ideas in some kind of expository database.

♦ Concerning structure, many workers feel the need for some format for various ministries to report what they are doing and their results, so that strategies could be both developed and evaluated.

All the opportunities, the vision, the needs, the challenge, and the joy of working with Muslims in North America are a fulfillment of prayer over many, many years. As volunteers and professional workers alike continue to offer their deeply heartfelt prayers to God on behalf of their dear Muslim friends, may God continue to grant them wisdom and discernment and the help they need to reap the harvest.

*Section 5*

# *How to Respond*
# *to Muslims*

# CHAPTER 13

# How to Respond to Muslims

*Sam Elisha*

## Background

I am a layman. I come from a part of the world that is home to many religions of the world. That is my heritage. So I will draw from that heritage and bare a bit of my soul to tell you how Islam connects with my life, and at the same time look at some of the Scripture to throw some light on the subject.

I was born into a Christian family. My paternal grandparents came from a Muslim background and my maternal grandparents had a Hindu heritage. My wife also grew up in a Christian home though her parentage goes in the opposite direction from mine: on her father's side they were Hindus and on her mother's side they descended from a chief Imam of a famous Muslim holy shrine. Needless to say, the Imam's conversion was no ordinary event.

When I was a small boy, one of seven children, our family lived in a predominantly Muslim village in the Punjab. My father was first a schoolteacher and then became a pastor. Being a Punjabi, he was a bit passionate about his faith. He had a modest formal education. In spite of that, he was able to interact with his Muslim neighbors with tact and boldness, a character trait with which he was naturally endowed. In fact, many Muslims and Hindus came to him for counsel, which was a surprise considering that Christians in that society were looked down upon by non-Christians. As children, we not only played with our friends from different faith backgrounds, but also argued with them about matters of faith.

## The Religious Landscape

Taking a long view of history we find that Hinduism claims to be more than 4,000 years old. Buddhism has been around for about 2500 years, and Jainism just about the same. All three of these religions came out of India, but Islam entered India toward the end of the first millennium after Christ.

As a young man, and even now as a layman, I have often asked myself: "Why did God allow Satan to deceive Adam and Eve in the Garden of Eden?" Why did He not "nip the evil in the bud" right then? Why were false religions, which today control the lives and minds of billions of people, allowed to grow and survive? Maybe we are not supposed to ask questions like these, but such thoughts do cross our minds from time to time.

## Searching the Scriptures

The story of how humanity fell into sin is given in Gen. 3:1–5.

> Now the serpent was more cunning than any beast of the field which the Lord God had made. And he said to the woman, "Has God indeed said, 'you shall not eat of every tree of the garden'?" And the woman said to the serpent, "We may eat the fruit of the trees of the garden, but of the fruit of the tree which is in the midst of the garden God has said, 'you shall not eat it, nor shall you touch it lest you die.'" And the serpent said to the woman, "You will not surely die. For God knows that in the day you eat of it your eyes will be opened, and you will be like God, knowing good and evil" (New KJV).

This is a familiar story, but in it we can begin to understand in a new way that God has *allowed* some things to happen. Adam and Eve were created sinless, just as God is sinless. But right into the Garden of Eden the Devil came to do his dirty work of deception by raising doubts in the minds of the first couple: "Has God indeed said…?" He took the truth of God's word and changed it around. As we look through history, we find that Satan has never given up. He is out there trying to oppose everything that God has done or wants to do. This explains how false religions have come into being and continue to flourish today.

In order to thwart God's plan of redemption, which He has had in place before the beginning of time, the Devil has encouraged what could be called "the Bible plus" doctrine—the idea that we need to supplement the Bible with other "truths," interpretations, or revelations. Hence Jehovah's Witnesses create their own version, the Mormons add the Book of Mormon, and the Muslims say the Qur'an must be accepted alongside the Bible, in fact revered above it as the "final" word of God!

How can we then sustain our faith as Christians in the light of these claims by the followers of other religions? Only by going back again and again to the Word of God—the Bible.

## The Window and the Chamber

While we know that we are not dealing with an ordinary foe, and that he will be with us until such a time that Christ will finally defeat and bind him, we are often not prepared for the pain and suffering that he can cause and is causing to God's elect.

Since we are involved closely with the plight of the persecuted church worldwide, we are regularly able to look inside the so-called 10/40 Window. And what do we find there? A chamber of horrors. Most of the people in the Window countries are either Hindu, Muslim, or Buddhist. They may react violently to the Gospel, killing, maiming, and murdering Christians, burning and destroying churches, and doing everything possible to suppress the message of the Gospel.

Take, for instance, the story of nine or so southern Sudanese Christian children, ages 6-13 or thereabouts, who were abducted by a raiding party from the north. They were beaten and threatened with dire consequences if they did not convert to Islam. Upon their persistent refusal to do so, they were brought near a burning fire and again asked to deny Jesus and convert. When they still would not submit, the youngest children, five of them, were held by their arms and feet, one after the other, and slowly lowered over the fire until they died excruciating deaths.

In spite of the fact that such horrendous atrocities are being committed against our brothers and sisters in the faith, as Christians we cannot hate any of these people, no matter what they do. We may find it hard or impossible to forgive them, but our Lord asks us to do so. Not only that, He is asking us to partner with Him in reaching all people everywhere—Muslims, Hindus, Sikhs, and others—with his message of love and hope. He is calling us, even the most ordinary and insignificant of us, to spread the Good News to those who have not yet heard.

## Uncompromising Truth

In Matthew 10:5–16, we find the story of the twelve Apostles whom Christ sends out on an evangelistic mission to the neighboring villages. The story ends with these startling words: "Behold, I send you out as sheep in the midst of wolves." The Truth must be preached, but it must be done in love. The environment in which we are asked to operate, however, is outright hostile and implacable. No wonder every minister of the gospel wrestles with this tension between the message and the method.

But the tension is resolved in his next statement: "Therefore be wise as serpents and harmless as doves." Whether we come from the laid-back culture of the East or the go-getter culture of the West, as followers of Christ we must operate in light of this divine principle.

## Call to Ministry

We started our ministry about seven years ago when we moved to Columbia, South Carolina, from Canada. We were ostensibly leaving Canada because my wife felt we needed to move to a warmer place. But the Lord had a different reason for moving us down south. He was calling us to reflect on all I had learned about Hinduism and Islam from my childhood on, and then use it to instruct and educate the American people about these two world religions which together comprise over two billion followers. Also we were being asked to find ways to engage them in some kind of dialogue through which the claims of Christ could be presented plainly and forthrightly to them. This dual challenge forced us to make prayer and intercession a central focus of our ministry.

During our very first year in Columbia, I was able to share this insight with a pastor who faced the challenge of advising his congregation as to how to deal with the impending construction of a Hindu temple near their town. They were told to build up their own spiritual defenses rather than resort to some reaction based on fear of the unknown. Very reluctantly he and his congregation agreed to have a night of prayer, at the end of which the members felt powerfully impacted and rejuvenated, to the extent that they left their traditional denomination and started a new Evangelical church.

## Ministry to Muslims

When we think today about what steps to take to reach Muslims for Christ, in my humble experience, the first thing is to start a prayer ministry. One can do prayer walks, prayer nights, concerts of prayer in any shape or form.

The purpose is to get Christian brothers and sisters in North America to go down on their knees, possibly for an hour or two or three, or even a whole night. Admittedly it is a tough road to travel, since most people are not in the habit of spending a substantial portion of their weekly schedules in times of prayer. They get tired very soon; they need snacks and coffee or other soft drinks; they want long breaks; they would like to have music playing in the background. However, the plain truth is that if we have not learned the basic lesson of seeking power from on high, we would not have much success in touching immigrant cultures here. That is why we have built an extensive network of praying partners in the city, state, and even in other parts of this country.

Our next step was to develop contacts with the Muslim community. Being aware of their great desire to be properly understood by the American people and to remove their misunderstandings about Islam, we developed the format of engaging them in "dialogues of understanding."

Such dialogues were not smooth sailing at the beginning. When we announced the very first event of this nature, we almost started a riot. I had invited an Arabic-speaking brother from the Middle East to be the speaker, without realizing that his presence would ignite such a passionate response from the Muslim community of this area.

About 500 Muslims showed up, and they persistently disrupted his lecture the first night and demanded that their Imam be allowed to engage in a debate with him the next night, to which we agreed. Again, there were some shouts, a few angry words, and rising emotions, but no severe problems. We could sense that the Holy Spirit was also there as a result of the prayer offensive that we had launched the previous night. To our surprise, rather than becoming a disaster, the event led to many lasting friendships among Muslims and Christians, and opened doors of future ministry for us.

We have had about ten such dialogues with them, without serious problems, even when some of our speakers have been somewhat insensitive in presenting facts or opinions. We have been able to have long discussions with them about every conceivable theological or other topic. We have also been able to freely share apologetic literature with them, present the claims of Christ to them, make friends with them, and visit their homes.

To sum up, the task of Muslim evangelism is not easy but we should not allow fear to keep us from attempting to share the gospel with them. We must continuously pray for them, create opportunities to dialogue with them, befriend them, and share the love of Jesus with them.

# Bibliography

Abdul-Raymond. 1983. Personal conversation with A. AbDat-Isa.

Accad, Fouad. 1997. *Building Bridges: Christianity and Islam*. Colorado Springs: NavPress.

Al-Ghazali, 1058-1111. 1970. *Ninety-nine Names of God in Islam: A Translation of the Major Portion of Al-Ghazali's Al-Maqsad Al-Asna*. Selections. Trans. Robert Charles Stade. Ibadan, Nigeria: Daystar Press.

*Alliance Video Magazine*. 1998. Vol. 12, #1.

Aulen, Gustaf. 1937. *Christus Victor: An Historical Study of the Three Maine Types of the Idea of the Atonement*, Translated by A. G. Hebert. New York: The Macmillan Co.

Bagby, Ihsan, Paul M. Perl, and Bryan T. Froehle. 2001. *The Mosque in America: A National Portrait*. A Report from the Mosque Study Project. Washington, DC: Council on American-Islamic Relations.

Bailey, Kenneth. 1973. *The Cross and the Prodigal*. St. Louis: Concordia Publishing House.

Bakus, Yunas. 1985. Presentation at the West Coast regional conference for the Islamic Society of North America, July.

Beaver, A. P. 1968. *American Protestant Women in World Mission: A History of the First Feminist Movement in North America*. Grand Rapids, MI: Eerdmans Publishing Company.

Blincoe, Robert. 1998. *Ethnic Realities and the Church: Lessons from Kurdistan.* Pasadena, CA: Presbyterian Center for Mission Studies.

Boulos, M. 1997. Personal conversation with A. AbDat-Isa.

Boyd, Gregory A. 1997. *God at War: The Bible and Spiritual Conflict.* Downers Grove, IL: Intervarsity Press.

"Bringing Back the Gospel." 1995. *Bright Side.* Campus Crusade for Christ, November.

Chapman, Colin. 1995. *Cross and Crescent: Responding to the Challenge of Islam.* Downers Grove, IL: InterVarsity Press.

Cooper, Anne, ed. 1985. *Ishmael My Brother: A Biblical Course on Islam.* London: Evangelical Missionary Alliance.

Dashti, Ali. 1985. *23 Years: A Study of the Prophetic Career of Mohammad.* London: George Allen & Unwin.

Galifianakis, Nick. 1994. "U.S. Muslim Population Grows." *Rockland Journal News,* Nyack, NY (10 February): C4.

Geisler, Norman L., and Abdul Saleeb. 1993. *Answering Islam: The Crescent in the Light of the Cross.* Grand Rapids, MI: Baker.

Gilliland, Dean S. 1990. History of the Muslim-Christian Encounter. Course notes, Fuller Theological Seminary.

————. 1991. Islam in Sub-Sahara Africa. Course notes, Fuller Theological Seminary.

Goldsmith, Martin. 1983. Lectures on Islam. Operation Mobilization Leadership Conference. Leuven, Belgium, September.

————. 1983. *Islam and Christian Witness.* Downers Grove, IL: InterVarsity Press.

Haddad, Yvonne Yazbeck, and Jane Idleman Smith. 1993. *Mission to America: Five Islamic Sectarian Communities in North America.* Gainesville, FL: University Press of Florida.

Haines, John F. 1998. *Good News for Muslims.* Philadelphia: Middle East Resources.

Hansen, J., with M. Powers. 1997. *Fashioned for Intimacy: Reconciling Men and Women to God's Original Design.* Ventura, CA: Regal.

Hodgson, Marshall G. S. 1974. *The Venture of Islam.* 3 vol. Chicago: University of Chicago Press.

*The Holy Quran.* 1989. Text, Translation, and Commentary by 'Abdullah Yusuf 'Ali. New Revised Edition. Brentwood, NM: Amana Corporation.

Johnstone, Patrick, John Hanna, and Marti Smith, eds. 1996. *Praying through the Window III: The Unreached Peoples.* Seattle, WA: YWAM Publishing.

Kantiok, J. 1997. Presentation on prayer for Muslim issues in Nigeria, West Africa, at a prayer meeting for the Muslim world, May.

Kraft, Charles. 1991. Intercultural Communication. Course notes, Fuller Theological Seminary.

Larson, W. 1996. "Islamic Fundamentalism in Pakistan: Its Implications for Conversion to Christianity." Doctoral dissertation, Fuller Theological Seminary. U.M.I. #U.M.9621987.

Lawlor, R. 1983. Teachings on Muslim Evangelism. Operation Mobilization Summer Campaign Orientation, June-July.

Lewis, C. S. 1950. *The Lion, the Witch and the Wardrobe.* New York: Macmillan.

Livingstone, Greg. 1993. *Planting Churches in Muslim Cities: A Team Approach.* Grand Rapids, MI: Baker.

Loewen, Arley. 1997. "Refreshing the Stranger: Celebrating God's Hospitality." In *Canada's New Harvest: Helping Christians Touch Newcomers*, ed., Brian Seim. Ontario, CAN: SIM Canada.

Love, F. 2000. "Developing Women Leaders in Muslim Background Believer Churches." In Love, F., and J. Eckheart, eds. *Ministry to Muslim Women: Longing to Call Them Sisters*. Pasadena, CA: William Carey Library, 199–221.

McCloud, Aminah. 1995. *African-American Islam*. Los Angeles: Routledge.

McCurry, Don M. 1982. *Sharing the Gospel with Iranians*. Altadena, CA: Samuel Zwemer Institute.

McDowell, Bruce A., and Anees Zaka. 1999. *Muslims and Christians at the Table: Promoting Biblical Understanding among North American Muslims*. Phillipsburg, NJ: P&R Publications.

Miller, William M. 1976. *A Christian Response to Islam*. Philadelphia: Presbyterian and Reformed Publishing Co.

———. 1975. *The Beliefs and Practices of Christians*, 3rd ed. Lahore, Pakistan: Masihi Isha'at Khana.

———. 1969; reprint 1987. *Ten Muslims Meet Christ*. Grand Rapids, MI: Eerdmans.

MISG. 1982. Malaysian Islamic Study Group's annual conference. St. Charles, IL, December.

Muhammed, Warith Uddin. 1986. Speech given at a Baptist church in Newark, NJ.

Mujtaba, Sayid, and Rukni Musawi Lari. 1977. *Western Civilization through Muslim Eyes*. Qum, Iran: Ansariyan Publications.

Musk, Bill. 1989. *The Unseen Face of Islam*. London: MARC.

Nasr, Seyyed Hossein. 1994. *A Young Muslim's Guide to the Modern World*. Chicago: Kazi Publications.

Parshall, Phil. 1994. *Inside the Community: Understanding Muslims through Their Traditions.* Grand Rapids, MI: Baker.

———. 1989. *The Cross and the Crescent: Understanding the Muslim Mind and Heart.* Wheaton, IL: Tyndale.

———. 1983. *Bridges to Islam: A Christian Perspective on Folk Islam.* Grand Rapids, MI: Baker.

Pierson, Paul. 1993. History of the World Christian Movement. Course notes, Fuller Theological Seminary.

Poston, Larry. 1994. "Islamic *Dawah:* Offensive Strategy or Defensive Posture?" Unpublished paper.

Poston, Larry A., and Carl F. Ellis, Jr. 2000. *The Changing Face of Islam in America.* Camp Hill, PA: Horizon Books.

Rahman, Fazlur. 1979. *Islam.* 2nd ed. Chicago: University of Chicago Press.

———. 1980. *Major Themes of the Quran.* Chicago: Bibliotheca Islamica.

Saal, William J. 1991. *Reaching Muslims for Christ.* Chicago: Moody Press.

Scott, Katherine Hutt. 2000. "New System Tracks Foreign Students." *USA Today,* April 19.

Stacey, Vivienne. 1997. Women in Islam. Course notes, Fuller Theological Seminary.

Tanbunaan, G. 1997. Doctoral dissertation, Fuller Theological Seminary.

*10/40 Window Reporter.* 1998. Christian Information Network, Winter.

Voll, John Obert. 1982. *Islam: Continuity and Change in the Modern World.* Boulder, CO: Westview Press.

Woodberry, J. Dudley. 1999. Current Trends in Islam. Course notes, Fuller Theological Seminary.

Woodberry, J. Dudley, and Dean S. Gilliland, eds. Forthcoming. *Muslims and Christians in Africa*. Pasadena, CA: William Carey Library.

Yung, A. 1993. Personal conversation with A. AbDat-Isa.

# Select List of Organizations
## Active in Ministry to Muslims in North America

The following 2 criteria were applied in deciding whom to include in the list:
1) The organization's Muslim ministry in North America must be larger than one worker. Many organizations with 2–5 active workers in North America are not listed.
2) The organization must have a larger mandate than a specific city or small region in North America.

It is important to notice that:
1) There is no significantly sized organization that has reaching Muslims in North America as its only purpose.
2) Some of the very large organizations listed below have no organized effort to reach Muslims in North America, but in spite of this, some of their workers are doing significant part-time work here.

### Answering Islam
c/o Horizons Int.
P.O. Box 18478
Boulder, CO 80308–1478

Email: jochen@answering-islam.org
Website: http://answering-islam.org
Contact Person: Jochen Katz

### Arab World Ministries
Box 3398
Cambridge, Ontario N3H 4T3
CANADA

Phone(s): 519–653–3170 (off.)
Contact Person: Abe Wiebe
Email: wiebe@1primus.ca

P.O. Box 96
Upper Darby, PA 19082
Email: usa@awm.org
Phone(s): 1–800–447–3566   610-352-2652 (fax)
Website: www.awm.org
Contact Person: E. J. Gibson
Email: ej@awm.org

## Christian & Missionary Alliance (C&MA)

Intercultural Ministries
P.O. Box 3500
Colorado Springs, CO 80935–3500

Phone(s): 719–599–5999 (off.)
Email: KongJ@CMAlliance.org
Website: www.cmalliance.org
Contact Person: Joseph Kong

## C&MA Canada

30 Carrier Dr., Suite 100
Etobicoke, Ontario, M2K 2R6
CANADA

Phone(s): 905–771–6747 (off.)    905–771–9874(fax)
Email: Nationaloffice@CMAcan.org
Website: www.cmacan.org
Contact Person: Dr. Franklin Pyles

## Campus Crusade For Christ

306 Westwood Dr.
Ames, IA  50014

Phone(s): 515–292–0156
Email: deggert@ames.net
Contact Person: David Eggert

## Center for Ministry to Muslims—CMM
2032 East Kearney, Suite 205
Springfield, MI 65803–4662

Phone(s): 417–866–3313 (off.)   417–866–3733 (fax)
Email: 76243.2762@compuserve.com
Website: www.cmmequip.org
Contact Person: Tommy Hodum, US Representative

## Christar (Formerly International Missions)
Att: North American Field
P.O. Box 14866
Reading, PA 19612

Phone(s): 800–755–7955 (off.)   610–375–6862 (fax)
Email: info@christar.org
Contact Person: Steve Coffey

## Church Without Walls
P.O. Box 27276
Philadelphia, PA 19118

Phone(s): 215–887–1195 (off.)   215–887–1195 (fax)
Email: cww.biis@juno.com
Contact Person: Dr. Anees Zaka

## Columbia Institute of Muslim Studies
P.O. Box 3122
Columbia, SC 29230–3122

7435 Monticello Rd.
Columbia, SC 29230–3122

Phone(s): 800–777–2227 x3325 (off.)   803–754–4100 x3710 (off.)
803–754–9119 (fax)
Email: muslimstudies@ciu.edu   extoff@ciu.edu
Website: http://www.ciu.edu/muslimstudies
www.ciuextension.com
Contact Person: Dr. Warren Larson

## Ethnic Focus Ministries (SIM)

857 Niagara St.
Carol Stream, IL 60188

Phone(s): 630–260–1845    630–752–5953 (off.)    630–871–7697 (fax)
Email: simesm@aol.com
Contact Person: Dr. David Ripley

## Fellowship of Faith for Muslims (FFM)

P.O. Box 65214
Toronto
Ontario, M4K 3Z2
CANADA

746 Pape Ave.
Toronto
Ontario, M4K 3Z2
CANADA

Phone(s): 416–778–6702 (off.)    416–466–3324 (fax)
Email: ffm.toronto@sympatico.ca
Contact Person: Norine Love

## Friends of the Kurds

P.O. Box 58319
Seattle, WA 98138–1319

Email: friends_of_kurds@home.com

## Frontiers

P.O. Box 31177
Mesa, AZ  85275

Phone(s): 480-834-1500    480-834-1974 (fax)
Email: info@us.frontiers.org
Website: www.frontiers.org

## Frontiers (Canada)

P.O. Box 9090
Edmonton, AB T5P 4K1
CANADA

Phone(s): 780–421–9090 (off.)   780-421-9292 (fax)
Email: nelson.wolf@ca.frontiers.org
Contact Person: Nelson Wolf

## Gospel Missionary Union (GMU)

1000 N. Oak
Kansas City, MO 64155

Phone(s): 816–734–8500 (off.)  816–734–4601 (fax)
Email: Hpeters@gmu.org
Website: www.gmu.org
Contact Person: Harold Peters

## Inter Varsity Christian Fellowship

6400 Schroeder Road,  P.O. Box 7895
Madison, WI  53707–7895

Phone(s): 608–274–9001 (off.)   608–274–7882 (fax)
Email: tgvd18a@prodigy.com
Website: www.ivcf.org
Contact Person: Ned Hale

## International Students Incorporated (ISI)

Box C
Colorado Springs, CO  80901–2901

Phone(s): 719–576–2700 x145 (off.)   719–576–5363 (fax)
800–474–4147 (off.)
Email: dhalverson@isionline.org
Website: www.isionline.org
Contact Person: Dean Halverson

## Iranian Christians International

P.O. Box 25607
Colorado Springs, CO 80936

Phone(s): 719–596–0010 (off.)    719–574–1141 (fax)
Email: 74521.230@compuserve.com
IranianChristiansInternational@compuserve.com
Website: www//farsinet.com/ICI
Contact Person: Abe Ghaffari

## Navigators

Phone(s): 765–497–2625
Email: abusenitz@juno.com
Contact Person: Allen Busenitz

## School of World Mission (SWM)

135 N. Oakland Ave.
Pasadena, CA 91182

Phone(s): 800–235–2222 x5260 (off.)
Email: swmadvis@fuller.edu   swm-reception@fuller.edu
Website: http://www.missionfrontiers.org
Contact Person: Dr. J. Dudley Woodberry

## SIM

P.O. Box 7900
Charlotte, NC 28241–8819

Phone(s): 704–552–1765 (off.)    704–587–1518 (fax)
Email: Gerefm@aol.com
Contact Person: Gerry Johnson

## SIM (Canada)

81 Carondale Crescent
Scarborough
Ontario, M1W 2A9
CANADA

Phone(s): 416–497–2424    416–497–2444 (fax)
Email: 102752.3222@compuserve.com
Contact Person: Jim Snell

## Southern Baptist Convention: North American Mission Board
4200 N. Point Parkway
Alpharetta, GA  30022–4176

Phone(s): 770–410–6000 (off.)    770–410–6018 (fax)
800–233–1123 (off.)
Email: interfaith@namb.net
Contact Person: Dr. Phil Roberts

## Summer Institute of Muslim Studies
Ministry To Muslims, 5215 Quasar Court
Colorado Springs, CO  80917

Horizons Int., P.O. Box 18478
Boulder, CO  80308

Phone(s): 800–554–5669    719–597–0609 (off.)    719–597–0712 (fax)
Email: 76361.3344@compuserve.com
Contact Person: Dr. Don McCurry

## Summer Training and Outreach Program (STOP)
c/o Christar
P.O. Box 14866
Reading, PA  19612–4866

Phone(s): 800–755–7955 (off.)    610–375–7862 (fax)
Email: info@christar.org
Contact Person: Paul Troper

## Turkish World Outreach (TWO)
508 Fruitvale Court
Grand Junction, CO  81504–5768

Phone(s): 970–434–1942 (off.)   970–434–1461 (fax)
997–434–4194 (off.)
Email: two@onlinecol.com   TWOSteve@onlinecol.com
Contact Person: Steve Hagerman

## Voice of the Truth
P.O. Box 15013
Colorado Springs, CO  80935

Phone(s): 719–597–7562   719–574–5900 (off.)
Email: vot@kktv.com
Contact Person: Jadallah Ghrayyeb

## World Relief
655 Village Square Dr.
Stone Mountain, GA 30083

Phone(s): 404–294–4352  X252
Website: www.worldrelief.org
Email: Hsnedden@wr.org
Contact Person: Herb Snedden

## Zwemer Institute
6600 North Clinton St.
Fort Wayne, IN  46825–4996

Phone(s): 219–452–2245 (off.)   219–452–2121 (fax)
Email: zwemer@ctsfw.edu
Contact Person: Dr. Jim Dretke